ABOUT THIS PUBLICATION

FOR SERVICE ASSISTANCE

Customer Service Department
704.898.0770

North Carolina General Statues is published by The Muliti-Media Group of Greater Charlotte in Charlotte, North Carolina. Copyright 2015 by the Multi-Media Group of Greater Charlotte. This book or parts thereof may not be reproduced in any form, stored in a retrieval system, or transmitted in any form by any means—electronic, mechanical, photocopy, recording or otherwise—without prior written permission of the publisher, except as provided by United States of America copyright law.

The records required by U.S. Code 2257(a) through (c) and the pertinent regulations 28 C.F.R. Cli. 1, Part 75 with respect to this publication and all materials associated with such records are maintained by The Multi-Media Group of Greater Charlotte, Publisher and available for review by Attorney General.

www.visionbooks.org

Copyright © 2015 by MMGGC
All rights reserved!

TID: 4988964
ISBN (10) digit: 1502301695
ISBN (13) digit: 978-1502301697

123-4-56789-01235-Paperback
123-4-56789-01235-Hardback

First Edition

090520140547

Printed in the United States of America

2015 EDITION

North Carolina Criminal Law And Procedure-Pamphlet # 2

Printed In conjunction with the Administration of the Courts

North Carolina Criminal Law and Procedure
Pamphlet Reference Guide

Chapters	Pamphlet
Chapter 1 Civil Procedure	1
Chapter 1 Civil Procedure (Continue)	2
Chapter 1A Rules of Civil Procedure	2
Chapter 1B Contribution.	2
Chapter 1C Enforcement of Judgments.	2
Chapter 1D Punitive Damages.	2
Chapter 1E Eastern Band of Cherokee Indians.	2
Chapter 1F North Carolina Uniform Interstate Depositions and Discovery Act.	2
Chapter 2 - Clerk of Superior Court [Repealed and Transferred.]	3
Chapter 3 - Commissioners of Affidavits and Deeds [Repealed.]	3
Chapter 4 - Common Law	3
Chapter 5 - Contempt [Repealed.]	3
Chapter 5A - Contempt	3
Chapter 6 - Liability for Court Costs	3
Chapter 7 - Courts [Repealed and Transferred.]	3
Chapter 7A – Judicial Department	3
Chapter 7A – Continuation (7A) Judicial Department	4
Chapter 7A – Continuation (Judicial Department)	5
Chapter 7B - Juvenile Code	5
Chapter 8 - Evidence	6
Chapter 8A - Interpreters for Deaf Persons [Recodified.]	6
Chapter 8B - Interpreters for Deaf Persons	6
Chapter 8C - Evidence Code	6
Chapter 9 - Jurors	6
Chapter 10 - Notaries [Repealed.]	6
Chapter 10A - Notaries [Recodified.]	6
Chapter 10B - Notaries	6
Chapter 11 - Oaths	6
Chapter 12 - Statutory Construction	6
Chapter 13 - Citizenship Restored	6
Chapter 14 - Criminal Law	7
Chapter 14 –Criminal Law (Continuation)	8
Chapter 15 - Criminal Procedure	9
Chapter 15A - Criminal Procedure Act (Continuation)	10
Chapter 15A - Criminal Procedure Act (Continuation)	11
Chapter 15B - Victims Compensation	11
Chapter 15C - Address Confidentiality Program	11
Chapter 16 - Gaming Contracts and Futures	11
Chapter 17 - Habeas Corpus	11

Chapter 17A - Law-Enforcement Officers [Recodified.]	11
Chapter 17B - North Carolina Criminal Justice Education and Training System [Recodified.] Chapter 17C - North Carolina Criminal Justice Education and Training Standards Commission	11
	11
Chapter 17D - North Carolina Justice Academy	11
Chapter 17E - North Carolina Sheriffs' Education and Training Standards Commission	11
Chapter 18 - Regulation of Intoxicating Liquors [Repealed.]	12
Chapter 18A - Regulation of Intoxicating Liquors [Repealed.]	12
Chapter 18B - Regulation of Alcoholic Beverages	12
Chapter 18C - North Carolina State Lottery	12
Chapter 19 - Offenses against Public Morals	12
Chapter 19A - Protection of Animals	12
Chapter 20 - Motor Vehicles	13
Chapter 20 - Motor Vehicles (Continuation)	14
Chapter 20 - Motor Vehicles (Continuation)	15
Chapter 20 - Motor Vehicles (Continuation)	16
Chapter 21 - Bills of Lading	17
Chapter 22 - Contracts Requiring Writing	17
Chapter 22A - Signatures	17
Chapter 22B - Contracts Against Public Policy	17
Chapter 22C - Payments to Subcontractors	17
Chapter 23 - Debtor and Creditor	17
Chapter 24 – Interest	17
Chapter 25 – Uniform Commercial Code	18
Chapter 25 – Uniform Commercial Code (Continuation)	19
Chapter 25A – Retail Installment Sales Act	20
Chapter 25B - Credit	20
Chapter 25C - Sales of Artwork	20
Chapter 26 - Suretyship	20
Chapter 27 - Warehouse Receipts [Repealed.]	20
Chapter 28 - Administration [Repealed.]	20
Chapter 28A - Administration of Decedents' Estates	20
Chapter 28B - Estates of Absentees in Military Service	20
Chapter 28C - Estates of Missing Persons	20
Chapter 29 - Intestate Succession	21
Chapter 30 - Surviving Spouses	21
Chapter 31 - Wills	21
Chapter 31A - Acts Barring Property Rights	21
Chapter 31B - Renunciation of Property and Renunciation of Fiduciary Powers Act	21
Chapter 31C - Uniform Disposition of Community Property Rights at Death Act	21
Chapter 32 - Fiduciaries	21
Chapter 32A - Powers of Attorney	21
Chapter 33 - Guardian and Ward [Repealed and Recodified.]	21

Chapter 33A - North Carolina Uniform Transfers to Minors Act	21
Chapter 33B - North Carolina Uniform Custodial Trust Act	21
Chapter 34 - Veterans' Guardianship Act	22
Chapter 35 - Sterilization Procedures	22
Chapter 35A - Incompetency and Guardianship	22
Chapter 36 - Trusts and Trustees [Repealed.]	22
Chapter 36A - Trusts and Trustees	22
Chapter 36B - Uniform Management of Institutional Funds Act [Repealed.]	22
Chapter 36C - North Carolina Uniform Trust Code	22
Chapter 36D - North Carolina Community Third Party Trusts, Pooled Trusts	23
Chapter 36E - Uniform Prudent Management of Institutional Funds Act	23
Chapter 37 - Allocation of Principal and Income [Repealed.]	23
Chapter 37A - Uniform Principal and Income Act	23
Chapter 38 - Boundaries	23
Chapter 38A - Landowner Liability	23
Chapter 39 - Conveyances	23
Chapter 39A - Transfer Fee Covenants Prohibited	23
Chapter 40 - Eminent Domain [Repealed.]	23
Chapter 40A - Eminent Domain	23
Chapter 41 - Estates	23
Chapter 41A - State Fair Housing Act	23
Chapter 42 - Landlord and Tenant	23
Chapter 42A - Vacation Rental Act	23
Chapter 43 - Land Registration	23
Chapter 44 - Liens	24
Chapter 44A - Statutory Liens and Charges	24
Chapter 45 - Mortgages and Deeds of Trust	24
Chapter 45A - Good Funds Settlement Act	24
Chapter 46 - Partition	24
Chapter 47 - Probate and Registration	25
Chapter 47A - Unit Ownership	25
Chapter 47B - Real Property Marketable Title Act	25
Chapter 47C - North Carolina Condominium Act	25
Chapter 47D - Notice of Settlement Act [Expired.]	25
Chapter 47E - Residential Property Disclosure Act	25
Chapter 47F - North Carolina Planned Community Act	25
Chapter 47G - Option to Purchase Contracts	25
Chapter 47H - Contracts for Deed	25
Chapter 48 - Adoptions	26
Chapter 48A - Minors	26
Chapter 49 - Bastardy	26
Chapter 49A - Rights of Children	26
Chapter 50 - Divorce and Alimony	26
Chapter 50A - Uniform Child-Custody Jurisdiction and	

Enforcement Act	26
Chapter 50B - Domestic Violence	26
Chapter 50C - Civil No-Contact Orders	26
Chapter 51 - Marriage	26
Chapter 52 - Powers and Liabilities of Married Persons	27
Chapter 52A - Uniform Reciprocal Enforcement of Support Act [Repealed.]	27
Chapter 52B - Uniform Premarital Agreement Act	27
Chapter 52C - Uniform Interstate Family Support Act	27
Chapter 53 - Banks	27
Chapter 53A - Business Development Corporations and North Carolina Capital Resource Corporations	28
Chapter 53B - Financial Privacy Act	28
Chapter 54 - Cooperative Organizations	28
Chapter 54A - Capital Stock Savings and Loan Associations [Repealed.]	28
Chapter 54B - Savings and Loan Associations	29
Chapter 54C - Savings Banks	29
Chapter 55 - North Carolina Business Corporation Act	30
Chapter 55A - North Carolina Nonprofit Corporation Act	31
Chapter 55B - Professional Corporation Act	31
Chapter 55C - Foreign Trade Zones	31
Chapter 55D - Filings, Names, and Registered Agents for Corporations, Nonprofit Corporations, and Partnerships	31
Chapter 56 - Electric, Telegraph and Power Companies [Repealed.]	31
Chapter 57 - Hospital, Medical and Dental Service Corporations [Recodified.]	31
Chapter 57A - Health Maintenance Organization Act [Recodified.]	31
Chapter 57B - Health Maintenance Organization Act [Recodified.]	31
Chapter 57C - North Carolina Limited Liability Company Act.	31
Chapter 58 - Insurance.	32
Chapter 58 - Insurance (Continuation)	33
Chapter 58 - Insurance (Continuation)	34
Chapter 58 - Insurance (Continuation)	35
Chapter 58 - Insurance (Continuation)	36
Chapter 58 - Insurance (Continuation)	37
Chapter 58 - Insurance (Continuation)	38
Chapter 58A - North Carolina Health Insurance Trust Commission [Recodified.]	38
Chapter 59 - Partnership.	39
Chapter 59 - Partnership.	39
Chapter 59B - Uniform Unincorporated Nonprofit Association Act.	39
Chapter 60 - Railroads and Other Carriers [Repealed and Transferred.]	39
Chapter 61 - Religious Societies	39

Chapter 62 - Public Utilities	39
Chapter 62 - Public Utilities (Continuation)	40
Chapter 62A - Public Safety Telephone Service And Wireless Telephone Service	40
Chapter 63 - Aeronautics	40
Chapter 63A - North Carolina Global TransPark Authority	40
Chapter 64 - Aliens	40
Chapter 65 – Cemeteries	40
Chapter 66 - Commerce and Business	41
Chapter 67 - Dogs	41
Chapter 68 - Fences and Stock Law	41
Chapter 69 - Fire Protection	41
Chapter 70 - Indian Antiquities, Archaeological Resources and Unmarked Human Skeletal Remains Protection	42
Chapter 71 - Indians [Repealed.]	42
Chapter 71A - Indians	42
Chapter 72 - Inns, Hotels and Restaurants	42
Chapter 73 - Mills	42
Chapter 74 - Mines and Quarries	42
Chapter 74A - Company Police [Repealed.]	42
Chapter 74B - Private Protective Services Act [Repealed.]	42
Chapter 74C - Private Protective Services	42
Chapter 74D - Alarm Systems	42
Chapter 74E - Company Police Act	42
Chapter 74F - Locksmith Licensing Act	42
Chapter 74G - Campus Police Act	42
Chapter 75 - Monopolies, Trusts and Consumer Protection	42
Chapter 75A - Boating and Water Safety	43
Chapter 75B - Discrimination in Business	43
Chapter 75C - Motion Picture Fair Competition Act	43
Chapter 75D - Racketeer Influenced and Corrupt Organizations	43
Chapter 75E - Unlawful Activities in Connection With Certain Corporate Transactions	43
Chapter 76 - Navigation	43
Chapter 76A - Navigation and Pilotage Commissions	43
Chapter 77 - Rivers, Creeks, and Coastal Waters	43
Chapter 78 - Securities Law [Repealed.]	43
Chapter 78A - North Carolina Securities Act	43
Chapter 78B - Tender Offer Disclosure Act [Repealed.]	43
Chapter 78C - Investment Advisers	43
Chapter 78D - Commodities Act	43
Chapter 79 - Strays [Repealed.]	43
Chapter 80 - Trademarks, Brands, etc.	44
Chapter 81 - Weights and Measures [Recodified.]	44
Chapter 81A - Weights and Measures Act of 1975.	44
Chapter 82 - Wrecks [Repealed.]	44

Chapter 83 - Architects [Recodified.]	44
Chapter 83A - Architects	44
Chapter 84 - Attorneys-at-Law	44
Chapter 84A - Foreign Legal Consultants	44
Chapter 85 - Auctions and Auctioneers [Repealed.]	44
Chapter 85A - Bail Bondsmen and Runners [Recodified.]	44
Chapter 85B - Auctions and Auctioneers	44
Chapter 85C - Bail Bondsmen and Runners [Recodified.]	44
Chapter 86 - Barbers [Recodified.]	44
Chapter 86A - Barbers	44
Chapter 87 - Contractors	44
Chapter 88 - Cosmetic Art [Repealed.]	44
Chapter 88A - Electrolysis Practice Act	44
Chapter 88B - Cosmetic Art	45
Chapter 89 - Engineering and Land Surveying [Recodified.]	45
Chapter 89A - Landscape Architects	45
Chapter 89B - Foresters	45
Chapter 89C - Engineering and Land Surveying	45
Chapter 89D - Landscape Contractors	45
Chapter 89E - Geologists Licensing Act	45
Chapter 89F - North Carolina Soil Scientist Licensing Act	45
Chapter 89G - Irrigation Contractors	45
Chapter 90 - Medicine and Allied Occupations	45
Chapter 90 - Medicine and Allied Occupations (Continuation)	46
Chapter 90 - Medicine and Allied Occupations (Continuation)	47
Chapter 90 - Medicine and Allied Occupations (Continuation)	48
Chapter 90A - Sanitarians and Water and Wastewater Treatment Facility Operators	48
Chapter 90B - Social Worker Certification and Licensure Act	48
Chapter 90C - North Carolina Recreational Therapy Licensure Act	48
Chapter 90D - Interpreters and Transliterators	48
Chapter 91 - Pawnbrokers [Repealed.]	48
Chapter 91A - Pawnbrokers Modernization Act of 1989	48
Chapter 92 - Photographers [Deleted.]	48
Chapter 93 - Certified Public Accountants	48
Chapter 93A - Real Estate License Law	49
Chapter 93B - Occupational Licensing Boards	49
Chapter 93C - Watchmakers [Repealed.]	49
Chapter 93D - North Carolina State Hearing Aid Dealers and Fitters Board.	49
Chapter 93E - North Carolina Appraisers Act	49
Chapter 94 - Apprenticeship	49
Chapter 95 - Department of Labor and Labor Regulations	49
Chapter 95 - Department of Labor and Labor Regulations (Continuation)	50
Chapter 96 - Employment Security	50
Chapter 97 - Workers' Compensation Act	50

Chapter 97 - Workers' Compensation Act (Continuation)	51
Chapter 98 - Burnt and Lost Records	51
Chapter 99 - Libel and Slander	51
Chapter 99A - Civil Remedies for Criminal Actions	51
Chapter 99B - Products Liability	51
Chapter 99C - Actions Relating to Winter Sports Safety and Accidents	51
Chapter 99D - Civil Rights	51
Chapter 99E - Special Liability Provisions	51
Chapter 100 - Monuments, Memorials and Parks	51
Chapter 101 - Names of Persons	51
Chapter 102 - Official Survey Base	51
Chapter 103 - Sundays, Holidays and Special Days	51
Chapter 104 - United States Lands	51
Chapter 104A - Degrees of Kinship	51
Chapter 104B - Hurricanes or Other Acts of Nature	51
Chapter 104C - Atomic Energy, Radioactivity and Ionizing Radiation [Repealed and Recodified.]	51
Chapter 104D - Southern States Energy Compact	51
Chapter 104E - North Carolina Radiation Protection Act	51
Chapter 104F - Southeast Interstate Low-Level Radioactive Waste Management Compact [Repealed]	51
Chapter 104G - North Carolina Low-Level Radioactive Waste Management Authority Act of 1987 [Repealed]	51
Chapter 105 - Taxation	51
Chapter 105 - Taxation (Continuation)	52
Chapter 105 - Taxation (Continuation)	53
Chapter 105 - Taxation (Continuation)	54
Chapter 105A - Setoff Debt Collection Act	55
Chapter 105B - Defaulted Student Loan Recovery Act	55
Chapter 106 - Agriculture	55
Chapter 106 - Agriculture (Continue)	56
Chapter 106 - Agriculture (Continue)	57
Chapter 107 - Agricultural Development Districts [Repealed.]	57
Chapter 108 - Social Services [Repealed and Recodified.]	57
Chapter 108A - Social Services	57
Chapter 108B - Community Action Programs	58
Chapter 108C Medicaid and Health Choice Provider Requirements.	58
Chapter 108D Medicaid Managed Care for Behavioral Health Services.	58
Chapter 109 - Bonds [Recodified.]	58
Chapter 110 - Child Welfare	58
Chapter 111 - Aid to the Blind	58
Chapter 112 - Confederate Homes and Pensions [Repealed.]	58
Chapter 113 - Conservation and Development	58

Chapter 113 - Conservation and Development (Continuation)	59
Chapter 113A - Pollution Control and Environment	59
Chapter 113A - Pollution Control and Environment (Continuation)	60
Chapter 113B - North Carolina Energy Policy Act of 1975	60
Chapter 114 - Department of Justice	60
Chapter 115 - Elementary and Secondary Education [Repealed.]	60
Chapter 115A - Community Colleges, Technical Institutes, and Industrial Education Centers [Repealed.]	60
Chapter 115B - Tuition and Fee Waivers	60
Chapter 115C - Elementary and Secondary Education	60
Chapter 115C - Elementary and Secondary Education (Continuation)	61
Chapter 115C - Elementary and Secondary Education (Continuation)	62
Chapter 115C - Elementary and Secondary Education (Continuation)	63
Chapter 115D - Community Colleges	63
Chapter 115E - Private Educational Facilities Finance Act [Recodified]	63
Chapter 116 - Higher Education	63
Chapter 116 - Higher Education (Continuation)	63
Chapter 116A - Escheats and Abandoned Property [Repealed.]	64
Chapter 116B - Escheats and Abandoned Property	64
Chapter 116C - Continuum of Education Programs	64
Chapter 116D - Higher Education Bonds	64
Chapter 116E -Education Longitudinal Data System	64
Chapter 117 - Electrification	64
Chapter 118 - Firemen's and Rescue Squad Workers' Relief and Pension Funds [Recodified.]	64
Chapter 118A - Firemen's Death Benefit Act [Repealed.]	64
Chapter 118B - Members of a Rescue Squad Death Benefit Act [Repealed.]	64
Chapter 119 - Gasoline and Oil Inspection and Regulation	64
Chapter 120 - General Assembly	65
Chapter 120 - General Assembly (Continuation)	66
Chapter 120 - General Assembly (Continuation)	67
Chapter 120C - Lobbying	67
Chapter 121 - Archives and History	67
Chapter 122 - Hospitals for the Mentally Disordered [Repealed.]	67
Chapter 122A - North Carolina Housing Finance Agency	67
Chapter 122B - North Carolina Agricultural Facilities Finance Act [Repealed.]	67
Chapter 122C - Mental Health, Developmental Disabilities, and Substance Abuse Act of 1985	67
Chapter 122C - Mental Health, Developmental	

Disabilities, and Substance Abuse Act of 1985 (Continuation)	68
Chapter 122D - North Carolina Agricultural Finance Act	68
Chapter 122E - North Carolina Housing Trust and Oil Overcharge Act	68
Chapter 123 - Impeachment	69
Chapter 123A - Industrial Development [Repealed.]	69
Chapter 124 - Internal Improvements	69
Chapter 125 - Libraries	69
Chapter 126 - State Personnel System	69
Chapter 127 - Militia [Repealed.]	69
Chapter 127A - Militia	69
Chapter 127B - Military Affairs	69
Chapter 127C - Advisory Commission on Military Affairs	69
Chapter 128 - Offices and Public Officers	69
Chapter 128 - Offices and Public Officers (Continuation)	70
Chapter 129 - Public Buildings and Grounds	70
Chapter 130 - Public Health [Repealed.]	70
Chapter 130A - Public Health	70
Chapter 130A - Public Health (Continuation)	71
Chapter 130A - Public Health (Continuation)	72
Chapter 130B - Hazardous Waste Management Commission [Repealed.]	72
Chapter 131 - Public Hospitals [Repealed.]	72
Chapter 131A - Health Care Facilities Finance Act	72
Chapter 131B - Licensing of Ambulatory Surgical Facilities [Repealed.]	72
Chapter 131C - Charitable Solicitation Licensure Act [Repealed.]	72
Chapter 131D - Inspection and Licensing of Facilities	72
Chapter 131E - Health Care Facilities and Services	72
Chapter 131E - Health Care Facilities and Services (Continuation)	73
Chapter 131F - Solicitation of Contributions	73
Chapter 132 - Public Records	73
Chapter 133 - Public Works	74
Chapter 134 - Youth Development [Recodified.]	74
Chapter 134A - Youth Services [Repealed.]	74
Chapter 135 - Retirement System for Teachers and State Employees; Social Security; Health Insurance Program for Children	74
Chapter 135 - Retirement System for Teachers and State Employees; Social Security; Health Insurance Program for Children	75
Chapter 136 - Transportation	75
Chapter 136 - Transportation (Continuation)	76
Chapter 137 - Rural Rehabilitation [Repealed.]	76
Chapter 138 - Salaries, Fees and Allowances	76

Chapter 138A - State Government Ethics Act	76
Chapter 139 - Soil and Water Conservation Districts	76
Chapter 140 - State Art Museum; Symphony and Art Societies	76
Chapter 140A - State Awards System	76
Chapter 141 - State Boundaries	76
Chapter 142 - State Debt	76
Chapter 143 - State Departments, Institutions, and Commissions	77
Chapter 143 - State Departments, Institutions, and Commissions (Continuation)	78
Chapter 143 - State Departments, Institutions, and Commissions (Continuation)	79
Chapter 143 - State Departments, Institutions, and Commissions (Continuation)	80
Chapter 143A - State Government Reorganization	80
Chapter 143B - Executive Organization Act of 1973	80
Chapter 143B - Executive Organization Act of 1973 (Continuation)	81
Chapter 143B - Executive Organization Act of 1973 (Continuation)	82
Chapter 143C - State Budget Act	83
Chapter 143D - The State Governmental Accountability and Internal Control Act	83
Chapter 144 - State Flag, Official Governmental Flags, Motto, and Colors	83
Chapter 145 - State Symbols and Other Official Adoptions.	83
Chapter 146 - State Lands	83
Chapter 147 - State Officers	83
Chapter 148 - State Prison System	84
Chapter 149 - State Song and Toast	84
Chapter 150 - Uniform Revocation of Licenses [Repealed.]	84
Chapter 150A - Administrative Procedure Act [Recodified.]	84
Chapter 150B - Administrative Procedure Act	84
Chapter 151 - Constables [Repealed.]	84
Chapter 152 - Coroners	84
Chapter 152A - County Medical Examiner [Repealed.]	84
Chapter 152A - County Medical Examiner [Repealed.] (Continuation)	85
Chapter 153 - Counties and County Commissioners [Repealed.]	85
Chapter 153A - Counties	85
Chapter 153B - Mountain Resources Planning Act	85
Chapter 153C - Uwharrie Regional Resources Act	85
Chapter 154 - County Surveyor [Repealed.]	85
Chapter 155 - County Treasurer [Repealed.]	85

Chapter 156 - Drainage	85
Chapter 156 – Drainage (Continuation)	86
Chapter 157 - Housing Authorities and Projects	86
Chapter 157A - Historic Properties Commissions [Transferred.]	86
Chapter 158 - Local Development	86
Chapter 159 - Local Government Finance	86
Chapter 159 - Local Government Finance (Continuation)	87
Chapter 159A - Pollution Abatement and Industrial Facilities Financing Act [Unconstitutional.]	87
Chapter 159B - Joint Municipal Electric Power and Energy Act	87
Chapter 159C - Industrial and Pollution Control Facilities Financing Act	87
Chapter 159D - The North Carolina Capital Facilities Financing Act	87
Chapter 159E - Registered Public Obligations Act	87
Chapter 159F - North Carolina Energy Development Authority [Repealed.]	87
Chapter 159G - Water Infrastructure	87
Chapter 159H - [Reserved.]	87
Chapter 159I - Solid Waste Management Loan Program and Local Government Special Obligation Bonds	87
Chapter 160 - Municipal Corporations [Repealed And Transferred.]	87
Chapter 160A - Cities and Towns	88
Chapter 160A - Cities and Towns (Continuation)	89
Chapter 160B - Consolidated City-County Act	89
Chapter 160C - Baseball Park Districts [Repealed.]	90
Chapter 161 - Register of Deeds	90
Chapter 162 - Sheriff	90
Chapter 162A - Water and Sewer Systems	90
Chapter 162B Continuity of Local Government in Emergency.	90
Chapter 163 Elections and Election Laws.	90
Chapter 163 Elections and Election Laws. (Continuation)	91
Chapter 164 Concerning the General Statutes of North Carolina.	92
Chapter 165 Veterans.	92
Chapter 166 Civil Preparedness Agencies [Repealed.]	92
Chapter 166A North Carolina Emergency Management Act.	92
Chapter 167 State Civil Air Patrol [Repealed.]	92
Chapter 168 Persons with Disabilities.	92
Chapter 168A Persons With Disabilities Protection Act.	92

§ 1-539.2B. Double damages for injury to agricultural commodities or production systems; define value of agricultural commodities grown for educational, testing, or research purposes.

(a) Any person who unlawfully and willfully injures or destroys any other person's agricultural commodities or production system is liable to the owner for double the value of the commodities or production system injured or destroyed.

(b) For purposes of this section, the value of agricultural commodities that are grown for educational, testing, or research purposes includes all of the following:

(1) The diminution in market value of the commodities when the commodities were grown for sale and the plaintiff is the entity who sold the commodities or would have sold the commodities but for their injury or destruction.

(2) Costs to the plaintiff for research and development of the injured or destroyed commodities.

(3) Other incidental and consequential damages proven to have been incurred by the plaintiff.

(c) For the purpose of this section, the following definitions apply:

(1) "Agricultural commodities" means:

a. Commodities produced for individual and public use, consumption, and marketing from one of the following:

1. The cultivation of soil or hydroponics or any other method of production for crops, including fruits, vegetables, flowers, and ornamental plants.

2. The planting and production of trees, timber, forests, or forest products.

3. The raising of livestock, poultry, and eggs.

4. Aquaculture as defined in G.S. 106-758.

b. Seed, genetic material, tissue cultures, and any research and development materials, information, and records related to items included in subdivision (1)a. of this subsection developed or used for educational, testing, or research purposes.

(2) "Production systems" means land, buildings, and equipment used in the production of agricultural commodities, including aquaculture facilities as defined in G.S. 106-758. (2001-290, s. 1.)

§ 1-539.2C. Damages for identity theft.

(a) Any person whose property or person is injured by reason of an act made unlawful by Article 19C of Chapter 14 of the General Statutes, or a violation of G.S. 75-66, may sue for civil damages. For each unlawful act, or each violation of G.S. 75-66, damages may be

(1) In an amount of up to five thousand dollars ($5,000), but no less than five hundred dollars ($500.00), or

(2) Three times the amount of actual damages,

whichever amount is greater. A person seeking damages as set forth in this section may also institute a civil action to enjoin and restrain future acts that would constitute a violation of this section. The court, in an action brought under this section, may award reasonable attorneys' fees to the prevailing party.

(b) If the identifying information of a deceased person is used in a manner made unlawful by Article 19C of Chapter 14 of the General Statutes, or by a violation of G.S. 75-66, the deceased person's estate shall have the right to recover damages pursuant to subsection (a) of this section.

(c) The venue for any civil action brought under this section shall be the county in which the plaintiff resides or any county in which any part of the alleged violation of G.S. 75-66, G.S. 14-113.20 or G.S. 14-113.20A took place, regardless of whether the defendant was ever actually present in that county. Civil actions under this section must be brought within three years from the date on which the identity of the wrongdoer was discovered or reasonably should have been discovered.

(d) Civil action under this section does not depend on whether or not a criminal prosecution has been or will be instituted under Article 19C of Chapter 14 of the General Statutes for the acts which are the subject of the civil action.

The rights and remedies provided by this section are in addition to any other rights and remedies provided by law. (2002-175, s. 8; 2005-414, s. 9; 2007-534, s. 3.)

Article 43A.

Adjudication of Small Claims in Superior Court.
§§ 1-539.3 through 1-539.8: Repealed by Session Laws 1971, c. 268, s. 34.

Article 43B.

Defense of Charitable Immunity Abolished; and Qualified Immunity for Volunteers.

§ 1-539.9. Defense abolished as to actions arising after September 1, 1967.

The common-law defense of charitable immunity is abolished and shall not constitute a valid defense to any action or cause of action arising subsequent to September 1, 1967. (1967, c. 856.)

§ 1-539.10. Immunity from civil liability for volunteers.

(a) A volunteer who performs services for a charitable organization or a volunteer engaged in providing emergency services is not liable in civil damages for any acts or omissions resulting in any injury, death, or loss to person or property arising from the volunteer services rendered if:

(1) The volunteer was acting in good faith and the services rendered were reasonable under the circumstances; and

(2) The acts or omissions do not amount to gross negligence, wanton conduct, or intentional wrongdoing.

(3) The acts or omissions did not occur while the volunteer was operating or responsible for the operation of a motor vehicle.

(b) To the extent that any charitable organization or volunteer has liability insurance, that charitable organization or volunteer shall be deemed to have waived the qualified immunity herein to the extent of indemnification by insurance for the negligence by any volunteer.

(c) Nothing herein shall be construed to alter the standard of care requirement or liability of persons rendering professional services. (1987, c. 505, s. 1(2); 2005-273, s. 1.)

§ 1-539.11. Definitions.

As used in this Article:

(1) "Charitable Organization" means an organization that has humane and philanthropic objectives, whose activities benefit humanity or a significant rather than limited segment of the community without expectation of pecuniary profit or reward and is exempt from taxation under either G.S. 105-130.11(a)(3) or G.S. 105-130.11(a)(5) or Section 501(c)(3) of the Internal Revenue Code of 1954.

(1a) "Emergency services" means the preparation for and the carrying out of functions to prevent, minimize, and repair injury and damage resulting from natural or man-made disasters and all other activities necessary or incidental to the preparation for and carrying out of these functions. These functions include firefighting services, police services, medical and health services, rescue services, engineering services, land surveying services, warning services and communications, radiological, chemical and other special weapons defense services, evacuation of persons from stricken areas, emergency welfare services, including providing emergency shelter, emergency transportation, and emergency resource management services, existing or properly assigned plant protection services, temporary restoration of public utility services, services performed as a function of a Medical Reserve Corps (MRC) unit or a Community Emergency Response Team (CERT), and other functions related to civilian protection, including the administration of approved State and federal disaster recovery and assistance programs.

(2) "Volunteer" means an individual, serving as a direct service volunteer performing services for a charitable, nonprofit organization, who does not receive compensation, or anything of value in lieu of compensation, for the services, other than reimbursement for expenses actually incurred or any person providing emergency services without any financial gain. (1987, c. 505, s. 1(2); 2005-273, s. 2.)

§ 1-539.12. Immunity from civil liability for employers disclosing information.

(a) An employer who discloses information about a current or former employee's job history or job performance to a prospective employer of the current or former employee upon request of the prospective employer or upon request of the current or former employee is immune from civil liability and is not liable in civil damages for the disclosure or any consequences of the disclosure. This immunity shall not apply when a claimant shows by a preponderance of the evidence both of the following:

(1) The information disclosed by the current or former employer was false.

(2) The employer providing the information knew or reasonably should have known that the information was false.

(b) For purposes of this section, "job performance" includes:

(1) The suitability of the employee for re-employment;

(2) The employee's skills, abilities, and traits as they may relate to suitability for future employment; and

(3) In the case of a former employee, the reason for the employee's separation.

(c) The provisions of this section apply to any employee, agent, or other representative of the current or former employer who is authorized to provide and who provides information in accordance with the provisions of this section. For the purposes of this section, "employer" also includes a job placement service but does not include a private personnel service as defined in G.S. 95-47.1 or a job listing service as defined in G.S. 95-47.19 except as provided hereinafter. The provisions of this section apply to a private personnel service as defined in G.S, 95-47.1 and a job listing service as defined in G.S. 95-47.19 only to the extent that the service conveys information derived from credit reports, court records, educational records, and information furnished to it by the employee or prior employers and the service identifies the source of the information.

(d) This section does not affect any privileges or immunities from civil liability established by another section of the General Statutes or available at common law. (1997-478, s. 1.)

§ 1-539.13. Reserved for future codification purposes.

§ 1-539.14. Reserved for future codification purposes.

Article 43C.

Actions Pertaining to Local Units of Government.

§ 1-539.15: Repealed by Session Laws 1981, c. 777, s. 1.

§ 1-539.16. Notice of claims against local units of government.

No local act, including city charters, shall require a notice to a local unit of government of any claim against it and prohibit suit against the local unit if notice is not given or limit the period during which an action may be brought on such a claim after notice has been given. (1981, c. 777, s. 2.)

§ 1-539.17. Reserved for future codification purposes.

§ 1-539.18. Reserved for future codification purposes.

§ 1-539.19. Reserved for future codification purposes.

§ 1-539.20. Reserved for future codification purposes.

Article 43D.

Abolition of Parent-Child Immunity in Motor Vehicle Cases.

§ 1-539.21. Abolition of parent-child immunity in motor vehicle cases.

The relationship of parent and child shall not bar the right of action by a person or his estate against his parent or child for wrongful death, personal injury, or property damage arising out of operation of a motor vehicle owned or operated by the parent or child. (1975, c. 685, s. 1; 1985, c. 201; 1989, c. 782, s. 2.)

§ 1-539.22. Reserved for future codification purposes.

§ 1-539.23. Reserved for future codification purposes.

§ 1-539.24. Reserved for future codification purposes.

Article 43E.

Affirmative Defense Based on Year 2000 Failure.

§ 1-539.25. Expired October 1, 2000 (see previous document versions for former law).

§ 1-539.26. Expired October 1, 2000. (see previous document versions for former law)

SUBCHAPTER XV. INCIDENTAL PROCEDURE IN CIVIL ACTIONS.

Article 44.

Compromise.

§ 1-540. By agreement receipt of less sum is discharge.

In all claims, or money demands, of whatever kind, and howsoever due, where an agreement is made and accepted for a less amount than that demanded or claimed to be due, in satisfaction thereof, the payment of the less amount according to such agreement in compromise of the whole is a full and complete discharge of the same. (1874-5, c. 178; Code, s. 574; Rev., s. 859; C.S., s. 895.)

§ 1-540.1. Effect of release of original wrongdoer on liability of physicians and surgeons for malpractice.

The compromise settlement or release of a cause of action against a person responsible for a personal injury to another shall not operate as a bar to an action by the injured party against a physician or surgeon or other professional practitioner treating such injury for the negligent treatment thereof, unless the express terms of the compromise, settlement or release agreement given by the injured party to the person responsible for the initial injury provide otherwise. (1961, c. 212.)

§ 1-540.2. Settlement of property damage claims arising from motor vehicle collisions or accidents; same not to constitute admission of liability, nor bar party seeking damages for bodily injury or death.

In any claim, civil action, or potential civil action which arises out of a motor vehicle collision or accident, settlement of any property damage claim arising from such collision or accident, whether such settlement be made by an individual, a self-insurer, or by an insurance carrier under a policy of insurance, shall not constitute an admission of liability on the part of the person, self-insurer or insurance carrier making such settlement, which arises out of the same motor vehicle collision or accident. It shall be incompetent for any claimant or party plaintiff in the said civil action to offer into evidence, either by oral testimony or paper writing, the fact that a settlement of the property damage claim arising from such collision or accident has been made; provided further, that settlement made of such property damage claim arising out of a motor vehicle collision or accident shall not in and of itself act as a bar, release, accord and satisfaction, or discharge of any claims other than the property damage claim, unless by the written terms of a properly executed settlement agreement it is specifically stated that the acceptance of said settlement constitutes full settlement of all claims and causes of action arising out of the said motor vehicle collision or accident. (1967, c. 662, s. 1.)

§ 1-540.3. Advance payments.

(a)   In any claim, potential civil action or action in which any person claims to have sustained bodily injuries, advance or partial payment or payments to any such person claiming to have sustained bodily injuries or to the personal representative of any person claimed to have sustained fatal injuries may be made to such person or such personal representative by the person or party against whom such claim is made or by the insurance carrier for the person, party, corporation, association or entity which is or may be liable for such injuries or death. Such advance or partial payment or payments shall not constitute an admission of liability on the part of the person, party, corporation, association or entity on whose behalf the payment or payments are made or by the insurance carrier making the payments. It shall be incompetent for any party in a civil action to offer into evidence, through any witness either by oral testimony or paper writing, the fact of the advance or partial payment or payments made by or on behalf of the opposing party. The receipt of the advance or partial payment or payments shall not in and of itself act as a bar, release, accord and satisfaction, or a discharge of any claims of the person or representative receiving the advance or partial payment or payments, unless by the terms of a properly executed settlement agreement it is specifically stated that the acceptance of said payment or payments constitutes full settlement of all claims and causes of action for personal injuries or wrongful death, as applicable.

(b) In any civil action for personal injuries or wrongful death the person or party against whom claim is made for such injuries or death and by or on whose behalf advance or partial payment or payments have been made to the party asserting the claim shall file with the Court and serve upon opposing counsel a motion setting out the date and amount of payment or payments and praying that said sums be credited upon any judgment recovered by the opposing party against the party on whose behalf the payment or payments were made. Prior to the entry of judgment, the trial judge shall conduct a hearing and may consider affidavits, oral testimony, depositions, and any other competent evidence, and shall enter his findings of fact and conclusions of law as to whether the advance or partial payment or payments were made by or on behalf of the person or party claiming to have made such payment(s) to the party asserting the claim for injuries or wrongful death. Upon a finding that the advance or partial payment or payments were made by or on behalf of the person or party claiming to have made such payment(s), all such payments shall be credited by the trial judge upon any judgment rendered in favor of the person or representative who received the payment or payments. Advance payments made by one joint tort-feasor shall not inure to the benefit or credit of any joint tort-feasor not making such payments.

No claim for reimbursement may be made or allowed by or on behalf of the person or party making such advance payment or payments against the person or party to whom such payment or payments are made except a claim based on fraud.

The making of any advance payment shall not affect in any way whatsoever the running of the statute of limitations. (1971, c. 854.)

§§ 1-541 through 1-543. Repealed by Session Laws 1967, c. 954, s. 4.

Article 44A

Tender.

§ 1-543.1. Service of order of tender; return.

In all matters in which it is proper or necessary to make or serve a tender, the clerk of the superior court in the county in which the tender is to be made shall, upon request of the tendering party, direct the sheriff of said county to serve an order of tender, together with the property to be tendered, upon the party or parties upon whom said tender is to be made. In the event said property is incapable of being manually tendered, said order of tender shall so state and service of said order tendering same shall have the same legal effect as if the property had been manually tendered. Within five days after receipt of the order, the sheriff shall make his return thereon, showing upon whom the same was served, the date and hour of service, the property tendered, and whether or not said tender was accepted, or that, after due diligence, the party or parties upon whom service was to be made could not be found within the county. He shall then return said order of tender to the clerk who issued it, and this shall constitute proper tender. Nothing in this section shall be construed to prevent other methods of tender or tender by any party to an action in open court upon any other party to said action. (1965, c. 699.)

§ 1-543.2. Reserved for future codification purposes.

§ 1-543.3. Reserved for future codification purposes.

§ 1-543.4. Reserved for future codification purposes.

§ 1-543.5. Reserved for future codification purposes.

§ 1-543.6. Reserved for future codification purposes.

§ 1-543.7. Reserved for future codification purposes.

§ 1-543.8. Reserved for future codification purposes.

§ 1-543.9. Reserved for future codification purposes.

Article 44B

Structured Settlement Protection Act.

§ 1-543.10. Title.

This Article may be cited as the North Carolina Structured Settlement Protection Act. (1999-367, s. 1.)

§ 1-543.11. Definitions.

For purposes of this Article:

(1) "Annuity issuer" means an insurer that has issued an annuity or insurance contract used to fund periodic payments under a structured settlement;

(2) "Discounted present value" means the fair present value of future payments, as determined by discounting such payments to the present utilizing the tables adopted in Article 5 of Chapter 8 of the General Statutes;

(3) "Independent professional advice" means advice of an attorney, certified public accountant, actuary, or other licensed or registered professional or financial adviser:

a. Who is engaged by a payee to render advice concerning the legal, tax, and financial implications of a transfer of structured settlement payment rights;

b. Who is not in any manner affiliated with or compensated by the transferee of such transfer; and

c. Whose compensation for rendering such advice is not affected by whether a transfer occurs or does not occur;

(4) "Interested parties" means, with respect to any structured settlement, the payee, any beneficiary designated under the annuity contract to receive payments following the payee's death, the annuity issuer, the structured settlement obligor, and any other party that has continuing rights or obligations under the terms of the structured settlement;

(5) "Payee" means an individual who is receiving tax-free damage payments under a structured settlement and proposes to make a transfer of payment rights thereunder;

(6) "Qualified assignment agreement" means an agreement providing for a qualified assignment within the meaning of section 130 of the Internal Revenue Code, United States Code Title 26, as amended from time to time;

(7) "Responsible administrative authority" means, with respect to a structured settlement, any government authority vested by law with exclusive jurisdiction over the settled claim resolved by such structured settlement;

(8) "Settled claim" means the original tort claim resolved by a structured settlement;

(9) "Structured settlement" means an arrangement for periodic payment of damages for personal injuries established by settlement or judgment in resolution of a tort claim;

(10) "Structured settlement agreement" means the agreement, judgment, stipulation, or release embodying the terms of a structured settlement, including the rights of the payee to receive periodic payments;

(11) "Structured settlement obligor" means, with respect to any structured settlement, the party that has the continuing periodic payment obligation to the payee under a structured settlement agreement or a qualified assignment agreement;

(12) "Structured settlement payment rights" means rights to receive periodic payments (including lump-sum payments) under a structured settlement, whether from the settlement obligor or the annuity issuer, where:

a. The payee is domiciled in this State;

b. The structured settlement agreement was approved by a court or responsible administrative authority in this State; or

c. The settled claim was pending before the courts of this State when the parties entered into the structured settlement agreement;

(13) "Terms of the structured settlement" include, with respect to any structured settlement, the terms of the structured settlement agreement, the annuity contract, any qualified assignment agreement, and any order or approval of any court or responsible administrative authority or other government authority authorizing or approving such structured settlement; and

(14) "Transfer" means any sale, assignment, pledge, hypothecation, or other form of alienation or encumbrance made by a payee for consideration;

(15) "Transfer agreement" means the agreement providing for transfer of structured settlement payment rights from a payee to a transferee. (1999-367, s. 1.)

§ 1-543.12. Structured settlement payment rights.

No direct or indirect transfer of structured settlement payment rights shall be effective, and no structured settlement obligor or annuity issuer shall be required to make any payment directly or indirectly to any transferee of structured settlement payment rights unless the transfer has been authorized in advance in a final order of a court of competent jurisdiction or a responsible administrative authority based on express findings by such court or responsible administrative authority that:

(1) The transfer complies with the requirements of this Article [of] law;

(2) Not less than 10 days prior to the date on which the payee first incurred any obligation with respect to the transfer, the transferee has provided to the payee a disclosure statement in bold type, no smaller than 14 point setting forth:

a. The amounts and due dates of the structured settlement payments to be transferred;

b. The aggregate amount of such payments;

c. The discounted present value of such payments;

d. The gross amount payable to the payee in exchange for such payments;

e. An itemized listing of all brokers' commissions, service charges, application fees, processing fees, closing costs, filing fees, administrative fees, legal fees, notary fees and other commissions, fees, costs, expenses, and charges payable by the payee or deductible from the gross amount otherwise payable to the payee;

f. The net amount payable to the payee after deduction of all commissions, fees, costs, expenses, and charges described in sub-subdivision e. of this subdivision;

g. The quotient (expressed as a percentage) obtained by dividing the net payment amount by the discounted present value of the payments;

h. The discount rate used by the transferee to determine the net amount payable to the payee for the structured settlement payments to be transferred; and

i. The amount of any penalty and the aggregate amount of any liquidated damages (inclusive of penalties) payable by the payee in the event of any breach of the transfer agreement by the payee;

(3) The transfer is in the best interest of the payee;

(4) The payee has received independent professional advice regarding the legal, tax, and financial implications of the transfer;

(5) The transferee has given written notice of the transferee's name, address, and taxpayer identification number to the annuity issuer and the structured settlement obligor and has filed a copy of such notice with the court or responsible administrative authority;

(6) The discount rate used in determining the net amount payable to the payee, as provided in subdivision (2) of this section, does not exceed an annual percentage rate of prime plus five percentage points calculated as if the net amount payable to the payee, as provided in sub-subdivision (2)f. of this

section, was the principal of a consumer loan made by the transferee to the payee, and if the structured settlement payments to be transferred to the transferee were the payee's payments of principal plus interest on such loan. For purposes of this subdivision, the prime rate shall be as reported by the Federal Reserve Statistical Release H.15 on the first Monday of the month in which the transfer agreement is signed by both the payee and the transferee, except when the transfer agreement is signed prior to the first Monday of that month then the prime rate shall be as reported by the Federal Reserve Statistical Release H.15 on the first Monday of the preceding month;

(7) Any brokers' commissions, service charges, application fees, processing fees, closing costs, filing fees, administrative fees, notary fees and other commissions, fees, costs, expenses, and charges payable by the payee or deductible from the gross amount otherwise payable to the payee do not exceed two percent (2%) of the net amount payable to the payee;

(8) The transfer of structured settlement payment rights is fair and reasonable; and

(9) Notwithstanding a provision of the structured settlement agreement prohibiting an assignment by the payee, the court may order a transfer of periodic payment rights provided that the court finds that the provisions of this Article are satisfied.

If the court or responsible administrative authority authorizes the transfer pursuant to this section, the court or responsible administrative authority shall order the structured settlement obligor to execute an acknowledgment of assignment letter on behalf of the transferee for the amount of the structured settlement payment rights to be transferred; provided, however, structured settlement payment rights arising from a claim pursuant to Chapter 97 shall not be authorized. (1999-367, s. 1; 1999-456, s. 67.)

§ 1-543.13. Jurisdiction

(a) Where the structured settlement agreement was entered into after commencement of litigation or administrative proceedings in this State, the court or administrative agency where the action was pending shall have exclusive jurisdiction over any application for authorization under this Article of a transfer of structured settlement payment rights.

(b) Where the structured settlement agreement was entered into prior to the commencement of litigation or administrative proceedings, or after the commencement of litigation outside this State, the Superior Court Division of the General Court of Justice shall have nonexclusive original jurisdiction over any application for authorization under this Article of a transfer of structured settlement payment rights. (1999-367, s. 1.)

§ 1-543.14. Procedure for approval of transfers

(a) Where the structured settlement agreement was entered into after the commencement of litigation or administrative proceedings in this State, the application for authorization of a transfer of structured settlement rights shall be filed with the court or administrative agency where the settled claim was pending as a motion in the cause.

(b) Where the structured settlement agreement was entered into prior to the commencement of litigation or administrative proceedings, or after the commencement of litigation or administrative proceedings outside this State, the application for authorization of a transfer of structured settlement payment rights shall be filed in the superior court with proper venue pursuant to Article 7 of this Chapter. The nature of the action shall be a special proceeding governed by the provisions of Article 33 of this Chapter.

(c) Not less than 30 days prior to the scheduled hearing on any application for authorization of a transfer of structured settlement payment rights under this Article, the transferee shall file with the proper court or responsible administrative authority and serve on any other government authority which previously approved the structured settlement, on all interested parties as defined in G.S. 1-543.11(4), and on the Attorney General, a notice of the proposed transfer and the application for its authorization, including in such notice:

(1) A copy of the transferee's application;

(2) A copy of the transfer agreement;

(3) A copy of the disclosure statement required under G.S. 1-543.12(a)(2);

(4) Notification that any interested party is entitled to support, oppose, or otherwise respond to the transferee's application, either in person or by counsel,

by submitting written comments to the court or responsible administrative authority or by participating in the hearing; and

(5)   Notification of the time and place of the hearing and notification of the manner in which and the time by which written responses to the application must be filed in order to be considered by the court or responsible administrative authority.

(d)   The Attorney General shall have standing to raise, appear, and be heard on any matter relating to an application for authorization of a transfer of structured settlement payment rights under this Article. (1999-367, s. 1.)

§ 1-543.15. No waiver; penalties.

(a)   The provisions of this Article may not be waived.

(b)   Any payee who has transferred structured settlement payment rights to a transferee without complying with this Article may bring an action against the transferee to recover actual monetary loss or for damages up to five thousand dollars ($5,000) for the violation by the transferee, or bring actions for both. The payee is entitled to attorneys' fees and costs incurred to enforce this Article. In addition, all unpaid structured settlement payment rights transferred in violation of this Article by any transferee shall be reconveyed to the payee.

(c)   No payee who proposes to make a transfer of structured settlement payment rights shall incur any penalty, forfeit any application fee or other payment, or otherwise incur any liability to the proposed transferee based on any failure of such transfer to satisfy the conditions of this Article. (1999-367, s. 1.)

Article 45.

Arbitration and Award.

§§ 1-544 through 1-567. Repealed by Session Laws 1973, c. 676, s. 1.

Article 45A.

Arbitration and Award.

§§ 1-567.1 through 1-567.20: Repealed by Session Laws 2003-345, s. 1, effective January 1, 2004, and applicable to agreements to arbitrate made on or after that date.

§ 1-567.21. Reserved for future codification purposes.

§ 1-567.22. Reserved for future codification purposes.

§ 1-567.23. Reserved for future codification purposes.

§ 1-567.24. Reserved for future codification purposes.

§ 1-567.25. Reserved for future codification purposes.

§ 1-567.26. Reserved for future codification purposes.

§ 1-567.27. Reserved for future codification purposes.

§ 1-567.28. Reserved for future codification purposes.

§ 1-567.29. Reserved for future codification purposes.

Article 45B.

International Commercial Arbitration and Conciliation.

Part 1. General Provisions.

§ 1-567.30. Preamble and short title.

It is the policy of the State of North Carolina to promote and facilitate international trade and commerce, and to provide a forum for the resolution of disputes that may arise from participation therein. Pursuant to this policy, the purpose of this Article is to encourage the use of arbitration or conciliation as a means of resolving such disputes, to provide rules for the conduct of arbitration or conciliation proceedings, and to assure access to the courts of this State for legal proceedings ancillary to such arbitration or conciliation. This Article shall be known as the North Carolina International Commercial Arbitration and Conciliation Act. (1991, c. 292, s. 1; 1997-368, ss. 1, 2, 5.)

§ 1-567.31. Scope of application.

(a) This Article applies to international commercial arbitration and conciliation, subject to any applicable international agreement in force between the United States of America and any other nation or nations, or any federal statute.

(b) The provisions of this Article, except G.S. 1-567.38, 1-567.39, and 1-567.65, apply only if the place of arbitration is in this State.

(c) An arbitration or conciliation is international if:

(1) The parties to the arbitration or conciliation agreement have their places of business in different nations when the agreement is concluded; or

(2) One or more of the following places is situated outside the nations in which the parties have their places of business:

a. The place of arbitration or conciliation if determined pursuant to the arbitration agreement;

b. Any place where a substantial part of the obligations of the commercial relationship is to be performed; or

c. The place with which the subject matter of the dispute is most closely connected; or

(3) The parties have expressly agreed that the subject matter of the arbitration or conciliation agreement relates to more than one nation.

(d) For the purposes of subsection (c) of this section:

(1) If a party has more than one place of business, the place of business is that which has the closest relationship to the arbitration or conciliation agreement;

(2) If a party does not have a place of business, reference is to be made to the party's domicile.

(e) An arbitration or conciliation, respectively, is deemed commercial for the purposes of this Article if it arises out of a relationship of a commercial nature, including, but not limited to the following:

(1) A transaction for the exchange of goods and services;

(2) A distribution agreement;

(3) A commercial representation or agency;

(4) An exploitation agreement or concession;

(5) A joint venture or other related form of industrial or business cooperation;

(6) The carriage of goods or passengers by air, sea, land, or road;

(7) A contract or agreement relating to construction, insurance, licensing, factoring, leasing, consulting, engineering, financing, or banking;

(8) The transfer of data or technology;

(9) The use or transfer of intellectual or industrial property, including trade secrets, trademarks, trade names, patents, copyrights, and software programs;

(10) A contract for the provision of any type of professional service, whether provided by an employee or an independent contractor.

(f) This Article shall not affect any other law in force by virtue of which certain disputes may not be submitted to arbitration, conciliation, or mediation, or may be submitted to arbitration, conciliation, or mediation only according to provisions other than those of this Article.

(g) This Article shall not apply to any agreement providing explicitly that it shall not be subject to the North Carolina International Commercial Arbitration and Conciliation Act. This Article shall not apply to any agreement executed prior to June 13, 1991. (1991, c. 292, s. 1; 1997-141, s. 1; 1997-368, s. 6.)

§ 1-567.32. Definitions and rules of interpretation.

(a) For the purposes of this Article:

(1) "Arbitral award" means any decision of an arbitral tribunal on the substance of a dispute submitted to it, and includes an interlocutory, or partial award;

(2) "Arbitral tribunal" means a sole arbitrator or a panel of arbitrators;

(3) "Arbitration" means any arbitration whether or not administered by a permanent arbitral institution;

(4) "Party" means a party to an arbitration agreement;

(5) "Superior court" means the superior court of any county in this State selected pursuant to G.S. 1-567.36.

(b) Where a provision of this Article, except G.S. 1-567.58, leaves the parties free to determine a certain issue, such freedom includes the right of the parties to authorize a third party, including an institution, to make that determination.

(c) Where a provision of this Article refers to the fact that the parties have agreed or that they may agree or in any other way refers to an agreement of the parties, such agreement includes any arbitration rules referred to in that agreement.

(d) Where a provision of this Article, other than in G.S. 1-567.55(1) and G.S. 1-567.62(b)(1), refers to a claim, it also applies to a counterclaim, and where it refers to a defense, it also applies to a defense to such counterclaim. (1991, c. 292.)

§ 1-567.33. Receipt of written communications or submissions.

(a) Unless otherwise agreed by the parties, any written communication or submission is deemed to have been received if it is delivered to the addressee personally or if it is delivered at the addressee's place of business, domicile or mailing address and the communication or submission is deemed to have been received on the day it is so delivered. Delivery by facsimile transmission shall constitute valid receipt if the communication or submission is in fact received.

(b) If none of the places referred to in subsection (a) can be found after making reasonable inquiry, a written communication or submission is deemed to have been received if it is sent to the addressee's last known place of business, domicile or mailing address by registered mail or any other means which provide a record of the attempt to deliver it.

(c) The provisions of this Article do not apply to a written communication or submission relating to a court, administrative or special proceeding. (1991, c. 292.)

§ 1-567.33A. Severability.

In the event any provision of this act is held to be invalid, the court's holding as to that provision shall not affect the validity or operation of other provisions of the act; and to that end the provisions of the act are severable. (1991, c. 292, s. 1; 1997-368, s. 3.)

Part 2. International Commercial Arbitration.

§ 1-567.34. Waiver of right to object.

A party who knows that any provision of this Article or any requirement under the arbitration agreement has not been complied with and yet proceeds with the arbitration without stating an objection to such noncompliance without undue delay or, if a time limit is provided therefor, within that period of time, shall be deemed to have waived any right to object. (1991, c. 292.)

§ 1-567.35. Extent of court intervention.

In matters governed by this Article, no court shall intervene except where so provided in this Article or applicable federal law or any applicable international agreement in force between the United States of America and any other nation or nations. (1991, c. 292.)

§ 1-567.36. Venue and jurisdiction of courts

(a) The functions referred to in G.S. 1-567.41(c) and (d), 1-567.43(a), 1-567.44(b), 1-567.46(c), and 1-567.57 shall be performed by the superior court in:

(1) The county where the arbitration agreement is to be performed or was made;

(2) If the arbitration agreement does not specify a county where the agreement is to be performed and the agreement was not made in any county in the State of North Carolina, the county where any party to the court proceeding resides or has a place of business;

(3) In any case not covered by subdivisions (1) or (2) of this subsection, in any county in the State of North Carolina.

(b) All other functions assigned by this Article to the superior court shall be performed by the superior court of the county in which the place of arbitration is located. (1991, c. 292.)

§ 1-567.37. Definition and form of arbitration agreement.

(a) An "arbitration agreement" is an agreement by the parties to submit to arbitration all or certain disputes which have arisen or which may arise between them in respect of a defined legal relationship, whether or not contractual. An arbitration agreement may be in the form of an arbitration clause in a contract or in the form of a separate agreement.

(b) The arbitration agreement shall be in writing. An agreement is in writing if it is contained in a document signed by the parties or in an exchange of letters, telex, telegrams, facsimile transmission, or other means of telecommunication which provide a record of the agreement, or in an exchange of statements of claim and defense in which the existence of an agreement is alleged by one party and not denied by another. The reference in a contract to a document containing an arbitration clause constitutes an arbitration agreement provided that the contract is in writing and the reference is such as to make that clause part of the contract.

(c) Such arbitration agreement shall be valid, enforceable and irrevocable, except with the consent of all the parties, without regard to the justiciable character of the controversy. (1991, c. 292.)

§ 1-567.38. Arbitration agreement and substantive claim before court.

(a)   When a party to an international commercial arbitration agreement as defined in this Article commences judicial proceedings seeking relief with respect to a matter covered by the agreement to arbitrate, any other party to the agreement may apply to the superior court for an order to stay the proceedings and compel arbitration.

(b)   Arbitration proceedings may begin or continue, and an award may be made, while an action described in subsection (a) is pending before the court. (1991, c. 292.)

§ 1-567.39. Interim relief and the enforcement of interim measures.

(a)   In the case of an arbitration where the arbitrator or arbitrators have not been appointed, or where the arbitrator or arbitrators are unavailable, a party may seek interim relief directly from the superior court as provided in subsection (c). Enforcement shall be granted as provided by the law applicable to the type of interim relief sought.

(b)   In all other cases, a party shall seek interim measures under G.S. 1-567.47 from the arbitral tribunal and shall have no right to seek interim relief from the superior court, except that a party to an arbitration governed by this Article may request from the superior court enforcement of an order of an arbitral tribunal granting interim measures under G.S. 1-567.47.

(c)   In connection with an agreement to arbitrate or a pending arbitration, the superior court may grant, pursuant to subsection (a) of this section:

(1)   An order of attachment or garnishment;

(2)   A temporary restraining order or preliminary injunction;

(3)   An order for claim and delivery;

(4)   The appointment of a receiver;

(5)   Delivery of money or other property into court;

(6) Any other order that may be necessary to ensure the preservation or availability either of assets or of documents, the destruction or absence of which would be likely to prejudice the conduct or effectiveness of the arbitration.

(d) In considering a request for interim relief or the enforcement of interim measures, the court shall give preclusive effect to any finding of fact of the arbitral tribunal in the proceeding, including the probable validity of the claim that is the subject of the interim relief sought or the interim measures granted.

(e) Where the arbitral tribunal has not ruled on an objection to its jurisdiction, the court shall not grant preclusive effect to the tribunal's findings until the court has made an independent finding as to the jurisdiction of the arbitral tribunal. If the court rules that the arbitral tribunal did not have jurisdiction, the application for interim relief or the enforcement of interim measures shall be denied. Such a ruling by the court that the arbitral tribunal lacks jurisdiction is not binding on the arbitral tribunal or subsequent judicial proceedings.

(f) The availability of interim relief under this section may be limited by prior written agreement of the parties. (1991, c. 292, s. 1.)

§ 1-567.40. Number of arbitrators.

There shall be one arbitrator unless the parties agree on a greater number of arbitrators. (1991, c. 292.)

§ 1-567.41. Appointment of arbitrators.

(a) A person of any nationality may be an arbitrator.

(b) The parties may agree on a procedure of appointing the arbitral tribunal subject to the provisions of subsections (d) and (e) of this section.

(c) (1) If an agreement is not made under subsection (b) of this section, in an arbitration with three arbitrators, each party shall appoint one arbitrator, and the two arbitrators thus appointed shall appoint the third arbitrator; if a party fails to appoint the arbitrator within 30 days of receipt of a request to do so from the other party, or if the two arbitrators fail to agree on the third arbitrator within

30 days of their appointment, the appointment shall be made, upon request of a party, by the superior court.

(2) In an arbitration with a sole arbitrator, if the parties are unable to agree on the arbitrator, a sole arbitrator shall be appointed, upon request of a party, by the superior court.

(3) In an arbitration involving more than two parties, if no agreement is reached under subsection (b) of this section, the superior court, on request of a party, shall appoint one or more arbitrators, as provided in G.S. 1-567.40.

(d) The superior court, on request of any party, may take the necessary measures, unless the agreement on the appointment procedure provides other means for securing the appointment, if, under an appointment procedure agreed upon by the parties:

(1) A party fails to act as required under such procedure; or

(2) The parties, or two arbitrators, are unable to reach an agreement expected of them under such procedure; or

(3) A third party, including an institution, fails to perform any function entrusted to it under such procedure.

(e) A decision of the superior court on a matter entrusted by subsection (c) or (d) of this section shall be final and not subject to appeal.

(f) The superior court, in appointing an arbitrator, shall consider:

(1) Any qualifications required of the arbitrator by the agreement of the parties;

(2) Such other considerations as are likely to secure the appointment of an independent and impartial arbitrator;

(3) In the case of a sole or third arbitrator, the advisability of appointing an arbitrator of a nationality other than those of the parties.

(g) The parties may agree to employ an established arbitration institution to conduct the arbitration. If they do not so agree, the superior court may in its discretion designate an established arbitration institution to conduct the arbitration.

(h)   Unless otherwise agreed, an arbitrator shall be entitled to compensation at an hourly or daily rate which reflects the size and complexity of the case, and the experience of the arbitrator. If the parties are unable to agree on such a rate, the rate shall be determined by the arbitral institution chosen pursuant to subsection (g) of this section or by the arbitral tribunal, in either case subject to the review of the superior court upon the motion of any dissenting party. (1991, c. 292; 1993, c. 553, s. 6.)

§ 1-567.42. Grounds for challenge.

(a)   Except as otherwise provided in this Article, all persons whose names have been submitted for consideration for appointment or designation as arbitrators, or who have been appointed or designated as such, shall make a disclosure to the parties within 15 days of such submission, appointment, or designation of any information which might cause their impartiality to be questioned including, but not limited to, any of the following instances:

(1)   The person has a personal bias or prejudice concerning a party, or personal knowledge of disputed evidentiary facts concerning the proceeding;

(2)   The person served as a lawyer in the matter in controversy, or the person is or has been associated with another who has participated in the matter during such association, or has been a material witness concerning it;

(3)   The person served as an arbitrator in another proceeding involving one or more of the parties to the proceeding;

(4)   The person, individually or as a fiduciary, or such person's spouse or minor child residing in such person's household, has a financial interest in the subject matter in controversy or in a party to the proceeding, or any other interest that could be substantially affected by the outcome of the proceeding;

(5)   The person, his or her spouse, or a person within the third degree of relationship to either of them, or the spouse of such a person meets any of the following conditions:

a. The person is or has been a party to the proceeding, or an officer, director, or trustee of a party;

b. The person is acting or has acted as a lawyer in the proceeding;

c. The person is known to have an interest that could be substantially affected by the outcome of the proceeding;

d. The person is likely to be a material witness in the proceeding;

(6) The person has a close personal or professional relationship with a person who meets any of the following conditions:

a. The person is or has been a party to the proceeding, or an officer, director, or trustee of a party;

b. The person is acting or has acted as a lawyer or representative in the proceeding;

c. The person is or expects to be nominated as an arbitrator or conciliator in the proceeding;

d. The person is known to have an interest that could be substantially affected by the outcome of the proceeding;

e. The person is likely to be a material witness in the proceeding.

(b) The obligation to disclose information set forth in subsection (a) of this section is mandatory and cannot be waived as to the parties with respect to persons serving either as sole arbitrator or as the chief or prevailing arbitrator. The parties may otherwise agree to waive such disclosure.

(c) From the time of appointment and throughout the arbitral proceedings, an arbitrator shall disclose to the parties without delay any circumstances referred to in subsection (a) of this section which were not previously disclosed.

(d) Unless otherwise agreed by the parties or the rules governing the arbitration, an arbitrator may be challenged only if circumstances exist that give rise to justifiable doubts as to his or her independence or impartiality, or as to his or her possession of the qualifications upon which the parties have agreed.

(e) A party may challenge an arbitrator appointed by it, or in whose appointment it has participated only for reasons of which it becomes aware after the appointment has been made. (1991, c. 292.)

§ 1-567.43. Challenge procedure.

(a) The parties may agree on a procedure for challenging an arbitrator, subject to the provisions of subsection (c) of this section.

(b) If there is no agreement under subsection (a) of this section, a party challenging an arbitrator shall, within 15 days after becoming aware of the constitution of the arbitral tribunal or after becoming aware of any circumstance referred to in G.S. 1-567.42(a), send a written statement of the reasons for the challenge to the arbitral tribunal. Unless the challenged arbitrator withdraws or the other party agrees to the challenge, the arbitral tribunal shall decide on the challenge.

(c) If a challenge under any procedure agreed upon by the parties or under the procedure of subsection (b) of this section is not successful, the challenging party may, within 30 days after having received notice of the decision rejecting the challenge, request the superior court to decide on the challenge, which decision shall be final and subject to no appeal. While such a request is pending, the arbitral tribunal, including the challenged arbitrator, may continue to conduct the arbitral proceedings and make an award. (1991, c. 292.)

§ 1-567.44. Failure or impossibility to act.

(a) The mandate of an arbitrator terminates if the arbitrator becomes unable to perform the arbitrator's functions or for other reasons fails to act without undue delay or the arbitrator withdraws or the parties agree to the termination.

(b) If a controversy remains concerning any of the grounds referred to in subsection (a) of this section, a party may request the superior court to decide on the termination of the mandate. The decision of the superior court shall be final and not subject to appeal.

(c) If under this section or under G.S. 1-567.43, an arbitrator withdraws or otherwise agrees to the termination of his or her mandate, no acceptance of the validity of any ground referred to in this section or G.S. 1-567.43(b) shall be implied in consequence of such action. (1991, c. 292.)

§ 1-567.45. Appointment of substitute arbitrator.

(a)   Where the mandate of an arbitrator terminates for any reason, a substitute arbitrator shall be appointed according to the rules that were applicable to the appointment of the arbitrator being replaced.

(b)   Unless otherwise agreed by the parties:

(1)   Where the number of arbitrators is less than three and an arbitrator is replaced, any hearings previously held shall be repeated;

(2)   Where the presiding arbitrator is replaced, any hearings previously held shall be repeated;

(3)   Where the number of arbitrators is three or more and an arbitrator other than the presiding arbitrator is replaced, any hearings previously held may be repeated at the discretion of the arbitral tribunal.

(c)   Unless otherwise agreed by the parties, an order or ruling of the arbitral tribunal made prior to the replacement of an arbitrator under this section is not invalid because there has been a change in the composition of the tribunal. (1991, c. 292.)

§ 1-567.46. Competence of arbitral tribunal to rule on its jurisdiction.

(a)   The arbitral tribunal may rule on its own jurisdiction, including any objections with respect to the existence or validity of the arbitration agreement. For that purpose, an arbitration clause which forms a part of a contract shall be treated as an agreement independent of the other terms of the contract. A decision by the arbitral tribunal that the contract is null and void shall not entail ipso jure the invalidity of the arbitration clause, unless the arbitral tribunal finds that the arbitration clause was obtained by fraud, whether in the inducement or in the factum.

(b)   A plea that the arbitral tribunal does not have jurisdiction shall be raised not later than the submission of the statement of defense. However, a party is not precluded from raising such a plea by the fact that the party has appointed, or participated in the appointment of, an arbitrator. A plea that the arbitral tribunal is exceeding the scope of its authority shall be raised as soon as the matter alleged to be beyond the scope of its authority is raised during the arbitral proceedings. In either case, the arbitral tribunal may admit a later plea if it considers the delay justified.

(c) The arbitral tribunal may rule on a plea referred to in subsection (b) of this section either as a preliminary question or in an award on the merits. If the arbitral tribunal rules as a preliminary question that it has jurisdiction, after having received notice of that ruling, any party may request the superior court to decide the matter. The decision of the superior court shall be final and not subject to appeal. While such a request is pending, the arbitral tribunal may continue the arbitral proceedings and make an award. (1991, c. 292.)

§ 1-567.47. Power of arbitral tribunal to order interim measures.

Unless otherwise agreed by the parties, the arbitral tribunal may, at the request of a party, order any party to take such interim measure of protection as the arbitral tribunal may consider necessary in respect of the subject matter of the dispute, including an interim measure analogous to any type of interim relief specified in G.S. 1-567.39(c). The arbitral tribunal may require any party to provide appropriate security, including security for costs as provided in G.S. 1-567.61(h)(2), in connection with such measure. (1991, c. 292.)

§ 1-567.48. Equal treatment of parties; representation by attorney.

(a) The parties shall be treated with equality and each party shall be given a full opportunity to present its case.

(b) A party has the right to be represented by an attorney at any proceeding or hearing under this Article. A waiver of this right prior to the proceeding or hearing is ineffective. (1991, c. 292, s. 1; 1997-141, s. 2.)

§ 1-567.49. Determination of rules of procedure.

(a) Subject to the provisions of this Article, the parties may agree on the procedure to be followed by the arbitral tribunal in conducting the proceedings.

(b) If there is no agreement under subsection (a) of this section, the arbitral tribunal may, subject to the provisions of this Article, conduct the arbitration in such manner as it considers appropriate. The power conferred upon the arbitral tribunal includes the power to order such discovery as it deems necessary and to determine the admissibility, relevance, materiality, and weight of any evidence. Evidence need not be limited by the rules of evidence applicable in judicial proceedings, except as to immunities and privilege. Each party shall have the burden of proving the facts relied on to support its claim, setoff, or defense. (1991, c. 292.)

§ 1-567.50. Place of arbitration.

(a) The parties may agree on the place of arbitration. If the parties do not agree, the place of arbitration shall be determined by the arbitral tribunal having regard to the circumstances of the case, including the convenience of the parties.

(b) Notwithstanding the provisions of subsection (a) of this section, the arbitral tribunal may, unless otherwise agreed by the parties, meet at any place it considers appropriate for consultation among its members, for hearing witnesses, experts or the parties, or for inspection of goods, other property, or documents. (1991, c. 292.)

§ 1-567.51. Commencement of arbitral proceedings.

Unless otherwise agreed by the parties, the arbitral proceedings in respect of a particular dispute shall commence on the date on which a request for that dispute to be referred to arbitration is received by the respondent. (1991, c. 292.)

§ 1-567.52. Language.

(a) The parties may agree on the language or languages to be used in the arbitral proceedings. If the parties do not agree, the arbitral tribunal shall determine the language or languages to be used in the proceedings. This agreement or determination, unless otherwise specified therein, shall apply to any written statement by a party, any hearing and any award, decision, or other communication by the arbitral tribunal.

(b)   The arbitral tribunal may order that any documentary evidence shall be accompanied by a translation into the language or languages agreed upon by the parties or determined by the arbitral tribunal.

(c)   The arbitral tribunal may employ one or more translators at the expense of the parties. (1991, c. 292.)

§ 1-567.53. Statements of claim and defense.

(a)   Within the period of time agreed by the parties or determined by the arbitral tribunal, the claimant shall state the facts supporting its claim, the points at issue and the relief or remedy sought, and the respondent shall state its defenses and counterclaims or setoffs in respect of these particulars, unless the parties have otherwise agreed as to the required elements of such statements. The parties may submit with their statements all documents they consider to be relevant or may add a reference to the documents or other evidence the party will submit.

(b)   Unless otherwise agreed by the parties, either party may amend or supplement a claim or defense during the course of the arbitral proceedings, unless the arbitral tribunal considers it inappropriate to allow such amendment having regard to the delay in making it.

(c)   If there are more than two parties to the arbitration, each party shall state its claims, setoffs, and defenses as provided in subsection (a) of this section. (1991, c. 292.)

§ 1-567.54. Hearings and written proceedings

(a)   Unless otherwise agreed by the parties, the arbitral tribunal shall decide whether to hold oral hearings for the presentation of evidence or for oral argument, or whether the proceedings shall be conducted on the basis of documents and other materials. Unless the parties have agreed that no hearings shall be held, the arbitral tribunal shall hold such hearings at an appropriate stage of the proceedings, if so requested by a party.

(b) The parties shall be given sufficient advance notice of any hearing and of any meeting of the arbitral tribunal for the purposes of inspection of goods, other property, or documents.

(c) All statements, documents, or other information supplied to the arbitral tribunal by one party shall be served on the other party and any expert report or evidentiary document on which the arbitral tribunal may rely in making its decision shall be served on the parties. The arbitral tribunal shall direct the timing of such service to protect the parties from undue surprise.

(d) Unless otherwise agreed by the parties, all oral hearings and meetings in arbitral proceedings shall be held in camera. Confidential information disclosed during the proceedings by the parties or by witnesses shall not be divulged by the arbitrator or arbitrators. Unless otherwise agreed by the parties, or required by applicable law, the arbitral tribunal and the parties shall keep confidential all matters relating to the arbitration and the award.

(e) The parties may agree on:

(1) The attendance of a court reporter,

(2) The creation of a transcript of proceedings, or

(3) The making of an audio or video record of proceedings, at the expense of the parties.

Any party may provide for any of the actions specified in subdivisions (1) through (3) of this subsection at that party's own expense.

(f) After asking the parties if they have any further testimony or evidentiary submissions and upon receiving negative replies or being satisfied that the record is complete, the arbitral tribunal may declare the hearings closed. The arbitral tribunal may reopen the hearings, upon terms it considers just, at any time before the award is made. (1991, c. 292.)

§ 1-567.55. Default of a party.

Unless otherwise agreed by the parties, where, without showing sufficient cause:

(1) The claimant fails to submit a statement of claim in accordance with G.S. 1-567.53(a), the arbitral tribunal shall terminate the proceedings;

(2) The respondent fails to submit a statement of defense in accordance with G.S. 1-567.53(c), the arbitral tribunal shall continue to conduct the proceedings without treating such failure in itself as an admission of the claimant's allegations;

(3) Any party fails to appear at a hearing or to produce documentary evidence as directed by the arbitral tribunal, the arbitral tribunal may continue to conduct the proceedings and make the award on the evidence before it. (1991, c. 292.)

§ 1-567.56. Expert appointed by arbitral tribunal.

(a) Unless otherwise agreed by the parties, the arbitral tribunal:

(1) May appoint one or more experts to report to it on specific issues to be determined by the arbitral tribunal;

(2) May require a party to give the expert any relevant information or to produce, or to provide access to, any relevant documents, goods, or other property for the expert's inspection.

(b) Unless otherwise agreed by the parties, if a party so requests or if the arbitral tribunal considers it necessary, the expert shall, after delivery of his written or oral report, participate in an oral hearing where the parties have the opportunity to question the expert and to present expert witnesses on the points at issue. (1991, c. 292.)

§ 1-567.57. Court assistance in obtaining discovery and taking evidence.

(a) The arbitral tribunal or a party with the approval of the arbitral tribunal may request from the superior court assistance in obtaining discovery and taking evidence. The court may execute the request within its competence and according to its rules on discovery and taking evidence, and may impose sanctions for failure to comply with its orders. A subpoena may be issued as provided by G.S. 8-59, in which case the witness compensation provisions of G.S. 6-51, 6-53, and 7A-314 shall apply.

(b) If the parties to two or more arbitration agreements agree, in their respective arbitration agreements or otherwise, to consolidate the arbitrations arising out of those agreements, the superior court, upon application by a party, may do any of the following:

(1) Order the arbitrations to be consolidated on terms the court considers just and necessary;

(2) If all the parties cannot agree on an arbitral tribunal for the consolidated arbitration, appoint an arbitral tribunal as provided by G.S. 1-567.41; and

(3) If all the parties cannot agree on any other matter necessary to conduct the consolidated arbitration, make any other order it considers necessary. (1991, c. 292, s. 1; 1999-185, s. 2.)

§ 1-567.58. Rules applicable to substance of dispute.

(a) The arbitral tribunal shall decide the dispute in accordance with such rules of law as are chosen by the parties as applicable to the substance of the dispute. Any designation of the law or legal system of a given country or political subdivision thereof shall be construed, unless otherwise expressed, as directly referring to the substantive law of that country or political subdivision and not to its conflict of laws rules.

(b) Failing any designation by the parties, the arbitral tribunal shall apply the law determined by the conflict of laws rules which it considers applicable.

(c) The arbitral tribunal shall decide ex aequo et bono (on the basis of fundamental fairness), or as amiable compositeur (as an "amiable compounder"), only if the parties have expressly authorized it to do so.

(d) In all cases, the arbitral tribunal shall decide in accordance with the terms of the contract and shall take into account the usages of the trade applicable to the transaction. (1991, c. 292, c. 761, s. 1.)

§ 1-567.59. Decision making by panel of arbitrators.

Unless otherwise agreed by the parties, in arbitral proceedings with more than one arbitrator, any decision of the arbitral tribunal shall be made by a majority of all its members. However, questions of procedure may be decided by a presiding arbitrator, if authorized by the parties or all members of the arbitral tribunal. (1991, c. 292, s. 1.)

§ 1-567.60. Settlement.

(a) An arbitral tribunal may encourage settlement of the dispute and, with the agreement of the parties, may use mediation, conciliation, or other procedures at any time during the arbitral proceedings to encourage settlement.

(b) If, during arbitral proceedings, the parties settle the dispute, the arbitral tribunal shall terminate the proceedings and, if requested by the parties and not objected to by the arbitral tribunal, record the settlement in the form of an arbitral award on agreed terms.

(c) An award on agreed terms shall be made in accordance with the provisions of G.S. 1-567.61 and shall state that it is an arbitral award. Such an award shall have the same status and effect as any other award on the substance of the dispute. (1991, c. 292.)

§ 1-567.61. Form and contents of award.

(a) The award shall be made in writing and shall be signed by the arbitrator or arbitrators. In arbitral proceedings with more than one arbitrator, the signatures of the majority of all members of the arbitral tribunal shall suffice, provided that the reason for any omitted signature is stated.

(b) The award shall not state the reasons upon which it is based, unless the parties have agreed that reasons are to be given.

(c) The award shall state its date and the place of arbitration as determined in accordance with G.S. 1-567.50. The award shall be considered to have been made at that place.

(d) After the award is made, a copy signed by the arbitrator or arbitrators in accordance with subsection (a) of this section shall be delivered to each party.

(e) The award may be denominated in foreign currency, by agreement of the parties or in the discretion of the arbitral tribunal if the parties are unable to agree.

(f) Unless otherwise agreed by the parties, the arbitral tribunal may award interest.

(g) The arbitral tribunal may award specific performance in its discretion to a party requesting an award of specific performance.

(h) (1) Unless otherwise agreed by the parties, the awarding of costs of an arbitration shall be at the discretion of the arbitral tribunal.

(2) In making an order for costs, the arbitral tribunal may include as costs:

a. The fees and expenses of the arbitrator or arbitrators, expert witnesses, and translators;

b. Fees and expenses of counsel and of the institution supervising the arbitration, if any; and

c. Any other expenses incurred in connection with the arbitral proceedings.

(3) In making an order for costs, the arbitral tribunal may specify:

a. The party entitled to costs;

b. The party who shall pay the costs;

c. The amount of costs or method of determining that amount; and

d. The manner in which the costs shall be paid. (1991, c. 292.)

§ 1-567.62. Termination of proceedings.

(a) The arbitral proceedings are terminated by the final award or by an order of the arbitral tribunal in accordance with subsection (b) of this section.

(b) The arbitral tribunal shall issue an order for the termination of the arbitral proceedings if:

(1) The claimant withdraws the claim, unless the respondent objects to the order and the arbitral tribunal recognizes a legitimate interest on the respondent's part in obtaining a final settlement of the dispute;

(2) The parties agree on the termination of the proceedings; or

(3) The arbitral tribunal finds that the continuation of the proceedings has for any other reason become unnecessary or impossible.

(c) Subject to the provisions of G.S. 1-567.63, the mandate of the arbitral tribunal terminates with the termination of the arbitral proceedings. (1991, c. 292.)

§ 1-567.63. Correction and interpretation of awards; additional awards.

(a) Within 30 days of receipt of the award, unless another period of time has been agreed upon by the parties:

(1) A party may request the arbitral tribunal to correct in the award any computation, clerical or typographical errors or other errors of a similar nature;

(2) A party may request the arbitral tribunal to give an interpretation of a specific point or part of the award.

If the arbitral tribunal considers such request to be justified, it shall make the correction or give the interpretation within 30 days of receipt of the request. Such correction or interpretation shall become part of the award.

(b) The arbitral tribunal may correct any error of the type referred to in subsection (a) on its own initiative within 30 days of the date of the award.

(c) Unless otherwise agreed by the parties, within 30 days of receipt of the award, a party may request the arbitral tribunal to make an additional award as to claims presented in the arbitral proceedings but omitted from the award. If the arbitral tribunal considers the request to be justified, it shall make the additional award within 60 days after the date of receipt of the request.

(d) The arbitral tribunal may extend, if necessary, the period within which it shall make a correction, interpretation, or an additional award under subsection (a) or (c).

(e) The provisions of G.S. 1-567.61 shall apply to a correction or interpretation of the award or to an additional award made under this section. (1991, c. 292.)

§ 1-567.64. Modifying or vacating of awards.

Subject to the relevant provisions of federal law or any applicable international agreement in force between the United States of America and any other nation or nations, an arbitral award may be vacated by a court only upon a showing that the award is tainted by illegality, or substantial unfairness in the conduct of the arbitral proceedings. In determining whether an award is so tainted, the superior court shall have regard to the provisions of this Article, and of G.S. 1-569.23 and G.S. 1-569.24, but shall not engage in de novo review of the subject matter of the dispute giving rise to the arbitration proceedings. (1991, c. 292, s. 1; 2003-345, s. 3.)

§ 1-567.65. Confirmation and enforcement of awards.

Subject to the relevant provisions of federal law or any applicable international agreement in force between the United States of America and any other nation or nations, upon application of a party, the superior court shall confirm an arbitral award, unless it finds grounds for modifying or vacating the award under G.S. 1-567.64. An award shall not be confirmed unless the time for correction and interpretation of awards prescribed by G.S. 1-567.63 shall have expired or been waived by all the parties. Upon the granting of an order confirming, modifying, or correcting an award, judgment or decree shall be entered in conformity therewith and enforced as any other judgment or decree. The superior court may award costs of the application and of the subsequent proceedings. (1991, c. 292.)

§ 1-567.66. Applications to superior court

Except as otherwise provided, an application to the superior court under this Article shall be by motion and shall be heard in the manner and upon the notice provided by law or rule of court for the making and hearing of motions. Unless the parties have agreed otherwise, notice of an initial application for an order shall be served in the manner provided by law for the service of a summons in an action. (1991, c. 292.)

§ 1-567.67. Appeals.

(a) An appeal may be taken from:

(1) An order denying an application to compel arbitration made under G.S. 1-567.38;

(2) An order granting an application to stay arbitration made under G.S. 1-567.38;

(3) An order confirming or denying confirmation of an award;

(4) An order modifying or correcting an award;

(5) An order vacating an award without directing a rehearing; or

(6) A judgment or decree entered pursuant to the provisions of this Article.

(b) The appeal shall be taken in the manner and to the same extent as from orders or judgments in a civil action. (1991, c. 292, s. 1.)

§ 1-567.68: Recodified as § 1-567.33A by Session Laws 1997-368, s. 3.

§ 1-567.69. Reserved for future codification purposes.

§ 1-567.70. Reserved for future codification purposes.

§ 1-567.71. Reserved for future codification purposes.

§ 1-567.72. Reserved for future codification purposes.

§ 1-567.73. Reserved for future codification purposes.

§ 1-567.74. Reserved for future codification purposes.

§ 1-567.75. Reserved for future codification purposes.

§ 1-567.76. Reserved for future codification purposes.

§ 1-567.77. Reserved for future codification purposes.

Part 3. International Commercial Conciliation.

§ 1-567.78. Appointment of conciliators.

(a) The parties may select or permit an arbitral tribunal or other third party to select one or more persons to serve as the conciliators.

(b) The conciliator shall assist the parties in an independent and impartial manner in the parties' attempt to reach an amicable settlement of their dispute. The conciliator shall be guided by principles of objectivity, fairness, and justice and shall give consideration to, among other things, the rights and obligations of the parties, the usages of the trade concerned, and the circumstances surrounding the dispute, including any previous practices between the parties.

(c) The conciliator may conduct the conciliation proceedings in a manner that the conciliator considers appropriate, considering the circumstances of the case, the wishes of the parties, and the desirability of a prompt settlement of the dispute. Except as otherwise provided by this Article, other provisions of the law of this State governing procedural matters do not apply to conciliation proceedings brought under this Part. (1997-368, s. 7.)

§ 1-567.79. Representation.

The parties may appear in person or be represented or assisted by any person of their choice. (1997-368, s. 7.)

§ 1-567.80. Report of conciliators.

(a) At any time during the proceedings, a conciliator may prepare a draft conciliation agreement and send copies to the parties, specifying the time within which the parties must signify their approval. The draft conciliation agreement may include the assessment and apportionment of costs between the parties.

(b) A party is not required to accept a settlement proposed by the conciliator. (1997-368, s. 7.)

§ 1-567.81. Confidentiality.

(a) Evidence of anything said or of an admission made in the course of a conciliation is not admissible, and disclosure of that evidence shall not be compelled in any arbitration or civil action in which, under law, testimony may be compelled to be given. This subsection does not limit the admissibility of evidence when all parties participating in conciliation consent to its disclosure.

(b) If evidence is offered in violation of this section, the arbitral tribunal or the court shall make any order it considers appropriate to deal with the matter, including an order restricting the introduction of evidence or dismissing the case.

(c) Unless the document otherwise provides, a document prepared for the purpose of, in the course of, or pursuant to the conciliation, or a copy of such document, is not admissible in evidence, and disclosure of the document shall not be compelled in any arbitration or civil action in which, under law, testimony may be compelled. (1997-368, s. 7.)

§ 1-567.82. Stay of arbitration; resort to other proceedings.

(a) The agreement of the parties to submit a dispute to conciliation is considered an agreement between or among those parties to stay all judicial or arbitral proceedings from the beginning of conciliation until the termination of conciliation proceedings.

(b) All applicable limitation periods, including periods of prescription, are tolled or extended on the beginning of conciliation proceedings under this Part as to all parties to the conciliation proceedings until the tenth day following the date of termination of the proceedings. For purposes of this section, conciliation proceedings are considered to have begun when the parties have all agreed to participate in the conciliation proceedings. (1997-368, s. 7.)

§ 1-567.83. Termination of conciliation.

(a) A conciliation proceeding may be terminated as to all parties by any one of the following means:

(1) On the date of the declaration, a written declaration of the conciliators that further efforts at conciliation are no longer justified.

(2) On the date of the declaration, a written declaration of the parties addressed to the conciliators that the conciliation proceedings are terminated.

(3) On the date of the agreement, a conciliation agreement signed by all of the parties.

(4) On the date of the order, order of the court when the matter submitted to conciliation is in litigation in the courts of this State.

(b) A conciliation proceeding may be terminated as to particular parties by any one of the following means:

(1) On the date of the declaration, a written declaration of the particular party to the other parties and the conciliators that the conciliation proceedings are to be terminated as to that party.

(2) On the date of the agreement, a conciliation agreement signed by some of the parties.

(3) On the date of the order, order of the court when the matter submitted to conciliation is in litigation in the courts of this State. (1997-368, s. 7.)

§ 1-567.84. Enforceability of decree.

If the conciliation proceeding settles the dispute and the result of the conciliation is in writing and signed by the conciliators and the parties or their representatives, the written agreement shall be treated as an arbitral award rendered by an arbitral tribunal under this Article and has the same force and effect as a final award in arbitration. (1997-368, s. 7.)

§ 1-567.85. Costs.
(a) On termination of the conciliation proceeding, the conciliators shall set the costs of the conciliation and give written notice of the costs to the parties. For purposes of this section, "costs" includes all of the following:

(1) A reasonable fee to be paid to the conciliators.

(2) Travel and other reasonable expenses of the conciliators.

(3) Travel and other reasonable expenses of witnesses requested by the conciliators, with the consent of the parties.

(4) The cost of any expert advice requested by the conciliators, with the consent of the parties.

(5) The cost of any court.

(b) Costs shall be borne equally by the parties unless a conciliation agreement provides for a different apportionment. All other expenses incurred by a party shall be borne by that party. (1997-368, s. 7.)

§ 1-567.86. Effect on jurisdiction.

Requesting conciliation, consenting to participate in the conciliation proceedings, participating in conciliation proceedings, or entering into a conciliation agreement does not constitute consenting to the jurisdiction of any court in this State if conciliation fails. (1997-368, s. 7.)

§ 1-567.87. Immunity of conciliators and parties.

(a) A conciliator, party, or representative of a conciliator or party, while present in this State for the purpose of arranging for or participating in conciliation under this Part, is not subject to service of process on any civil matter related to the conciliation.

(b) A person who serves as a conciliator shall have the same immunity as judges from civil liability for their official conduct in any proceeding subject to this Part. This qualified immunity does not apply to acts or omissions which occur with respect to the operation of a motor vehicle. (1997-368, s. 7.)

§ 1-568: Repealed by Session Laws 1951, c. 760, s. 2.

§§ 1-568.1 through 1-568.27. Repealed by Session Laws 1967, c. 954, s. 4.

§ 1-569. Repealed by Session Laws 1951, c. 760, s. 2.

Article 45C.

Revised Uniform Arbitration Act.

§ 1-569.1. Definitions.

The following definitions apply in this Article:

(1) "Arbitration organization" means an association, agency, board, commission, or other entity that is neutral and initiates, sponsors, or administers an arbitration proceeding or is involved in the appointment of an arbitrator.

(2) "Arbitrator" means an individual appointed to render an award, alone or with others, in a controversy that is subject to an agreement to arbitrate.

(3) "Court" means a court of competent jurisdiction in this State.

(4) "Knowledge" means actual knowledge.

(5) "Person" means an individual, corporation, business trust, estate, trust, partnership, limited liability company, association, joint venture, government; governmental subdivision, agency, or instrumentality; public corporation; or any other legal or commercial entity.

(6) "Record" means information that is inscribed on a tangible medium or that is stored in an electronic or other medium and is retrievable in perceivable form. (2003-345, s. 2)

§ 1-569.2. Notice.

(a) Except as otherwise provided in this Article, a person gives notice to another person by taking action that is reasonably necessary to inform the other person in the ordinary course, whether or not the other person acquires knowledge of the notice.

(b) A person has notice if the person has knowledge of the notice or has received notice.

(c) A person receives notice when it comes to the person's attention or the notice is delivered at the person's place of residence or place of business or at another location held out by the person as a place of delivery of communications. (2003-345, s. 2.)

§ 1-569.3. When Article applies.

(a) This Article governs an agreement to arbitrate made on or after January 1, 2004.

(b) This Article governs an agreement to arbitrate made before January 1, 2004, if all parties to the agreement or to the arbitration proceeding agree in a record that this Article applies.

(c) This Article does not govern arbitrations under Article 1H of Chapter 90 of the General Statutes. (1973, c. 676, s. 1; 2003-345, s. 2; 2007-541, s. 2.)

§ 1-569.4. Effect of agreement to arbitrate; nonwaivable provisions.

(a) Except as otherwise provided in subsections (b) and (c) of this section, a party to an agreement to arbitrate or to an arbitration proceeding may waive, or the parties may vary the effect of, the requirements of this Article to the extent provided by law.

(b) Before a controversy arises that is subject to an agreement to arbitrate, a party to the agreement may not:

(1) Waive or agree to vary the effect of the requirements of G.S. 1-569.5(a), 1-569.6(a), 1-569.8, 1-569.17(a), 1-569.17(b), 1-569.26, or 1-569.28;

(2) Agree to unreasonably restrict the right under G.S. 1-569.9 to notice of the initiation of an arbitration proceeding;

(3) Agree to unreasonably restrict the right under G.S. 1-569.12 to disclosure of any facts by a neutral arbitrator; or

(4) Waive the right under G.S. 1-569.16 of a party to an agreement to arbitrate to be represented by an attorney at any proceeding or hearing under

this Article, but an employer and a labor organization may waive the right to representation by a lawyer in a labor arbitration.

(c)   A party to an agreement to arbitrate or to an arbitration proceeding may not waive, or the parties shall not vary the effect of, the requirements of this section or G.S. 1-569.3(a), 1-569.7, 1-569.14, 1-569.18, 1-569.20(d), 1-569.20(e), 1-569.22, 1-569.23, 1-569.24, 1-569.25(a), 1-569.25(b), 1-569.29, 1-569.30, 1-569.31. Any waiver contrary to this section shall not be effective but shall not have the effect of voiding the agreement to arbitrate. (2003-345, s. 2.)

§ 1-569.5. Application for judicial relief.

(a)   Except as otherwise provided in G.S. 1-569.28, an application for judicial relief under this Article shall be made by motion to the court and heard in the manner provided by law or rule of court for making and hearing motions.

(b)   Unless a civil action involving the agreement to arbitrate is pending, notice of an initial motion to the court under this Article shall be served in the manner provided by law for the service of a summons in a civil action. Otherwise, notice of the motion shall be given in the manner prescribed by law or rule of court for serving motions in pending cases. (1927, c. 94, s. 5; 1973, c. 676, s. 1; 2003-345, s. 2.)

§ 1-569.6. Validity of agreement to arbitrate.

(a)   An agreement contained in a record to submit to arbitration any existing or subsequent controversy arising between the parties to the agreement is valid, enforceable, and irrevocable except upon a ground that exists at law or in equity for revoking a contract.

(b)   The court shall decide whether an agreement to arbitrate exists or a controversy is subject to an agreement to arbitrate.

(c)   An arbitrator shall decide whether a condition precedent to arbitrability has been fulfilled and whether a contract containing a valid agreement to arbitrate is enforceable.

(d)   If a party to a judicial proceeding challenges the existence of, or claims that a controversy is not subject to, an agreement to arbitrate, the arbitration proceeding may continue pending final resolution of the issue by the court, unless the court otherwise orders. (1927, c. 94, s. 1; 1973, c. 676, s. 1; 1975, c. 19, s. 1; 2003-345, s. 2.)

§ 1-569.7. Motion to compel or stay arbitration.

(a) On motion of a person showing an agreement to arbitrate and alleging another person's refusal to arbitrate pursuant to the agreement:

(1) If the refusing party does not appeal or does not oppose the motion, the court shall order the parties to arbitrate; and

(2) If the refusing party opposes the motion, the court shall proceed summarily to decide the issue and order the parties to arbitrate unless it finds that there is no enforceable agreement to arbitrate.

(b) On motion of a person alleging that an arbitration proceeding has been initiated or threatened but that there is no agreement to arbitrate, the court shall proceed summarily to decide the issue. If the court finds that there is an enforceable agreement to arbitrate, it shall order the parties to arbitrate.

(c) If the court finds that there is no enforceable agreement to arbitrate, it shall not, pursuant to subsection (a) or (b) of this section, order the parties to arbitrate.

(d) The court shall not refuse to order arbitration because the claim subject to arbitration lacks merit or because grounds for the claim have not been established.

(e) If a proceeding involving a claim referable to arbitration under an alleged agreement to arbitrate is pending in a court, a motion under this section shall be made in that court. Otherwise a motion under this section may be made in any court as provided in G.S. 1-569.27.

(f) If a party makes a motion to the court to order arbitration, the court on just terms shall stay any judicial proceeding that involves a claim alleged to be subject to the arbitration until the court renders a final decision under this section.

(g)   If the court orders arbitration, the court on just terms shall stay any judicial proceeding that involves a claim subject to the arbitration. If a claim subject to the arbitration is severable, the court may limit the stay to that claim. (1973, c. 676, s. 1; 2003-345, s. 2.)

§ 1-569.8. Provisional remedies.

(a)   Before an arbitrator is appointed and is authorized and able to act, the court, upon motion of a party to an arbitration proceeding and for good cause shown, may enter an order for provisional remedies to protect the effectiveness of the arbitration proceeding to the same extent and under the same conditions as if the controversy were the subject of a civil action.

(b)   After an arbitrator is appointed and is authorized and able to act:

(1)   The arbitrator may issue orders for provisional remedies, including interim awards, as the arbitrator finds necessary to protect the effectiveness of the arbitration proceeding and to promote the fair and expeditious resolution of the controversy, to the same extent and under the same conditions as if the controversy were the subject of a civil action; and

(2)   A party to an arbitration proceeding may move the court for a provisional remedy if the matter is urgent and the arbitrator is not able to act in a timely manner or the arbitrator cannot provide an adequate remedy.

(c)   A party does not waive the right to arbitrate by making a motion under subsection (a) or (b) of this section. (2003-345, s. 2.)

§ 1-569.9. Initiation of arbitration.

(a)   A person initiates an arbitration proceeding by giving notice in a record to the other parties to the agreement to arbitrate in the agreed manner between the parties or, in the absence of agreement, by certified or registered mail, return receipt requested, and obtained, or by service as authorized for the commencement of a civil action. The notice shall describe the nature of the controversy and the remedy sought.

(b)   Unless a person objects for lack or insufficiency of notice under G.S. 1-569.15(c) no later than the beginning of the arbitration hearing, the person, by appearing at the hearing, waives any objection to lack or insufficiency of notice. (2003-345, s. 2.)

§ 1569.10. Consolidation of separate arbitration proceedings.

(a)   Except as otherwise provided in subsection (c) of this section, upon motion of a party to an agreement to arbitrate or to an arbitration proceeding, the court may order consolidation of separate arbitration proceedings as to all or some of the claims if:

(1)   There are separate agreements to arbitrate or separate arbitration proceedings between the same persons or one of them is a party to a separate agreement to arbitrate or a separate arbitration with a third person;

(2)   The claims subject to the agreements to arbitrate arise in substantial part from the same transaction or series of related transactions;

(3)   The existence of a common issue of law or fact creates the possibility of conflicting decisions in the separate arbitration proceedings; and

(4)   Prejudice resulting from a failure to consolidate is not outweighed by the risk of undue delay or prejudice to the rights of or hardship to parties opposing consolidation.

(b)   The court may order consolidation of separate arbitration proceedings as to some claims and allow other claims to be resolved in separate arbitration proceedings.

(c)   The court shall not order consolidation of the claims of a party to an agreement to arbitrate if the agreement prohibits consolidation. (2003-345, s. 2.)

§ 1-569.11. Appointment of arbitrator; service as a neutral arbitrator.

(a)   If the parties to an agreement to arbitrate agree on a method for appointing an arbitrator, that method shall be followed, unless the method fails. If the parties have not agreed on a method, the agreed method fails, or an arbitrator appointed fails or is unable to act and a successor has not been appointed, the court, on motion of a party to the arbitration proceeding, shall appoint the arbitrator. An arbitrator so appointed has all the powers of an arbitrator designated in the agreement to arbitrate or appointed pursuant to the agreed method.

(b)   An individual who has a known, direct, and material interest in the outcome of the arbitration proceeding or a known, existing, and substantial relationship with a party shall not serve as an arbitrator required by an agreement to be neutral. (1927, c. 94, s. 4; 1973, c. 676, s. 1; 2003-345, s. 2.)

§ 1-69.12. Disclosure by arbitrator.

(a)   Before accepting appointment, an individual who is requested to serve as an arbitrator, after making a reasonable inquiry, shall disclose to all parties to the agreement to arbitrate and to the arbitration proceeding and to any other arbitrators any known facts that a reasonable person would consider likely to affect the impartiality of the arbitrator in the arbitration proceeding, including:

(1)   A financial or personal interest in the outcome of the arbitration proceeding; and

(2)   An existing or past relationship with any of the parties to the agreement to arbitrate or to the arbitration proceeding, their counsel or representatives, a witness, or other arbitrators.

(b)   An arbitrator has a continuing obligation to disclose to all parties to the agreement to arbitrate and to the arbitration proceeding and to any other arbitrators any facts that the arbitrator learns after accepting appointment which a reasonable person would consider likely to affect the impartiality of the arbitrator.

(c)   If an arbitrator discloses a fact required by subsection (a) or (b) of this section to be disclosed and a party timely objects to the appointment or continued service of the arbitrator based upon the fact disclosed, the objection may be a ground under G.S. 1-569.23(a)(2) for vacating an award made by the arbitrator.

(d)   If the arbitrator did not disclose a fact as required by subsection (a) or (b) of this section, upon timely objection by a party, the court under G.S. 1-569.23(a)(2) may vacate an award.

(e) An arbitrator appointed as a neutral arbitrator who does not disclose a known, direct, and material interest in the outcome of the arbitration proceeding or a known, existing, and substantial relationship with a party is presumed to act with evident partiality under G.S. 1-569.23(a)(2).

(f) If the parties to an arbitration proceeding agree to the procedures of an arbitration organization or any other procedures for challenges to arbitrators before an award is made, substantial compliance with those procedures is a condition precedent to a motion to vacate an award on that ground under G.S. 1-569.23(a)(2). (2003-345, s. 2.)

§ 1-569.13. Action by majority.

If there is more than one arbitrator, the powers of an arbitrator shall be exercised by a majority of the arbitrators, but all of them shall conduct the hearing under G.S. 1-569.15(c). (1973, c. 676, s. 1; 2003-345, s. 2.)

§ 1-569.14. Immunity of arbitrator; competency to testify; attorneys' fees and costs.

(a) An arbitrator or an arbitration organization acting in that capacity is immune from civil liability to the same extent as a judge of a court of this State acting in a judicial capacity.

(b) The immunity afforded by this section supplements any immunity under other law.

(c) The failure of an arbitrator to make a disclosure required by G.S. 1-569.12 shall not cause any loss of immunity under this section.

(d) In a judicial, administrative, or similar proceeding, an arbitrator or representative of an arbitration organization is not competent to testify and shall not be required to produce records as to any statement, conduct, decision, or ruling occurring during the arbitration proceeding to the same extent as a judge of a court of this State acting in a judicial capacity. This subsection shall not apply:

(1) To the extent necessary to determine the claim of an arbitrator, arbitration organization, or representative of the arbitration organization against a party to the arbitration proceeding; or

(2) To a hearing on a motion to vacate an award under G.S. 1-569.23(a)(1) or (a)(2) if the movant makes a prima facie showing that a ground for vacating the award exists.

(e) If a person commences a civil action against an arbitrator, arbitration organization, or representative of an arbitration organization arising from the services of the arbitrator, organization, or representative, or if a person seeks to compel an arbitrator or a representative of an arbitration organization to testify or produce records in violation of subsection (d) of this section, and the court decides that the arbitrator, arbitration organization, or representative of an arbitration organization is immune from civil liability or that the arbitrator or representative of the organization is not competent to testify, the court shall award to the arbitrator, organization, or representative reasonable attorneys' fees, costs, and other reasonable expenses of litigation.

(f) Immunity under this section shall not apply to acts or omissions that occur with respect to the operation of a motor vehicle. (2003-345, s. 2.)

§ 1-569.15. Arbitration process.

(a) An arbitrator may conduct an arbitration in the manner the arbitrator considers appropriate for a fair and expeditious disposition of the proceeding. The authority conferred upon the arbitrator includes the power to hold conferences with the parties to the arbitration proceeding before the hearing and, among other matters, determine the admissibility, relevance, materiality, and weight of any evidence.

(b) An arbitrator may decide a request for summary disposition of a claim or particular issue:

(1) If all interested parties agree; or
(2) Upon request of one party to the arbitration proceeding if that party gives notice to all other parties to the proceeding and the other parties have a reasonable opportunity to respond.

(c) If an arbitrator orders a hearing, the arbitrator shall set a time and place and give notice of the hearing not less than five days before the hearing begins. Unless a party to the arbitration proceeding objects to the lack or insufficiency of notice not later than the beginning of the hearing, the party's appearance at the hearing waives the objection. Upon request of a party to the arbitration proceeding and for good cause shown, or upon the arbitrator's own initiative, the arbitrator may adjourn the hearing from time to time as necessary but shall not postpone the hearing to a time later than that fixed by the agreement to arbitrate for making the award unless the parties to the arbitration proceeding consent to a later date. The arbitrator may hear and decide the controversy upon the evidence produced although a party who was duly notified did not appear. The court, upon request, may direct the arbitrator to conduct the hearing promptly and render a timely decision.

(d) At a hearing under subsection (c) of this section, a party to the arbitration proceeding may be heard, present evidence material to the controversy, and cross-examine witnesses appearing at the hearing.

(e) If an arbitrator ceases to or is unable to act during the arbitration proceeding, a replacement arbitrator shall be appointed in accordance with G.S. 1-569.11 to continue the proceeding and to resolve the controversy.

(f) The rules of evidence shall not apply in arbitration proceedings, except as to matters of privilege or immunities. (1927, c. 94, ss. 6, 7; 1973, c. 676, s. 1; 2003-345, s. 2.)

§ 1-569.16. Representation by lawyer.

A party to an arbitration proceeding may be represented by an attorney or attorneys. (1927, c. 94, s. 9; 1973, c. 676, s. 1; 2003-345, s. 2.)

§ 1-569.17. Witnesses; subpoenas; depositions; discovery.

(a) An arbitrator may issue a subpoena for the attendance of a witness and for the production of records and other evidence at any hearing and may administer oaths. A subpoena shall be served in the manner for service of subpoenas in a civil action and, upon motion to the court by a party to the arbitration proceeding or the arbitrator, enforced in the manner for enforcement of subpoenas in a civil action.

(b) In order to make the proceedings fair, expeditious, and cost-effective, upon request of a party to or a witness in an arbitration proceeding, an arbitrator may permit a deposition of any witness to be taken for use as evidence at the hearing, including a witness who cannot be subpoenaed for or is unable to attend a hearing. The arbitrator shall determine the conditions under which the deposition is taken.

(c) An arbitrator may permit any discovery the arbitrator decides is appropriate under the circumstances, taking into account the needs of the parties to the arbitration proceeding and other affected persons and the desirability of making the proceeding fair, expeditious, and cost-effective.

(d) If an arbitrator permits discovery under subsection (c) of this section, the arbitrator may order a party to the arbitration proceeding to comply with the arbitrator's discovery-related orders, issue subpoenas for the attendance of a witness and for the production of records and other evidence at a discovery proceeding, and take action against a noncomplying party to the extent a court could if the controversy were the subject of a civil action in this State.

(e) An arbitrator may issue a protective order to prevent the disclosure of privileged information, confidential information, trade secrets, and other information protected from disclosure to the extent a court could if the controversy were the subject of a civil action in this State.

(f) All laws compelling a person under subpoena to testify and all fees for attending a judicial proceeding, a deposition, or a discovery proceeding as a witness apply to an arbitration proceeding as if the controversy were the subject of a civil action in this State.

(g) The court may enforce a subpoena or discovery-related order for the attendance of a witness within this State and for the protection of records and other evidence issued by an arbitrator in connection with an arbitration proceeding in another state upon conditions determined by the court so as to make the arbitration proceeding fair, expeditious, and cost-effective. A subpoena or discovery-related order issued by an arbitrator in another state shall be served in the manner provided by law for service of subpoenas in a civil action in this State and, upon motion to the court by a party to the arbitration proceeding or the arbitrator, enforced in the manner provided by law for enforcement of subpoenas in a civil action in this State.

(h) An arbitrator shall not have the authority to hold a party in contempt of any order the arbitrator makes under this section. A court may hold parties in contempt for failure to obey an arbitrator's order, or an order made by the court, pursuant to this section, among other sanctions imposed by the arbitrator or the court. (1927, c. 94, ss. 10, 11; 1973, c. 676, s. 1; 2003-345, s. 2.)

§ 1-569.18. Judicial enforcement of preaward ruling by arbitrator.

(a) If an arbitrator makes a preaward ruling in favor of a party to the arbitration proceeding, the party may request the arbitrator to incorporate the ruling into an award under G.S. 1-569.19. A prevailing party may make a motion to the court for an expedited order to confirm the award under G.S. 1-569.22, in which case the court shall summarily decide the motion. The court shall issue an order to confirm the award unless the court vacates, modifies, or corrects the award under G.S. 1-569.23 or G.S. 1-569.24.

(b) An arbitrator's ruling under subsection (a) of this section that denies a request for a preaward ruling is not subject to trial court review. A party whose request under subsection (a) of this section for a preaward ruling has been denied by an arbitrator may seek relief under G.S. 1-569.20 and G.S. 1-569.21 from any final award the arbitrator renders.

(c) There is no right of appeal from trial court orders and judgments on preaward rulings by an arbitrator after a trial court award under this section, G.S. 1-569.19, and G.S. 1-569.28. (2003-345, s. 2.)

§ 1-569.19. Award.

(a) An arbitrator shall make a record of an award. The record shall be signed or otherwise authenticated as authorized by federal or State law by any arbitrator who concurs with the award. The arbitrator or the arbitration organization shall give notice of the award, including a copy of the award, to each party to the arbitration proceeding.

(b) An award shall be made within the time specified by the agreement to arbitrate or, if not specified therein, within the time ordered by the court. The court may extend or the parties to the arbitration proceeding may agree in a record to extend the time. The court or the parties may extend the time within or after the time specified or ordered. A party waives any objection that an award was not timely made unless that party gives notice of the objection to the arbitrator before receiving notice of the award. (1927, c. 94, ss. 8, 14; 1973, c. 676, s. 1; 2003-345, s. 2.)

§ 1-569.20. Change of award by arbitrator.

(a) On motion to an arbitrator by a party to an arbitration proceeding, the arbitrator may modify or correct an award:

(1) Upon a ground stated in G.S. 1-569.24(a)(1) or (a)(3);

(2) Because the arbitrator had not made a final and definite award upon a claim submitted by the parties to the arbitration proceeding; or

(3) To clarify the award.

(b) A motion under subsection (a) of this section shall be made and notice given to all parties within 20 days after the moving party receives notice of the award.

(c) A party to the arbitration proceeding shall give notice of any objection to the motion within 10 days after receipt of the notice.

(d) If a motion to the court is pending under G.S. 1-569.22, 1-569.23, or 1-569.24, the court may submit the claim to the arbitrator to consider whether to modify or correct the award:

(1) Upon a ground stated in G.S. 1-569.24(a)(1) or (a)(3);

(2) Because the arbitrator had not made a final and definite award upon a claim submitted by the parties to the arbitration proceeding; or

(3) To clarify the award.

(e) An award modified or corrected pursuant to this section is subject to G.S. 1-569.19(a), 1-569.22, 1-569.23, and 1-569.24. (1973, c. 676, s. 1; 2003-345, s. 2.)

§ 1-569.21. Remedies; fees and expenses of arbitration proceeding.

(a)   An arbitrator may award punitive damages or other exemplary relief if:

(1)   The arbitration agreement provides for an award of punitive damages or exemplary relief;

(2)   An award for punitive damages or other exemplary relief is authorized by law in a civil action involving the same claim; and

(3)   The evidence produced at the hearing justifies the award under the legal standards otherwise applicable to the claim.

(b)   An arbitrator may award reasonable expenses of arbitration if an award of expenses is authorized by law in a civil action involving the same claim or by the agreement of the parties to the arbitration proceeding. An arbitrator may award reasonable attorneys' fees if:

(1)   The arbitration agreement provides for an award of attorneys' fees; and

(2)   An award of attorneys' fees is authorized by law in a civil action involving the same claim.

(c)   As to all remedies other than those authorized by subsections (a) and (b) of this section, an arbitrator may order any remedies the arbitrator considers just and appropriate under the circumstances of the arbitration proceeding. The fact that a remedy could not or would not be granted by the court is not a ground for refusing to confirm an award under G.S. 1-569.22 or for vacating an award under G.S. 1-569.23.

(d)   An arbitrator's expenses and fees, together with other expenses, shall be paid as provided in the award.

(e)   If an arbitrator awards punitive damages or other exemplary relief under subsection (a) of this section, the arbitrator shall specify in the award the basis in fact justifying and the basis in law authorizing the award and state separately the amount of the punitive damages or other exemplary relief. (1973, c. 676, s. 1; 2003-345, s. 2.)

§ 1-569.22. Confirmation of award.

After a party to an arbitration receives notice of an award, the party may make a motion to the court for an order confirming the award. Upon motion of a party for an order confirming the award, the court shall issue a confirming order unless the award is modified or corrected pursuant to G.S. 1-569.20 or G.S. 1-569.24 or is vacated pursuant to G.S. 1-569.23. (1927, c. 94, s. 15; 1973, c. 676, s. 1; 2003-345, s. 2.)

§ 1-569.23. Vacating award.

(a) Upon motion to the court by a party to an arbitration proceeding, the court shall vacate an award made in the arbitration proceeding if:

(1) The award was procured by corruption, fraud, or other undue means;

(2) There was:

a. Evident partiality by an arbitrator appointed as a neutral arbitrator;

b. Corruption by an arbitrator; or

c. Misconduct by an arbitrator prejudicing the rights of a party to the arbitration proceeding;

(3) An arbitrator refused to postpone the hearing upon a showing of sufficient cause for postponement, refused to consider evidence material to the controversy, or otherwise conducted the hearing contrary to G.S. 1-569.15 so as to prejudice substantially the rights of a party to the arbitration proceeding;

(4) An arbitrator exceeded the arbitrator's powers;

(5) There was no agreement to arbitrate, unless the person participated in the arbitration proceeding without raising the objection under G.S. 1-569.15(c) no later than the beginning of the arbitration hearing; or

(6) The arbitration was conducted without proper notice of the initiation of an arbitration as required in G.S. 1-569.9 so as to prejudice substantially the rights of a party to the arbitration proceeding.

(b)   A motion under this section shall be filed within 90 days after the moving party receives notice of the award pursuant to G.S. 1-569.19 or within 90 days after the moving party receives notice of a modified or corrected award pursuant to G.S. 1-569.20, unless the moving party alleges that the award was procured by corruption, fraud, or other undue means, in which case the motion shall be made within 90 days after the ground is known, or by the exercise of reasonable care would have been known, by the moving party.

(c)   If the court vacates an award on a ground other than that set forth in subdivision (a)(5) of this section, it may order a rehearing. If the award is vacated on a ground stated in subdivision (1) or (2) of subsection (a) of this section, the rehearing shall be before a new arbitrator. If the award is vacated on a ground stated in subdivision (3), (4), or (6) of subsection (a) of this section, the rehearing may be held before the arbitrator who made the award or the arbitrator's successor. The arbitrator shall render the decision in the rehearing within the same time as the time provided in G.S. 1-569.19(b) for an award.

(d)   If the court denies a motion to vacate an award, it shall confirm the award unless a motion to modify or correct the award pursuant to G.S. 1-569.24 is pending. (1927, c. 94, s. 16; 1973, c. 676, s. 1; 2003-345, s. 2.)

§ 1-569.24. Modification or correction of award.

(a)   Upon motion made within 90 days after the moving party receives notice of the award pursuant to G.S. 1-569.19 or within 90 days after the moving party receives notice of a modified or corrected award pursuant to G.S. 1-569.20, the court shall modify or correct the award if:

(1)   There was an evident mathematical miscalculation or an evident mistake in the description of a person, thing, or property referred to in the award;

(2)   The arbitrator has made an award on a claim not submitted to the arbitrator, and the award may be corrected without affecting the merits of the decision on the claims submitted; or

(3)   The award is imperfect in a matter of form not affecting the merits of the decision on the claims submitted.

(b)   If a motion made under subsection (a) of this section is granted, the court shall modify and confirm the award as modified or corrected. Otherwise, unless a motion to vacate is pending, the court shall confirm the award.

(c)   A motion to modify or correct an award pursuant to this section may be joined with a motion to vacate the award. (1927, c. 94, s. 17; 1973, c. 676, s. 1; 2003-345, s. 2.)

§ 1-569.25. Judgment on award; attorneys' fees and litigation expenses.

(a)   Upon granting an order confirming, vacating without directing a rehearing, modifying, or correcting an award, the court shall enter a judgment in conformity with the order. The judgment may be recorded, docketed, and enforced as any other judgment in a civil action.

(b)   A court may allow reasonable costs of the motion and subsequent judicial proceedings.

(c)   On motion of a prevailing party to a contested judicial proceeding under G.S. 1-569.22, 1-569.23, or 1-569.24, the court may award reasonable attorneys' fees and other reasonable expenses of litigation incurred in a judicial proceeding after the award is made to a judgment confirming, vacating without directing a rehearing, modifying, or correcting an award. (1927, c. 94, ss. 19, 21; 1973, c. 676, s. 1; 2003-345, s. 2.)

§ 1-569.26. Jurisdiction.

(a)   A court of this State having jurisdiction over the controversy and the parties to an agreement to arbitrate may enforce the agreement to arbitrate.

(b)   An agreement to arbitrate providing for arbitration in this State confers exclusive jurisdiction on the court to enter judgment on an award under this Article. (1927, c. 94, s. 3; 1973, c. 676, s. 1; 2003-345, s. 2.)

§ 1-569.27. Venue.
A motion pursuant to G.S. 1-569.5 shall be made in the court of the county in which the agreement to arbitrate specifies the arbitration hearing is to be held or, if the hearing has been held, in the court of the county in which it was held.

Otherwise, the motion may be made in the court of any county in which an adverse party resides or has a place of business or, if no adverse party has a residence or place of business in this State, in the court of any county in this State. All subsequent motions shall be made in the court hearing the initial motion unless the court otherwise directs. (2003-345, s. 2.)

§ 1-569.28. Appeals.

(a) An appeal may be taken from:

(1) An order denying a motion to compel arbitration;

(2) An order granting a motion to stay arbitration;

(3) An order confirming or denying confirmation of an award;

(4) An order modifying or correcting an award;

(5) An order vacating an award without directing a rehearing; or

(6) A final judgment entered pursuant to this Article.

(b) An appeal under this section shall be taken as from an order or a judgment in a civil action. (1927, c. 94, s. 22; 1973, c. 676, s. 1; 2003-345, s. 2.)

§ 1-569.29. Uniformity of application and construction.

In applying and construing this Article, consideration shall be given to the need to promote uniformity of the law with respect to its subject matter among states that enact it. (1927, c. 94, s. 23; 1973, c. 676, s. 1; 2003-345, s. 2.)

§ 1-569.30. Relationship to federal Electronic Signatures in Global and National Commerce Act.

The provisions of this Article governing the legal effect, validity, and enforceability of electronic records or electronic signatures, and of contracts performed with the use of these records or signatures, conform to the requirements of section 102 of the Electronic Signatures in Global and National

Commerce Act, 15 U.S.C. § 7001, et seq., or as otherwise authorized by federal or State law governing these electronic records or electronic signatures. (2003-345, s. 2.)

§ 1-569.31. Short title.

This Article may be cited as the Revised Uniform Arbitration Act. (2003-345, s. 2.)

Article 47.

Motions and Orders.

§§ 1-577 through 1-584. Repealed by Session Laws 1967, c. 954, s. 4.

Article 48.

Notices.

§§ 1-585 through 1-589. Repealed by Session Laws 1967, c. 954, s. 4.

§ 1-589.1. Withholding information necessary for service on law-enforcement officer prohibited.

When service of subpoena, or any other court process, is sought upon any law-enforcement officer of the State or of any political subdivision thereof pursuant to the provisions of G.S. 1-589, or of any other statute, it shall be unlawful for any officer or employee of the agency by whom the officer sought to be served is employed willfully to withhold the address or telephone number of the officer sought to be served with subpoena or other process. (1967, c. 456.)

§§ 1-590 through 1-592. Repealed by Session Laws 1967, c. 954, s. 4.
Article 49.

Time.

§ 1-593. How computed.

The time within which an act is to be done, as provided by law, shall be computed in the manner prescribed by Rule 6(a) of the Rules of Civil Procedure. (C.C.P., s. 348; Code, s. 596; Rev., s. 887; C.S., s. 922; 1957, c. 141; 1967, c. 954, s. 3.)

§ 1-594. Computation in publication.

Except as otherwise expressly provided, the time for publication of legal notices shall be computed in the manner prescribed by Rule 6 of the North Carolina Rules of Civil Procedure. (C.C.P., s. 359; Code, s. 602; Rev., s. 888; C.S., s. 923; 1979, c. 579, s. 2.)

Article 50.

General Provisions as to Legal Advertising.

§ 1-595. Advertisement of public sales.

When a statute or written instrument stipulates that an advertisement of a sale shall be made for any certain number of weeks, a publication once a week for the number of weeks so indicated is a sufficient compliance with the requirement, unless contrary provision is expressly made by the terms of the instrument. (1909, cc. 794, 875; C.S., s. 924.)

§ 1-596. Charges for legal advertising.

The publication of all advertising required by law to be made in newspapers in this State shall be paid for at not to exceed the local commercial rate of the newspapers selected. Any public or municipal officer or board created by or existing under the laws of this State that is now or may hereafter be authorized by law to enter into contracts for the publication of legal advertisements is hereby authorized to pay therefor prices not exceeding said rates.
No newspaper in this State shall accept or print any legal advertising until said newspaper shall have first filed with the clerk of the superior court of the county in which it is published a sworn statement of its current commercial rate for the

several classes of advertising regularly carried by said publication, and any owner or manager of a newspaper violating the provisions of this section shall be guilty of a Class 1 misdemeanor. (1919, c. 45, ss. 1, 2; C.S., s. 2586; 1945, c. 635; 1949, c. 205, s. 1 1/2; 1993, c. 539, s. 3; 1994, Ex. Sess., c. 24, s. 14(c).)

§ 1-597. Regulations for newspaper publication of legal notices, advertisements, etc.

Whenever a notice or any other paper, document or legal advertisement of any kind or description shall be authorized or required by any of the laws of the State of North Carolina, heretofore or hereafter enacted, or by any order or judgment of any court of this State to be published or advertised in a newspaper, such publication, advertisement or notice shall be of no force and effect unless it shall be published in a newspaper with a general circulation to actual paid subscribers which newspaper at the time of such publication, advertisement or notice, shall have been admitted to the United States mails in the Periodicals class in the county or political subdivision where such publication, advertisement or notice is required to be published, and which shall have been regularly and continuously issued in the county in which the publication, advertisement or notice is authorized or required to be published, at least one day in each calendar week for at least 25 of the 26 consecutive weeks immediately preceding the date of the first publication of such advertisement, publication or notice; provided that in the event that a newspaper otherwise meeting the qualifications and having the characteristics prescribed by G.S. 1-597 to 1-599, should fail for a period not exceeding four weeks in any calendar year to publish one or more of its issues such newspaper shall nevertheless be deemed to have complied with the requirements of regularity and continuity of publication prescribed herein. Provided further, that where any city or town is located in two or more adjoining counties, any newspaper published in such city or town shall, for the purposes of G.S. 1-597 to 1-599, be deemed to be admitted to the mails, issued and published in all such counties in which such town or city of publication is located, and every publication, advertisement or notice required to be published in any such city or town or in any of the counties where such city or town is located shall be valid if published in a newspaper published, issued and admitted to the mails anywhere within any such city or town, regardless of whether the newspaper's plant or the post office where the newspaper is admitted to the mails is in such county or not, if the newspaper otherwise meets the qualifications and requirements of G.S. 1-597 to 1-599. This provision shall be retroactive to May 1, 1940, and all publications, advertisements and notices published in accordance with this provision since May 1, 1940, are hereby validated.

Notwithstanding the provisions of G.S. 1-599, whenever a notice or any other paper, document or legal advertisement of any kind or description shall be authorized or required by any of the laws of the State of North Carolina, heretofore or hereafter enacted, or by any order or judgment of any court of this State to be published or advertised in a newspaper qualified for legal advertising in a county and there is no newspaper qualified for legal advertising as defined in this section in such county, then it shall be deemed sufficient compliance with such laws, order or judgment by publication of such notice or any other such paper, document or legal advertisement of any kind or description in a newspaper published in an adjoining county or in a county within the same district court district as defined in G.S. 7A-133 or superior court district or set of districts as defined in G.S. 7A-41.1, as the case may be; provided, if the clerk of the superior court finds as a fact that such newspaper otherwise meets the requirements of this section and has a general circulation in such county where no newspaper is published meeting the requirements of this section. (1939, c. 170, s. 1; 1941, c. 96; 1959, c. 350; 1985, c. 689, s. 1; 1987 (Reg. Sess., 1988), c. 1037, s. 41; 1997-9, s. 1.)

§ 1-598. Sworn statement prima facie evidence of qualifications; affidavit of publication.

Whenever any owner, partner, publisher, or other authorized officer or employee of any newspaper which has published a notice or any other paper, document or legal advertisement within the meaning of G.S. 1-597 has made a written statement under oath taken before any notary public or other officer or person authorized by law to administer oaths, stating that the newspaper in which such notice, paper, document, or legal advertisement was published, was, at the time of such publication, a newspaper meeting all of the requirements and qualifications prescribed by G.S. 1-597, such sworn written statement shall be received in all courts in this State as prima facie evidence that such newspaper was at the time stated therein a newspaper meeting the requirements and qualifications of G.S. 1-597. When filed in the office of the clerk of the superior court of any county in which the publication of such notice, paper, document or legal advertisement was required or authorized, any such sworn statement shall be deemed to be a record of the court, and such record or a copy thereof duly certified by the clerk shall be prima facie evidence that the newspaper named was at the time stated therein a qualified newspaper within the meaning of G.S. 1-597. Nothing in this section shall preclude proof that a newspaper was or is a qualified newspaper within the meaning of G.S. 1-597 by any other competent evidence. Any such sworn written statement shall be prima facie evidence of the qualifications on any newspaper at the time of any publication of any notice, paper, document, or legal advertisement published in such newspaper at any time from and after the first day of May, 1940.

The owner, a partner, publisher or other authorized officer or employee of any newspaper in which such notice, paper, document or legal advertisement is published, when such newspaper is a qualified newspaper within the meaning of G.S. 1-597, shall include in the affidavit of publication of such notice, paper, document or legal advertisement a statement that at the time of such publication such newspaper was a qualified newspaper within the meaning of G.S. 1-597. (1939, c. 170, s. 1 1/2; 1947, c. 213, ss. 1, 2.)

§ 1-599. Application of two preceding sections.

The provisions of G.S. 1-597 and G.S. 1-598 shall not apply in counties wherein only one newspaper is published, although it may not be a newspaper having the qualifications prescribed by G.S. 1-597; nor shall the provisions of G.S. 1-597 and G.S. 1-598 apply in any county wherein none of the newspapers published in such county has the qualifications and characteristics prescribed in G.S. 1-597. (1939, c. 170, ss. 2, 4 1/2; 1941, c. 49; 1985, c. 609, s. 1.)

§ 1-600. Proof of publication of notice in newspaper; prima facie evidence.

(a) Publication of any notice permitted or required by law to be published in a newspaper may be proved by a printed copy of the notice together with an affidavit made before some person authorized to administer oaths, of the publisher, proprietor, editor, managing editor, business or circulation manager, advertising, classified advertising or any other advertising manager or foreman of the newspaper, showing that the notice has been printed therein and the date or dates of publication. If the newspaper is published by a corporation, the affidavit may be made by one of the persons hereinbefore designated or by the president, vice president, secretary, assistant secretary, treasurer, or assistant treasurer of the corporation.

(b) Such affidavit and copy of the notice shall constitute prima facie evidence of the facts stated therein concerning publication of such notice.

(c) The method of proof of publication of a notice provided for in this section is not exclusive, and the facts concerning such publication may be proved by any competent evidence. (1951, c. 1005, s. 2; 1957, c. 204.)

§ 1-601. Certain legal advertisements validated.

Legal advertisements published prior to June 1, 1983, by a newspaper that met every requirement for publication of legal notices and advertisements under G.S. 1-597 when the advertisement was published except that the newspaper had a second class United States mail permit in a county adjacent to the county in which the advertisement was published instead of the county in which it was published may not be held to be invalid because of the lack of a second class United States mail permit in the proper county. (1983, c. 582, s. 2.)

§ 1-602. Reserved for future codification purposes.

§ 1-603. Reserved for future codification purposes.

§ 1-604. Reserved for future codification purposes.

Article 51.

False Claims Act.

§ 1-605. Short title; purpose.

(a) This Article shall be known and may be cited as the False Claims Act.

(b) The purpose of this Article is to deter persons from knowingly causing or assisting in causing the State to pay claims that are false or fraudulent and to provide remedies in the form of treble damages and civil penalties when money is obtained from the State by reason of a false or fraudulent claim. (2009-554, s. 1.)

§ 1-606. Definitions.

The following words and phrases when used in this act have the following meanings, unless the context clearly indicates otherwise:

(1)   "Attorney General." – The Attorney General of North Carolina, or any deputy, assistant, or associate attorney general.

(2)   "Claim." – Any request or demand, whether under a contract or otherwise, for money or property and whether or not the State has title to the money or property that (i) is presented to an officer, employee, or agent of the State or (ii) is made to a contractor, grantee, or other recipient, if the money or property is to be spent or used on the State's behalf or to advance a State program or interest and if the State government:

a.   Provides or has provided any portion of the money or property that is requested or demanded; or

b.   Will reimburse such contractor, grantee, or other recipient for any portion of the money or property which is requested or demanded.

A claim does not include requests or demands for money or property that the State has paid to an individual as compensation for State employment or as an income subsidy with no restrictions on that individual's use of the money or property.

(3)   "Judiciary." – A justice or judge of the General Court of Justice or clerk of court.

(4)   "Knowing" and "knowingly." – Whenever a person, with respect to information, does any of the following:

a.   Has actual knowledge of the information.

b.   Acts in deliberate ignorance of the truth or falsity of the information.

c.   Acts in reckless disregard of the truth or falsity of the information.

Proof of specific intent to defraud is not required.

(5)   "Material" means having a natural tendency to influence, or be capable of influencing, the payment or receipt of money or property.

(6) "Obligation" means an established duty, whether or not fixed, arising from an express or implied contractual, grantor-grantee, or licensor-licensee relationship, from a fee-based or similar relationship, from statute or regulation, or from the retention of any overpayment.

(7) "Public employee," "public official," and "public employment" includes federal, State, and local employees and officials.

(8) "Senior executive branch official." – The Governor, Lieutenant Governor, member of the Council of State, or head of department as defined in G.S. 143B-3. (2009-554, s. 1.)

§ 1-607. False claims; acts subjecting persons to liability for treble damages; costs and civil penalties; exceptions.

(a) Liability. – Any person who commits any of the following acts shall be liable to the State for three times the amount of damages that the State sustains because of the act of that person. A person who commits any of the following acts also shall be liable to the State for the costs of a civil action brought to recover any of those penalties or damages and shall be liable to the State for a civil penalty of not less than five thousand five hundred dollars ($5,500) and not more than eleven thousand dollars ($11,000) for each violation:

(1) Knowingly presents or causes to be presented a false or fraudulent claim for payment or approval.

(2) Knowingly makes, uses, or causes to be made or used, a false record or statement material to a false or fraudulent claim.

(3) Conspires to commit a violation of subdivision (1), (2), (4), (5), (6), or (7) of this section.

(4) Has possession, custody, or control of property or money used or to be used by the State and knowingly delivers or causes to be delivered less than all of that money or property.

(5) Is authorized to make or deliver a document certifying receipt of property used or to be used by the State and, intending to defraud the State, makes or delivers the receipt without completely knowing that the information on the receipt is true.

(6) Knowingly buys, or receives as a pledge of an obligation or debt, public property from any officer or employee of the State who lawfully may not sell or pledge the property.

(7) Knowingly makes, uses, or causes to be made or used, a false record or statement material to an obligation to pay or transmit money or property to the State, or knowingly conceals or knowingly and improperly avoids or decreases an obligation to pay or transmit money or property to the State.

(b) Damages Limitation. – Notwithstanding the provisions of subsection (a) of this section, the court may limit the damages assessed under subsection (a) of this section to not less than two times the amount of damages that the State sustains because of the act of the person described in that subsection and may assess no civil penalty if the court finds all of the following:

(1) The person committing the violation furnished officials of the State who are responsible for investigating false claims violations with all information known to that person about the violation within 30 days after the date on which the person first obtained the information.

(2) The person fully cooperated with any investigation of the violation by the State.

(3) At the time the person furnished the State with information about the violation, no criminal prosecution, civil action, or administrative action has commenced with respect to the violation, and the person did not have actual knowledge of the existence of an investigation into the violation.

(c) Exclusion. – This section does not apply to claims, records, or statements made under Chapter 105 of the General Statutes. (2009-554, s. 1.)

§ 1-608. Civil actions for false claims.

(a) Responsibilities of the Attorney General. – The Attorney General diligently shall investigate a violation under G.S. 1-607. If the Attorney General finds that a person has violated or is violating G.S. 1-607, the Attorney General may bring a civil action under this section against that person.

(b)   Actions by Private Persons. – A person may bring a civil action for a violation of G.S. 1-607 for the person and for the State, as follows:

(1)   The action shall be brought in the name of the State, and the person bringing the action shall be referred to as the qui tam plaintiff. Once filed, the action may be dismissed voluntarily by the person bringing the action only if the court and Attorney General have given written consent to the dismissal.

(2)   A copy of the complaint and written disclosure of substantially all material evidence and information the person possesses shall be served on the Attorney General pursuant to applicable rules of the North Carolina Rules of Civil Procedure. The complaint shall be filed in camera, shall remain under seal for at least 120 days, and shall not be served on the defendant until the court so orders. The State may elect to intervene and proceed with the action within 120 days after it receives both the complaint and the material evidence and information.

(3)   The State may, for good cause shown, move the court for extensions of the time during which the complaint remains under seal under subdivision (2) of this subsection. Any such motions may be supported by affidavits or other submissions in camera. The defendant shall not be required to respond to any complaint filed under this section until 30 days after the complaint is unsealed and served upon the defendant pursuant to the North Carolina Rules of Civil Procedure.

(4)   Before the expiration of the 120-day period or any extensions obtained under subdivision (3) of this subsection, the State shall:

a.   Proceed with the action, in which case the action shall be conducted by the State; or

b.   Notify the court that it declines to take over the action, in which case the person bringing the action shall have the right to conduct the action.

(5)   When a person brings an action under this subsection, the federal False Claims Act, 31 U.S.C. § 3729 et seq., or any similar provision of law in any other state, no person other than the State may intervene or bring a related action based on the facts underlying the pending action; provided, however, that nothing in this subdivision prohibits a person from amending a pending action in another jurisdiction to allege a claim under this subsection.

(c)   The Attorney General may retain a portion of the damages recovered for a State agency out of the proceeds of the action or settlement under this Article as reimbursement for costs incurred by the Attorney General in investigating and bringing a civil action under this Article, including reasonable attorneys' fees and investigative costs. Retained funds shall be used by the Attorney General to carry out the provisions of this Article. (2009-554, s. 1; 2010-96, s. 25(a).)

§ 1-609. Rights of the parties to qui tam actions.

(a)   If the State proceeds with an action under G.S. 1-608(b), it shall have the primary responsibility for prosecuting the action and shall not be bound by an act of the qui tam plaintiff. The qui tam plaintiff shall have the right to continue as a party to the action, subject to the limitations set forth in subsections (b) through (e) of this section.

(b)   The State may dismiss the action for good cause notwithstanding the objections of the qui tam plaintiff if the qui tam plaintiff has been notified by the State of the filing of the motion and the court has provided the qui tam plaintiff with an opportunity for a hearing on the motion.

(c)   The State may settle the action with the defendant, notwithstanding the objections of the qui tam plaintiff, if the court determines, after a hearing, that the proposed settlement is fair, adequate, and reasonable under all the circumstances. Upon a showing of good cause, the hearing may be heard in camera.

(d)   Upon a showing by the State that the qui tam plaintiff's unrestricted participation during the course of the litigation would interfere with or unduly delay the State's prosecution of the case or would be repetitious, irrelevant, or for purposes of harassment, the court may, in its discretion, impose limitations on the person's participation, such as any of the following:

(1)   Limiting the number of witnesses the qui tam plaintiff may call.

(2)   Limiting the length of the testimony of those witnesses.

(3)   Limiting the qui tam plaintiff's cross-examination of witnesses.
(4)   Otherwise limiting the participation by the qui tam plaintiff in the litigation.

(e) Upon a showing by the defendant that the qui tam plaintiff's unrestricted participation during the course of the litigation would be for purposes of harassment or would cause the defendant undue burden or unnecessary expense, the court may limit the participation by the qui tam plaintiff in the litigation.

(f) If the State elects not to proceed with the action, the qui tam plaintiff shall have the right to conduct the action. If the State so requests, it shall be served with copies of all pleadings filed in the action and shall be supplied with copies of all deposition transcripts at the State's expense. When a qui tam plaintiff proceeds with the action, the court, without limiting the status and rights of the qui tam plaintiff, may permit the State to intervene at a later date upon a showing of good cause.

(g) Whether or not the State proceeds with the action, upon a showing by the State that certain actions of discovery by the qui tam plaintiff would interfere with the State's investigation or prosecution of a criminal or civil matter arising out of the same facts, the court may stay such discovery for a period of not more than 120 days. Such a showing shall be conducted in camera. The court may extend the 120‑day period upon a further showing in camera that the State has pursued the criminal or civil investigation or proceedings with reasonable diligence and any proposed discovery in the civil action will interfere with the ongoing criminal or civil investigations or proceedings.

(h) Notwithstanding the provisions of G.S. 1-608(b), the State may elect to pursue its claim through any alternate remedy available to the State, including any administrative proceeding to determine a civil money penalty. If any such alternate remedy is pursued in another proceeding, the qui tam plaintiff shall have the same rights in that proceeding as the qui tam plaintiff would have had if the action had continued under this section. Any finding of fact or conclusion of law made in the other proceeding that has become final shall be conclusive on all parties to an action under this section. For purposes of this subsection, a finding or conclusion is final if it has been finally determined on appeal to the appropriate court of the State, if all time for filing such an appeal with respect to the finding or conclusion has expired, or if the finding or conclusion is not subject to judicial review. (2009‑554, s. 1.)

§ 1-610. Award to qui tam plaintiff.

(a) Except as otherwise provided in this section, if the State proceeds with an action brought by a qui tam plaintiff under G.S. 1-608(b), the qui tam plaintiff shall receive at least fifteen percent (15%) but not more than twenty-five percent (25%) of the proceeds of the action or settlement of the claim, depending upon the extent to which the qui tam plaintiff substantially contributed to the prosecution of the action.

(b) Where the action is one which the court finds to be based primarily on disclosures of specific information, other than information provided by the qui tam plaintiff, relating to allegations or transactions (i) in a criminal, civil, or administrative hearing at the State or federal level, (ii) in a congressional, legislative, administrative, General Accounting Office, or State Auditor's report, hearing, audit, or investigation, or (iii) from the news media, the court may award such sums as it considers appropriate, but in no case more than ten percent (10%) of the proceeds, taking into account the significance of the information and the role of the qui tam plaintiff in advancing the case to litigation.

(c) Any payment to a qui tam plaintiff under subsection (a) or (b) of this section shall be made from the proceeds.

(d) The qui tam plaintiff also shall receive an amount for reasonable expenses that the court finds to have been necessarily incurred, plus reasonable attorneys' fees and costs. All such expenses, fees, and costs shall be awarded against the defendant.

(e) If the State does not proceed with an action under this Article, the qui tam plaintiff shall receive an amount which the court decides is reasonable for collecting the civil penalty and damages. The amount shall not be less than twenty-five percent (25%) and not more than thirty percent (30%) of the proceeds of the action or settlement and shall be paid out of the proceeds. The qui tam plaintiff also shall receive an amount for reasonable expenses that the court finds to have been necessarily incurred, plus reasonable attorneys' fees and costs. All such expenses, fees, and costs shall be awarded against the defendant.

(f) Whether or not the State proceeds with the action, if the court finds that the qui tam plaintiff planned and initiated the violation of G.S. 1-607 upon which the action was brought, then the court may, to the extent the court considers appropriate, reduce the share of the proceeds of the action which the qui tam plaintiff would otherwise receive under subsection (a), (b), or (e) of this section, taking into account the role of the qui tam plaintiff in advancing the case to litigation and any relevant circumstances pertaining to the violation. If the qui tam plaintiff is convicted of criminal conduct arising from his or her role in the violation of G.S. 1-607, the qui tam plaintiff shall be dismissed from the civil action and shall not receive any share of the proceeds of the action. Such a dismissal shall not prejudice the right of the State to continue the action.

(g)   If the State does not proceed with the action and the qui tam plaintiff conducts the action, the court may award to the defendant its reasonable attorneys' fees and expenses if the defendant prevails in the action and the court finds that the claim of the qui tam plaintiff was clearly frivolous, clearly vexatious, or brought primarily for purposes of harassment. (2009-554, s. 1.)

§ 1-611. Certain actions barred.

(a)   No court shall have jurisdiction over an action brought under G.S. 1-608(b) against a member of the General Assembly, a member of the judiciary, or a senior executive branch official acting in their official capacity if the action is based on evidence or information known to the State when the action was brought.

(b)   In no event may a person bring an action under G.S. 1-608(b) that is based upon allegations or transactions that are the subject of a civil suit or an administrative civil money penalty proceeding in which the State is already a party.

(c)   No civil action may be brought under this Article by a person who is or was a public employee or public official if the allegations of such action are based substantially upon either of the following:

(1)   Allegations of wrongdoing or misconduct which such person had a duty or obligation to report or investigate within the scope of his or her public employment or office.

(2)   Information or records to which the person had access as a result of his or her public employment or office.

(d)   No court shall have jurisdiction over an action under G.S. 1-608(b) based upon the public disclosure of allegations or transactions (i) in a criminal, civil, or administrative hearing at the State or federal level, (ii) in a congressional, legislative, administrative, General Accounting Office, or State Auditor's report, hearing, audit, or investigation, or (iii) from the news media, unless the action is brought by the Attorney General, or the person bringing the action is an original source of the information. For purposes of this section, "original source" means an individual who has direct and independent knowledge of the information on which the allegations are based and has voluntarily provided the information to the State before filing an action under G.S. 1-608(b) that is based on the information. (2009-554, s. 1; 2010-96, s. 25(b).)

§ 1-612. State not liable for certain expenses.

The State is not liable for expenses that a person incurs in bringing an action under G.S. 1-608(b). (2009-554, s. 1.)

§ 1-613. Private action for retaliation action.

Any employee, contractor, or agent who is discharged, demoted, suspended, threatened, harassed, or in any other manner discriminated against in the terms and conditions of employment because of lawful acts done by the employee, contractor, or agent on behalf of the employee, contractor, or agent or associated others in furtherance of an action under this Article, or in furtherance of other efforts to stop one or more violations of G.S. 1-607, including investigation for, initiation of, testimony for, or assistance in an action filed or to be filed under this Article, shall be entitled to all relief necessary to make the employee whole. Such relief shall include reinstatement with the same seniority status the employee, contractor, or agent would have had but for the discrimination, two times the amount of back pay, interest on the back pay, and compensation for any special damages sustained as a result of the discrimination, including litigation costs and reasonable attorneys' fees. An employee, contractor, or agent may bring an action in superior court for the relief provided in this section. (2009-554, s. 1.)

§ 1-614. Civil investigative demand.

(a)   A civil investigative demand is an administrative subpoena. Whenever the Attorney General has reason to believe that a person has information or is in possession, custody, or control of any document or other object relevant to an investigation or that would lead to the discovery of relevant information in an investigation of a violation of G.S. 1-607, the Attorney General may issue in writing and cause to be served upon the person, before bringing or intervening or making an election in an action under G.S. 1-608 or other false claims law, a civil investigative demand requiring the person to produce any documents or objects for their inspection and copying.

(b) The civil investigative demand shall comply with all of the following:

(1) Be served upon the person in the manner required for service of process in civil actions and may be served by the Attorney General or investigator assigned to the North Carolina Department of Justice.

(2) Describe the nature of the conduct constituting the violation under investigation.

(3) Describe the class or classes of any documents or objects to be produced with sufficient definiteness to permit them to be fairly identified.

(4) Prescribe a reasonable date and time at which the person shall produce any document or object.

(5) Advise the person that objections to or reasons for not complying with the demand may be filed with the Attorney General on or before that date and time.

(6) Designate a person to whom any document or object shall be produced.

(7) Contain a copy of subsections (b) and (c) of this section.

(c) The date within which any document or object must be produced shall be more than 30 days after the civil investigative demand has been served upon the person.

(d) A civil investigative demand may include an express demand for any product of discovery. A product of discovery includes the original or duplicate of any deposition, interrogatory, document, thing, examination, or admission, that is obtained by any method of discovery in any judicial or administrative proceeding of an adversarial nature, and any digest, compilation, and index of any product of discovery. Whenever a civil investigative demand is an express demand for any product of discovery, a copy of the demand shall be served on the person from whom the discovery was obtained, and the Attorney General shall notify the person to whom the demand is issued of the date on which the copy was served. A demand for a product of discovery shall not be returned or returnable until 30 days after a copy of the demand has been served on the person from whom the discovery was obtained. Within 30 days after service of the demand, the person from whom the discovery was obtained or the person on whom the demand was served will serve on the Attorney General a copy of any protective order that prevents or restrains disclosure of the product of discovery to the Attorney General. The Attorney General may petition the court that issued the protective order to modify the order to allow compliance with the demand. Disclosure of any product of discovery pursuant to any express demand does not constitute a waiver of any right or privilege that the person making the disclosure may be entitled to invoke to resist discovery of trial preparation materials.

(e)   The production of documents and objects in response to a civil investigative demand served under this section shall be made under a sworn certificate by the person to whom the demand is directed, or in the case of a person other than a natural person, a person having knowledge of the facts and circumstances relating to the production and authorized to act on behalf of the person. The certificate shall state that all of the documentary material required by the demand and in the possession, custody, or control of the person to whom the demand is directed has been produced and made available. Upon written agreement between the person served with the civil investigative demand and the Attorney General, the person may substitute copies for originals of all or any part of the documents requested.

(f)   If a person objects to or otherwise fails to comply with a civil investigative demand served upon the person under subsection (a) of this section, the Attorney General may file an action in superior court for an order to enforce the demand. Venue for the action to enforce the demand shall be in either Wake County or the county in which the person resides, is found, or transacts business. Notice of a hearing on the action to enforce the demand and a copy of the action shall be served upon the person in the same manner as prescribed in the Rules of Civil Procedure. If the court finds that the demand is proper, that there is reasonable cause to believe that there may have been a violation of G.S. 1-607, and that the information sought or document or object demanded is relevant to the violation, the court shall order the person to comply with the demand, subject to modifications the court may prescribe.

(g) If the person fails to comply with an order entered pursuant to subsection (f) of this section, the court may do any of the following:

(1) Adjudge the person to be in contempt of court.

(2) Grant injunctive relief against the person to whom the demand is issued to restrain the conduct which is the subject of the investigation.

(3) Grant any other relief as the court may deem proper.

(h) A petition for an order of the court to modify or set aside a civil investigative demand issued under this section may be filed by any person who has received a civil investigative demand or in the case of an express demand for any product of discovery, the person on whom the discovery was obtained. The petition may be filed in superior court in either Wake County or the county in which the person resides, is found, or transacts business, or, in the case of a petition to modify an express demand for any product of discovery, the petition shall be filed in the court in which the proceeding was pending when the product of discovery was obtained. Any petition under this subsection must be filed within 30 days after the date of service of the civil investigative demand or before the return date specified in the demand, whichever date is earlier, or within a longer period as may be prescribed in writing by the investigator identified in the demand. The petition shall specify each ground upon which the petitioner relies in seeking relief and may be based upon any failure to comply with the provisions of this section or upon any constitutional or other legal right or privilege of the person. During the pendency of the petition in the court, the court may stay, as it deems proper, the running of the time allowed for compliance with the demand, in whole or in part, except that the person filing the petition shall comply with any portions of the demand not sought to be modified or set aside.

(i) Any documents and objects produced pursuant to this section may be used in connection with any civil action brought under G.S. 1-608 and for any use that is consistent with the law, and the regulations and policies of the Attorney General, including use in connection with internal Attorney General memoranda and reports; communications between the Attorney General and a federal, State, or local governmental agency, or a contractor of a federal, State, or local governmental agency, undertaken in furtherance of an Attorney General investigation or prosecution of a case; interviews of any qui tam relator or other witness; oral examinations; depositions; preparation for and response to civil discovery requests; introduction into the record of a case or proceeding applications, motions, memoranda, and briefs submitted to a court or other tribunal; and communications with government investigators, auditors, consultants and experts, the counsel of other parties, arbitrators and mediators, concerning an investigation, case, or proceeding. Any documents and objects obtained by the Attorney General under this section may be shared with any qui tam relator if the Attorney General determines it is necessary as part of any false claims act investigation. Before using or sharing documents and objects obtained by the Attorney General under this section with any person, the Attorney General may require that the person agree to an order of the court protecting the documents or objects, or any information contained in the documents or objects, from disclosure by that person. In the case of documents or objects the producing party has designated as a trade secret or other confidential research, development, or commercial information, the Attorney General shall either (i) require that the person with whom documents or objects are shared be prohibited from disclosing the documents or objects, or any information contained in the documents or objects, or (ii) petition the court for an order directing the producing party to either appear and support the designation or withdraw the designation.

(j)   The Attorney General may designate an employee of the North Carolina Department of Justice to serve as a custodian of documents and objects.

(k)   Except as otherwise provided in this section, no documents or objects, or copies thereof, while in the possession of the North Carolina Department of Justice, shall be available for examination by any person other than an employee of the North Carolina Department of Justice. The prohibition in the preceding sentence on the availability of documents or objects shall not apply if consent is given by the person who produced the documents or objects, or, in the case of any product of discovery produced pursuant to an express demand, consent is given by the person from whom the discovery was obtained, or prevent disclosure to any other federal or State agency for use by that agency in furtherance of its statutory responsibilities upon application made by the Attorney General to the superior court showing substantial need for the use of the documents or objects by any agency in furtherance of its statutory responsibilities.

(l)   While in the possession of the custodian and under reasonable terms and conditions as the Attorney General shall prescribe, documents or objects shall be available for examination by the person who produced the documents or objects, or by a representative of that person authorized by that person to examine the documents or objects.

(m) If any documents or objects have been produced by any person in the course of any investigation pursuant to a civil investigative demand under this section, and any case or proceeding before any court arising out of the investigation, or any proceeding before any agency involving the documents or objects, has been completed, or no case or proceeding in which the documents or objects may be used has been commenced within a reasonable time after completion of the investigation, the custodian shall, upon written request of the person who produced the documents or objects, return to the person any documents or objects that have not passed into the control of any court or agency.

(n) The North Carolina Rules of Civil Procedure shall apply to this section to the extent that the rules are not inconsistent with the provisions of this section. (2009-554, s. 1.)

§ 1-615. False claims procedure.

(a) Statute of Limitations. – A civil action under G.S. 1-608 may not be brought (i) more than six years after the date on which the violation of G.S. 1-607 was committed or (ii) more than three years after the date when facts material to the right of action are known or reasonably should have been known by the official of the State of North Carolina charged with responsibility to act in the circumstances, but in no event more than 10 years after the date on which the violation is committed, whichever occurs last.

(b) If the Attorney General elects to intervene and proceed with an action brought under G.S. 1-608(b), the State may file its own complaint or amend the complaint of a person who has brought an action under G.S. 1-608(b) to clarify or add detail to the claims with respect to which the State is intervening and to add any additional claims with respect to which the State contends it is entitled to relief. For statute of limitations purposes, any such State pleading shall relate back to the filing date of the complaint of the person who originally brought the action, to the extent that the claim of the State arises out of the conduct, transactions, or occurrences set forth, or attempted to be set forth, in the prior complaint of that person.

(c) Burden of Proof. – In any action brought under G.S. 1-608, the State or the qui tam plaintiff shall be required to prove all essential elements of the cause of action, including damages, by a preponderance of the evidence.

(d) Estoppel. – Notwithstanding any other provision of law, a final judgment rendered in favor of the State in a criminal proceeding charging false statements or fraud, whether upon a verdict after trial or upon a plea of guilty or nolo contendere, shall estop the defendant from denying the essential elements of the offense in any action that involves the same transaction as in the criminal proceeding and which is brought under G.S. 1-608.

(e) Venue. – Venue for any action brought pursuant to G.S. 1-608 shall be in either Wake County or in any county in which a claim originated, or in which any statement or record was made, or acts done, or services or property rendered in connection with any act constituting part of the violation of this Article.

(f) Service on Federal, State, or Local Authorities. – With respect to the United States or any State or local government that is named as a co-plaintiff in an action brought under G.S. 1-608, a seal on the action ordered by the court under G.S. 1-608(b) shall not preclude the State or the person bringing the action from serving the complaint, any other pleadings, or the written disclosure of substantially all material evidence and information possessed by the person bringing the action on the law enforcement authorities that are authorized under the law of the co-plaintiff government to investigate and prosecute such actions on behalf of that co-plaintiff government, except that the seal applies to the law enforcement authorities so served to the same extent as the seal applies to other parties in the action.

(g) A civil action may not be brought under both this Article and Part 7 of Article 2 of Chapter 108A of the General Statutes. (2009-554, s. 1.)

§ 1-616. Remedies under other laws; severability of provisions; liberality of legislative construction; adoption of legislative history.

(a) Remedies Under Other Laws. – The provisions of this Article are not exclusive, and the remedies provided for in this Article shall be in addition to any other remedies provided for in any other law or available under common law. No criminal or administrative action need be brought against any person as a condition for establishing civil liability under this section.
(b) If any provision of this Article or the application of this Article to any person or circumstance is held to be unconstitutional, the remainder of this

Article and the application of the provision to other persons or circumstances shall not be affected by that holding.

(c) This Article shall be interpreted and construed so as to be consistent with the federal False Claims Act, 31 U.S.C. § 3729, et seq., and any subsequent amendments to that act. (2009-554, s. 1.)

§ 1-617. Reporting.

(a) In reporting on the terms and disbursements set forth in any settlement agreement or final order or judgment in a case filed under this Article as required by G.S. 114-2.5, the report shall include the percentage of the proceeds and the amount paid to any qui tam plaintiff under G.S. 1-610.

(b) On or before February 1 of each year, the Attorney General shall submit to the Joint Legislative Commission on Governmental Operations and the Chairs of the Appropriations Subcommittees on Justice and Public Safety of the House of Representatives and the Senate a report on the number of qui tam cases under this Article pending in the State and the number of qui tam cases pending in other jurisdictions involving the State, the number of qui tam cases under this Article that were settled, the number of qui tam cases in which judgment was entered, and the amount of proceeds paid to qui tam plaintiffs during the previous calendar year. (2009-554, s. 1.)

§ 1-618. Rules.

The Attorney General may adopt rules necessary to carry out the purposes set forth in this Article. (2009-554, s. 1.)

Article 52.

Limited Civil Liability of Domestic Violence Shelters and Persons Associated With the Shelters.

§ 1-630. Definitions.

As used in this Article, the following terms mean:

(1) Client. – A person who is the victim of domestic violence, as defined in Chapter 50B of the General Statutes, or of nonconsensual sexual conduct or stalking, as defined in Chapter 50C of the General Statutes, and is using services or facilities of a shelter.

(2) Conduct. – One or more actions or omissions.

(3) Harm. – Injury, death, or loss to person or property.

(4) Perpetrator. – A person who has committed domestic violence and who bears one of the personal relationships specified in G.S. 50B-1(b) to the victim of domestic violence, or a person who has committed nonconsensual sexual conduct or stalking as defined in Chapter 50C of the General Statutes.

(5) Person associated with the shelter. – A person who is a director, owner, trustee, officer, employee, victim advocate, or volunteer connected with the shelter.

(6) Shelter. – A facility that meets the criteria set forth in G.S. 50B-9 and is funded through the Domestic Violence Center Fund providing shelter to victims of domestic violence, nonconsensual sexual conduct, or stalking.

(7) Victim advocate. – A person from a crime victim service organization who provides support and assistance for a victim of a crime during court proceedings and recovery efforts related to the crime.

(8) Volunteer. – An individual who provides any service at a shelter without expectation of receiving and without receiving any compensation or other form of remuneration, directly or indirectly, for the provision of the service. (2010-5, s. 2.)

§ 1-631. Immunity of a domestic violence shelter and any person associated with the shelter concerning torts committed on the shelter's premises.

(a) Except as provided in subsection (b) of this section, no shelter and no person associated with the shelter is liable in damages in a tort action for any harm that a client or other person who is on the premises of the shelter sustains as a result of tortious conduct of a perpetrator that is committed on the premises of the shelter if the perpetrator is not a person associated with the shelter.

(b) The immunity established by this section does not extend to gross negligence, wanton conduct, or intentional wrongdoing that would otherwise be actionable. (2010-5, s. 2.)

Chapter 1A.

Rules of Civil Procedure.

§ 1A-1. Rules of Civil Procedure.

The Rules of Civil Procedure are as follows:

Article 1.

Scope of Rules–One Form of Action.

Rule 1. Scope of rules.

These rules shall govern the procedure in the superior and district courts of the State of North Carolina in all actions and proceedings of a civil nature except when a differing procedure is prescribed by statute. They shall also govern the procedure in tort actions brought before the Industrial Commission except when a differing procedure is prescribed by statute. (1967, c. 954, s. 1; 1971, c. 818.)

Rule 2. One form of action.

There shall be in this State but one form of action for the enforcement or protection of private rights or the redress of private wrongs, which shall be denominated a civil action. (1967, c. 954, s. 1.)

Article 2.

Commencement of Action; Service of Process, Pleadings, Motions, and Orders.

Rule 3. Commencement of action.

(a) A civil action is commenced by filing a complaint with the court. The clerk shall enter the date of filing on the original complaint, and such entry shall be prima facie evidence of the date of filing.

A civil action may also be commenced by the issuance of a summons when

(1) A person makes application to the court stating the nature and purpose of his action and requesting permission to file his complaint within 20 days and

(2) The court makes an order stating the nature and purpose of the action and granting the requested permission.

The summons and the court's order shall be served in accordance with the provisions of Rule 4. When the complaint is filed it shall be served in accordance with the provisions of Rule 4 or by registered mail if the plaintiff so elects. If the complaint is not filed within the period specified in the clerk's order, the action shall abate. (b) The clerk shall maintain as prescribed by the Administrative Office of the Courts a separate index of all medical malpractice actions, as defined in G.S. 90-21.11. Upon the commencement of a medical malpractice action, the clerk shall provide a current copy of the index to the senior regular resident judge of the district in which the action is pending. (1967, c. 954, s. 1; 1987, c. 859, s. 2.)

Rule 4. Process.

(a) Summons – Issuance; who may serve. – Upon the filing of the complaint, summons shall be issued forthwith, and in any event within five days. The complaint and summons shall be delivered to some proper person for service. In this State, such proper person shall be the sheriff of the county where service is to be made or some other person duly authorized by law to serve summons. Outside this State, such proper person shall be anyone who is not a party and is not less than 21 years of age or anyone duly authorized to serve summons by the law of the place where service is to be made. Upon request of the plaintiff separate or additional summons shall be issued against any defendants. A summons is issued when, after being filled out and dated, it is signed by the officer having authority to do so. The date the summons bears shall be prima facie evidence of the date of issue.

(b) Summons – Contents. – The summons shall run in the name of the State and be dated and signed by the clerk, assistant clerk, or deputy clerk of the court in the county in which the action is commenced. It shall contain the title of the cause and the name of the court and county wherein the action has been commenced. It shall be directed to the defendant or defendants and shall notify each defendant to appear and answer within 30 days after its service upon him and further that if he fails so to appear, the plaintiff will apply to the court for the relief demanded in the complaint. It shall set forth the name and address of plaintiff's attorney, or if there be none, the name and address of plaintiff. If a request for admission is served with the summons, the summons shall so state.

(c) Summons – Return. – Personal service or substituted personal service of summons as prescribed by Rule 4(j)(1) a and b must be made within 60 days after the date of the issuance of summons. When a summons has been served upon every party named in the summons, it shall be returned immediately to the clerk who issued it, with notation thereon of its service.

Failure to make service within the time allowed or failure to return a summons to the clerk after it has been served on every party named in the summons shall not invalidate the summons. If the summons is not served within the time allowed upon every party named in the summons, it shall be returned immediately upon the expiration of such time by the officer to the clerk of the court who issued it with notation thereon of its nonservice and the reasons therefor as to every such party not served, but failure to comply with this requirement shall not invalidate the summons.

(d) Summons – Extension; endorsement, alias and pluries. – When any defendant in a civil action is not served within the time allowed for service, the action may be continued in existence as to such defendant by either of the following methods of extension:

(1) The plaintiff may secure an endorsement upon the original summons for an extension of time within which to complete service of process. Return of the summons so endorsed shall be in the same manner as the original process. Such endorsement may be secured within 90 days after the issuance of summons or the date of the last prior endorsement, or

(2) The plaintiff may sue out an alias or pluries summons returnable in the same manner as the original process. Such alias or pluries summons may be sued out at any time within 90 days after the date of issue of the last preceding summons in the chain of summonses or within 90 days of the last prior endorsement.

Provided, in tax and assessment foreclosures under G.S. 47-108.25 and G.S. 105-374, the first endorsement may be made at any time within two years after the issuance of the original summons, and subsequent endorsements may thereafter be made as in other actions; or an alias or pluries summons may be sued out at any time within two years after the issuance of the original summons, and after the issuance of such alias or pluries summons, the chain of summonses may be kept up as in any other action.

Provided, for service upon a defendant in a place not within the United States, the first endorsement may be made at any time within two years after the issuance of the original summons, and subsequent endorsements may thereafter be made at least once every two years; or an alias or pluries summons may be sued out at any time within two years after the issuance of the original summons, and after the issuance of such alias or pluries summons, the chain of summonses may be kept up as in any other action if sued out within two years of the last preceding summons in the chain of summonses or within two years of the last prior endorsement.

Provided, further, the methods of extension may be used interchangeably in any case and regardless of the form of the preceding extension.

(e) Summons – Discontinuance. – When there is neither endorsement by the clerk nor issuance of alias or pluries summons within the time specified in Rule 4(d), the action is discontinued as to any defendant not theretofore served with summons within the time allowed. Thereafter, alias or pluries summons may issue, or an extension be endorsed by the clerk, but, as to such defendant, the action shall be deemed to have commenced on the date of such issuance or endorsement.

(f) Summons – Date of multiple summonses. – If the plaintiff shall cause separate or additional summonses to be issued as provided in Rule 4(a), the date of issuance of such separate or additional summonses shall be considered the same as that of the original summons for purposes of endorsement or alias summons under Rule 4(d).

(g) Summons – Docketing by clerk. – The clerk shall keep a record in which he shall note the day and hour of issuance of every summons, whether original, alias, pluries, or endorsement thereon. When the summons is returned, the clerk shall note on the record the date of the return and the fact as to service or non-service.

(h) Summons – When proper officer not available. – If at any time there is not in a county a proper officer, capable of executing process, to whom summons or other process can be delivered for service, or if a proper officer refuses or neglects to execute such process, or if such officer is a party to or otherwise interested in the action or proceeding, the clerk of the issuing court, upon the facts being verified before him by written affidavit of the plaintiff or his agent or attorney, shall appoint some suitable person who, after he accepts such process for service, shall execute such process in the same manner, with like effect, and subject to the same liabilities, as if such person were a proper officer regularly serving process in that county.

(h1) Summons – When process returned unexecuted. – If a proper officer returns a summons or other process unexecuted, the plaintiff or his agent or attorney may cause service to be made by anyone who is not less than 21 years of age, who is not a party to the action, and who is not related by blood or marriage to a party to the action or to a person upon whom service is to be made. This subsection shall not apply to executions pursuant to Article 28 of Chapter 1 or summary ejectment pursuant to Article 3 of Chapter 42 of the General Statutes.

(i) Summons – Amendment. – At any time, before or after judgment, in its discretion and upon such terms as it deems just, the court may allow any process or proof of service thereof to be amended, unless it clearly appears that material prejudice would result to substantial rights of the party against whom the process issued.

(j) Process – Manner of service to exercise personal jurisdiction. – In any action commenced in a court of this State having jurisdiction of the subject matter and grounds for personal jurisdiction as provided in G.S. 1-75.4, the manner of service of process within or without the State shall be as follows:

(1) Natural Person. – Except as provided in subdivision (2) below, upon a natural person by one of the following:

a. By delivering a copy of the summons and of the complaint to the natural person or by leaving copies thereof at the defendant's dwelling house or usual place of abode with some person of suitable age and discretion then residing therein.
b. By delivering a copy of the summons and of the complaint to an agent authorized by appointment or by law to be served or to accept service of

process or by serving process upon such agent or the party in a manner specified by any statute.

c. By mailing a copy of the summons and of the complaint, registered or certified mail, return receipt requested, addressed to the party to be served, and delivering to the addressee.

d. By depositing with a designated delivery service authorized pursuant to 26 U.S.C. § 7502(f)(2) a copy of the summons and complaint, addressed to the party to be served, delivering to the addressee, and obtaining a delivery receipt. As used in this sub-subdivision, "delivery receipt" includes an electronic or facsimile receipt.

e. By mailing a copy of the summons and of the complaint by signature confirmation as provided by the United States Postal Service, addressed to the party to be served, and delivering to the addressee.

(2) Natural Person under Disability. – Upon a natural person under disability by serving process in any manner prescribed in this section (j) for service upon a natural person and, in addition, where required by paragraph a or b below, upon a person therein designated.

a. Where the person under disability is a minor, process shall be served separately in any manner prescribed for service upon a natural person upon a parent or guardian having custody of the child, or if there be none, upon any other person having the care and control of the child. If there is no parent, guardian, or other person having care and control of the child when service is made upon the child, then service of process must also be made upon a guardian ad litem who has been appointed pursuant to Rule 17.

b. If the plaintiff actually knows that a person under disability is under guardianship of any kind, process shall be served separately upon his guardian in any manner applicable and appropriate under this section (j). If the plaintiff does not actually know that a guardian has been appointed when service is made upon a person known to him to be incompetent to have charge of his affairs, then service of process must be made upon a guardian ad litem who has been appointed pursuant to Rule 17.

(3) The State. – Upon the State by personally delivering a copy of the summons and of the complaint to the Attorney General or to a deputy or assistant attorney general; by mailing a copy of the summons and of the

complaint, registered or certified mail, return receipt requested, addressed to the Attorney General or to a deputy or assistant attorney general; or by depositing with a designated delivery service authorized pursuant to 26 U.S.C. § 7502(f)(2) a copy of the summons and complaint, addressed to the Attorney General or to a deputy or assistant attorney general, delivering to the addressee, and obtaining a delivery receipt. As used in this subdivision, "delivery receipt" includes an electronic or facsimile receipt.

(4) An Agency of the State. –

a. Upon an agency of the State by personally delivering a copy of the summons and of the complaint to the process agent appointed by the agency in the manner hereinafter provided; by mailing a copy of the summons and of the complaint, registered or certified mail, return receipt requested, addressed to said process agent; or by depositing with a designated delivery service authorized pursuant to 26 U.S.C. § 7502(f)(2) a copy of the summons and complaint, addressed to the process agent, delivering to the addressee, and obtaining a delivery receipt. As used in this sub-subdivision, "delivery receipt" includes an electronic or facsimile receipt.

b. Every agency of the State shall appoint a process agent by filing with the Attorney General the name and address of an agent upon whom process may be served.

c. If any agency of the State fails to comply with paragraph b above, then service upon such agency may be made by personally delivering a copy of the summons and of the complaint to the Attorney General or to a deputy or assistant attorney general; by mailing a copy of the summons and of the complaint, registered or certified mail, return receipt requested, addressed to the Attorney General, or to a deputy or assistant attorney general; or by depositing with a designated delivery service authorized pursuant to 26 U.S.C. § 7502(f)(2) a copy of the summons and complaint, addressed to the Attorney General or to a deputy or assistant attorney general, delivering to the addressee, and obtaining a delivery receipt. As used in this sub-subdivision, "delivery receipt" includes an electronic or facsimile receipt.

d. For purposes of this rule, the term "agency of the State" includes every agency, institution, board, commission, bureau, department, division, council, member of Council of State, or officer of the State government of the State of North Carolina, but does not include counties, cities, towns, villages, other municipal corporations or political subdivisions of the State, county or city boards of education, other local public districts, units, or bodies of any kind, or private corporations created by act of the General Assembly.

(5) Counties, Cities, Towns, Villages and Other Local Public Bodies. –

a. Upon a city, town, or village by personally delivering a copy of the summons and of the complaint to its mayor, city manager or clerk; by mailing a copy of the summons and of the complaint, registered or certified mail, return receipt requested, addressed to its mayor, city manager or clerk; or by depositing with a designated delivery service authorized pursuant to 26 U.S.C. § 7502(f)(2) a copy of the summons and complaint, addressed to the mayor, city manager, or clerk, delivering to the addressee, and obtaining a delivery receipt. As used in this sub-subdivision, "delivery receipt" includes an electronic or facsimile receipt.

b. Upon a county by personally delivering a copy of the summons and of the complaint to its county manager or to the chairman, clerk or any member of the board of commissioners for such county; by mailing a copy of the summons and of the complaint, registered or certified mail, return receipt requested, addressed to its county manager or to the chairman, clerk, or any member of this board of commissioners for such county; or by depositing with a designated delivery service authorized pursuant to 26 U.S.C. § 7502(f)(2) a copy of the summons and complaint, addressed to the county manager or to the chairman, clerk, or any member of the board of commissioners of that county, delivering to the addressee, and obtaining a delivery receipt. As used in this sub-subdivision, "delivery receipt" includes an electronic or facsimile receipt.

c. Upon any other political subdivision of the State, any county or city board of education, or other local public district, unit, or body of any kind (i) by personally delivering a copy of the summons and of the complaint to an officer or director thereof, (ii) by personally delivering a copy of the summons and of the complaint to an agent or attorney-in-fact authorized by appointment or by statute to be served or to accept service in its behalf, (iii) by mailing a copy of the summons and of the complaint, registered or certified mail, return receipt requested, addressed to the officer, director, agent, or attorney-in-fact as specified in (i) and (ii), or (iv) by depositing with a designated delivery service authorized pursuant to 26 U.S.C. § 7502(f)(2) a copy of the summons and complaint, addressed to the officer, director, agent, or attorney-in-fact as specified in (i) and (ii), delivering to the addressee, and obtaining a delivery receipt. As used in this sub-subdivision, "delivery receipt" includes an electronic or facsimile receipt.

d.   In any case where none of the officials, officers or directors specified in paragraphs a, b and c can, after due diligence, be found in the State, and that fact appears by affidavit to the satisfaction of the court, or a judge thereof, such court or judge may grant an order that service upon the party sought to be served may be made by personally delivering a copy of the summons and of the complaint to the Attorney General or any deputy or assistant attorney general of the State of North Carolina; by mailing a copy of the summons and of the complaint, registered or certified mail, return receipt requested, addressed to the Attorney General or any deputy or assistant attorney general of the State of North Carolina; or by depositing with a designated delivery service authorized pursuant to 26 U.S.C. § 7502(f)(2) a copy of the summons and complaint, addressed to the Attorney General or any deputy or assistant attorney general of the State of North Carolina, delivering to the addressee, and obtaining a delivery receipt. As used in this sub-subdivision, "delivery receipt" includes an electronic or facsimile receipt.

(6)   Domestic or Foreign Corporation. – Upon a domestic or foreign corporation by one of the following:

a.   By delivering a copy of the summons and of the complaint to an officer, director, or managing agent of the corporation or by leaving copies thereof in the office of such officer, director, or managing agent with the person who is apparently in charge of the office.

b.   By delivering a copy of the summons and of the complaint to an agent authorized by appointment or by law to be served or to accept service of process or by serving process upon such agent or the party in a manner specified by any statute.

c.   By mailing a copy of the summons and of the complaint, registered or certified mail, return receipt requested, addressed to the officer, director or agent to be served as specified in paragraphs a and b.

d.   By depositing with a designated delivery service authorized pursuant to 26 U.S.C. § 7502(f)(2) a copy of the summons and complaint, addressed to the officer, director, or agent to be served as specified in paragraphs a. and b., delivering to the addressee, and obtaining a delivery receipt. As used in this sub-subdivision, "delivery receipt" includes an electronic or facsimile receipt.

(7) Partnerships. – Upon a general or limited partnership:

a. By delivering a copy of the summons and of the complaint to any general partner, or to any attorney-in-fact or agent authorized by appointment or by law to be served or to accept service of process in its behalf; by mailing a copy of the summons and of the complaint, registered or certified mail, return receipt requested, addressed to any general partner, or to any attorney-in-fact or agent authorized by appointment or by law to be served or to accept service of process in its behalf; or by depositing with a designated delivery service authorized pursuant to 26 U.S.C. § 7502(f)(2) a copy of the summons and complaint, addressed to any general partner or to any attorney-in-fact or agent authorized by appointment or by law to be served or to accept service of process in its behalf, delivering to the addressee, and obtaining a delivery receipt; or by leaving copies thereof in the office of such general partner, attorney-in-fact or agent with the person who is apparently in charge of the office. As used in this sub-subdivision, "delivery receipt" includes an electronic or facsimile receipt.

b. If relief is sought against a partner specifically, a copy of the summons and of the complaint must be served on such partner as provided in this section (j).

(8) Other Unincorporated Associations and Their Officers. – Upon any unincorporated association, organization, or society other than a partnership by one of the following:

a. By delivering a copy of the summons and of the complaint to an officer, director, managing agent or member of the governing body of the unincorporated association, organization or society, or by leaving copies thereof in the office of such officer, director, managing agent or member of the governing body with the person who is apparently in charge of the office.

b. By delivering a copy of the summons and of the complaint to an agent authorized by appointment or by law to be served or to accept service of process or by serving process upon such agent or the party in a manner specified by any statute.

c. By mailing a copy of the summons and of the complaint, registered or certified mail, return receipt requested, addressed to the officer, director, agent or member of the governing body to be served as specified in paragraphs a and b.

d. By depositing with a designated delivery service authorized pursuant to 26 U.S.C. § 7502(f)(2) a copy of the summons and complaint, addressed to the officer, director, agent, or member of the governing body to be served as specified in paragraphs a. and b., delivering to the addressee, and obtaining a delivery receipt. As used in this sub-subdivision, "delivery receipt" includes an electronic or facsimile receipt.

(9) Foreign States and Their Political Subdivisions, Agencies, and Instrumentalities. – Upon a foreign state or a political subdivision, agency, or instrumentality thereof, pursuant to 28 U.S.C. § 1608.

(j1) Service by publication on party that cannot otherwise be served. – A party that cannot with due diligence be served by personal delivery, registered or certified mail, or by a designated delivery service authorized pursuant to 26 U.S.C. § 7502(f)(2) may be served by publication. Except in actions involving jurisdiction in rem or quasi in rem as provided in section (k), service of process by publication shall consist of publishing a notice of service of process by publication once a week for three successive weeks in a newspaper that is qualified for legal advertising in accordance with G.S. 1-597 and G.S. 1-598 and circulated in the area where the party to be served is believed by the serving party to be located, or if there is no reliable information concerning the location of the party then in a newspaper circulated in the county where the action is pending. If the party's post-office address is known or can with reasonable diligence be ascertained, there shall be mailed to the party at or immediately prior to the first publication a copy of the notice of service of process by publication. The mailing may be omitted if the post-office address cannot be ascertained with reasonable diligence. Upon completion of such service there shall be filed with the court an affidavit showing the publication and mailing in accordance with the requirements of G.S. 1-75.10(a)(2), the circumstances warranting the use of service by publication, and information, if any, regarding the location of the party served.

The notice of service of process by publication shall (i) designate the court in which the action has been commenced and the title of the action, which title may be indicated sufficiently by the name of the first plaintiff and the first defendant; (ii) be directed to the defendant sought to be served; (iii) state either that a pleading seeking relief against the person to be served has been filed or has been required to be filed therein not later than a date specified in the notice; (iv) state the nature of the relief being sought; (v) require the defendant being so served to make defense to such pleading within 40 days after a date stated in the notice, exclusive of such date, which date so stated shall be the date of the first publication of notice, or the date when the complaint is required to be filed, whichever is later, and notify the defendant that upon his failure to do so the party seeking service of process by publication will apply to the court for the relief sought; (vi) in cases of attachment, state the information required by G.S. 1-440.14; (vii) be subscribed by the party seeking service or his attorney and give the post-office address of such party or his attorney; and (viii) be substantially in the following form:

NOTICE OF SERVICE OF PROCESS BY PUBLICATION

STATE OF NORTH CAROLINA _____COUNTY

In the _____ Court

[Title of action or special proceeding] [To Person to be served]:

Take notice that a pleading seeking relief against you (has been filed) (is required to be filed not later than _____, ____) in the above-entitled (action) (special proceeding). The nature of the relief being sought is as follows:

(State nature.)

You are required to make defense to such pleading not later than (_____, ____) and upon your failure to do so the party seeking service against you will apply to the court for the relief sought.

This, the _____ day of _____, ____

(Attorney) (Party)

(Address)

(j2) Proof of service. – Proof of service of process shall be as follows:

(1) Personal Service. – Before judgment by default may be had on personal service, proof of service must be provided in accordance with the requirements of G.S. 1-75.10(a)(1).

(2) Registered or Certified Mail, Signature Confirmation, or Designated Delivery Service. – Before judgment by default may be had on service by registered or certified mail, signature confirmation, or by a designated delivery service authorized pursuant to 26 U.S.C. § 7502(f)(2) with delivery receipt, the serving party shall file an affidavit with the court showing proof of such service in accordance with the requirements of G.S. 1-75.10(a)(4), 1-75.10(a)(5), or 1-75.10(a)(6), as appropriate. This affidavit together with the return receipt, copy of the proof of delivery provided by the United States Postal Service, or delivery receipt, signed by the person who received the mail or delivery if not the addressee raises a presumption that the person who received the mail or delivery and signed the receipt was an agent of the addressee authorized by appointment or by law to be served or to accept service of process or was a person of suitable age and discretion residing in the addressee's dwelling house or usual place of abode. In the event the presumption described in the preceding sentence is rebutted by proof that the person who received the receipt at the addressee's dwelling house or usual place of abode was not a person of suitable age and discretion residing therein, the statute of limitation may not be pleaded as a defense if the action was initially commenced within the period of limitation and service of process is completed within 60 days from the date the service is declared invalid. Service shall be complete on the day the summons and complaint are delivered to the address. As used in this subdivision, "delivery receipt" includes an electronic or facsimile receipt provided by a designated delivery service.

(3) Publication. – Before judgment by default may be had on service by publication, the serving party shall file an affidavit with the court showing the circumstances warranting the use of service by publication, information, if any, regarding the location of the party served which was used in determining the area in which service by publication was printed and proof of service in accordance with G.S. 1-75.10(a)(2).

(j3) Service in a foreign country. – Unless otherwise provided by federal law, service upon a defendant, other than an infant or an incompetent person, may be effected in a place not within the United States:

(1) By any internationally agreed means reasonably calculated to give notice, such as those means authorized by the Hague Convention on the Service Abroad of Judicial and Extrajudicial Documents; or

(2) If there is no internationally agreed means of service or the applicable international agreement allows other means of service, provided that service is reasonably calculated to give notice:

a. In the manner prescribed by the law of the foreign country for service in that country in an action in any of its courts of general jurisdiction;

b. As directed by the foreign authority in response to a letter rogatory or letter of request; or

c. Unless prohibited by the law of the foreign country, by

1. Delivery to the individual personally of a copy of the summons and the complaint and, upon a corporation, partnership, association or other such entity, by delivery to an officer or a managing or general agent;

2. Any form of mail requiring a signed receipt, to be addressed and dispatched by the clerk of the court to the party to be served; or

(3) By other means not prohibited by international agreement as may be directed by the court.

Service under subdivision (2)c.1. or (3) of this subsection may be made by any person authorized by subsection (a) of this Rule or who is designated by order of the court or by the foreign court.

On request, the clerk shall deliver the summons to the plaintiff for transmission to the person or the foreign court or officer who will make the service. Proof of service may be made as prescribed in G.S. 1-75.10, by the order of the court, or by the law of the foreign country.

Proof of service by mail shall include an affidavit or certificate of addressing and mailing by the clerk of court.

(j4) Process or judgment by default not to be attacked on certain grounds. – No party may attack service of process or a judgment of default on the basis that service should or could have been effected by personal service rather than service by registered or certified mail. No party that receives timely actual notice may attack a judgment by default on the basis that the statutory requirement of due diligence as a condition precedent to service by publication was not met.

(j5) Personal jurisdiction by acceptance of service. – Any party personally, or through the persons provided in Rule 4(j), may accept service of process by notation of acceptance of service together with the signature of the party accepting service and the date thereof on an original or copy of a summons, and such acceptance shall have the same force and effect as would exist had the process been served by delivery of copy and summons and complaint to the person signing said acceptance.

(j6) Service by electronic mailing not authorized. – Nothing in subsection (j) of this section authorizes the use of electronic mailing for service on the party to be served.

(k) Process – Manner of service to exercise jurisdiction in rem or quasi in rem. – In any action commenced in a court of this State having jurisdiction of the subject matter and grounds for the exercise of jurisdiction in rem or quasi in rem as provided in G.S. 1-75.8, the manner of service of process shall be as follows:

(1) Defendant Known. – If the defendant is known, he may be served in the appropriate manner prescribed for service of process in section (j), or, if otherwise appropriate section (j1); except that the requirement for service by publication in (j1) shall be satisfied if made in the county where the action is pending and proof of service is made in accordance with section (j2).

(2) Defendant Unknown. – If the defendant is unknown, he may be designated by description and process may be served by publication in the manner provided in section (j1), except that the requirement for service by publication in (j1) shall be satisfied if made in the county where the action is pending and proof of service is made in accordance with section (j2). (1967, c. 954, s. 1; 1969, c. 895, ss. 1-4; 1971, c. 962; c. 1156, s. 2; 1975, cc. 408, 609; 1977, c. 910, ss. 1-3; 1981, c. 384, s. 3; c. 540, ss. 1-8; 1983, c. 679, ss. 1, 2; 1989, c. 330; c. 575, ss. 1, 2; 1995, c. 275, s. 1; c. 389, ss. 2, 3; c. 509, s. 135.1(e), (f); 1997-469, s. 1; 1999-456, s. 59; 2001-379, ss. 1, 2, 2.1, 2.2; 2005-221, ss. 1, 2; 2008-36, ss. 1-3, 5.)

Rule 5. Service and filing of pleadings and other papers.

(a) Service of orders, subsequent pleadings, discovery papers, written motions, written notices, and other similar papers – When required. – Every order required by its terms to be served, every pleading subsequent to the original complaint unless the court otherwise orders because of numerous defendants, every paper relating to discovery required to be served upon a party unless the court otherwise orders, every written motion other than one which may be heard ex parte, and every written notice, appearance, demand, offer of judgment and similar paper shall be served upon each of the parties, but no service need be made on parties in default for failure to appear except that pleadings asserting new or additional claims for relief against them shall be served upon them in the manner provided for service of summons in Rule 4.

(a1) Service of briefs or memoranda in support or opposition of certain dispositive motions. – In actions in superior court, every brief or memorandum in support of or in opposition to a motion to dismiss, a motion for judgment on the pleadings, a motion for summary judgment, or any other motion seeking a final determination of the rights of the parties as to one or more of the claims or parties in the action shall be served upon each of the parties at least two days before the hearing on the motion. If the brief or memorandum is not served on the other parties at least two days before the hearing on the motion, the court may continue the matter for a reasonable period to allow the responding party to prepare a response, proceed with the matter without considering the untimely served brief or memorandum, or take such other action as the ends of justice require. The parties may, by consent, alter the period of time for service. For the purpose of this two-day requirement only, service shall mean personal delivery, facsimile transmission, or other means such that the party actually receives the brief within the required time.

(b) Service – How made. – A pleading setting forth a counterclaim or cross claim shall be filed with the court and a copy thereof shall be served on the party against whom it is asserted or on the party's attorney of record. With respect to all pleadings subsequent to the original complaint and other papers required or permitted to be served, service with due return may be made in the manner provided for service and return of process in Rule 4 and may be made upon either the party or, unless service upon the party personally is ordered by the court, upon the party's attorney of record. With respect to such other pleadings and papers, service upon the attorney or upon a party may also be made by delivering a copy to the party or by mailing it to the party at the party's last known address or, if no address is known, by filing it with the clerk of court. Delivery of a copy within this rule means handing it to the attorney or to the party, leaving it at the attorney's office with a partner or employee, or by sending it to the attorney's office by a confirmed telefacsimile transmittal for receipt by 5:00 P.M. Eastern Time on a regular business day, as evidenced by a telefacsimile receipt confirmation. If receipt of delivery by telefacsimile is after 5:00 P.M., service will be deemed to have been completed on the next business day. Service by mail shall be complete upon deposit of the pleading or paper enclosed in a post-paid, properly addressed wrapper in a post office or official depository under the exclusive care and custody of the United States Postal Service.

A certificate of service shall accompany every pleading and every paper required to be served on any party or nonparty to the litigation, except with respect to pleadings and papers whose service is governed by Rule 4. The certificate shall show the date and method of service or the date of acceptance of service and shall show the name and service address of each person upon whom the paper has been served. If one or more persons are served by facsimile transmission, the certificate shall also show the telefacsimile number of each person so served. Each certificate of service shall be signed in accordance with and subject to Rule 11 of these rules.

(c)   Service – Numerous defendants. – In any action in which there are unusually large numbers of defendants, the court, upon motion or of its own initiative, may order that service of the pleadings of the defendants and replies thereto need not be made as between the defendants and that any crossclaim, counterclaim, or matter constituting an avoidance or affirmative defense contained therein shall be deemed to be denied or avoided by all other parties and that the filing of any such pleading and service thereof upon the plaintiff constitutes due notice of it to the parties. A copy of every such order shall be served upon the parties in such manner and form as the court directs.

(d)   Filing. – The following papers shall be filed with the court, either before service or within five days after service:

(1)   All pleadings, as defined by Rule 7(a) of these rules, subsequent to the complaint, whether such pleadings are original or amended.

(2)   Written motions and all notices of hearing.

(3)   Any other application to the court for an order that may affect the rights of or in any way commands any individual, business entity, governmental agency, association, or partnership to act or to forego action of any kind.

(4) Notices of appearance.

(5) Any other paper required by rule or statute to be filed.

(6) Any other paper so ordered by the court.

(7) All orders issued by the court.

All other papers, regardless of whether these rules require them to be served upon a party, should not be filed with the court unless (i) the filing is agreed to by all parties, or (ii) the papers are submitted to the court in relation to a motion or other request for relief, or (iii) the filing is permitted by another rule or statute. Briefs or memoranda provided to the court may not be filed with the clerk of court unless ordered by the court. The party taking a deposition or obtaining material through discovery is responsible for its preservation and delivery to the court if needed or so ordered.

(e) (1) Filing with the court defined. – The filing of pleadings and other papers with the court as required by these rules shall be made by filing them with the clerk of the court, except that the judge may permit the papers to be filed with him, in which event he shall note thereon the filing date and forthwith transmit them to the office of the clerk.

(2) Filing by electronic means. – If, pursuant to G.S. 7A-34 and G.S. 7A-343, the Supreme Court and the Administrative Officer of the Courts establish uniform rules, regulations, costs, procedures and specifications for the filing of pleadings or other court papers by electronic means, filing may be made by the electronic means when, in the manner, and to the extent provided therein. (1967, c. 954, s. 1; 1971, c. 538; c. 1156, s. 2.5; 1975, c. 762, s. 1; 1983, c. 201, s. 1; 1985, c. 546; 1991, c. 168, s. 1; 2000-127, s. 1; 2001-379, s. 3; 2001-388, s. 1; 2001-487, s. 107.5(a); 2004-199, s. 5(a); 2005-138, ss. 1, 2; 2006-187, s. 2(a).)

Rule 6. Time.

(a) Computation. – In computing any period of time prescribed or allowed by these rules, by order of court, or by any applicable statute, including rules, orders or statutes respecting publication of notices, the day of the act, event, default or publication after which the designated period of time begins to run is not to be included. The last day of the period so computed is to be included, unless it is a Saturday, Sunday or a legal holiday when the courthouse is closed for transactions, in which event the period runs until the end of the next day which is not a Saturday, Sunday, or a legal holiday when the courthouse is closed for transactions. When the period of time prescribed or allowed is less than seven days, intermediate Saturdays, Sundays, and holidays shall be excluded in the computation. A half holiday shall be considered as other days and not as a holiday.

(b)   Enlargement. – When by these rules or by a notice given thereunder or by order of court an act is required or allowed to be done at or within a specified time, the court for cause shown may at any time in its discretion with or without motion or notice order the period enlarged if request therefor is made before the expiration of the period originally prescribed or as extended by a previous order. Upon motion made after the expiration of the specified period, the judge may permit the act to be done where the failure to act was the result of excusable neglect. Notwithstanding any other provisions of this rule, the parties may enter into binding stipulations without approval of the court enlarging the time, not to exceed in the aggregate 30 days, within which an act is required or allowed to be done under these rules, provided, however, that neither the court nor the parties may extend the time for taking any action under Rules 50(b), 52, 59(b), (d), (e), 60(b), except to the extent and under the conditions stated in them.

(c)   Unaffected by expiration of session. – The period of time provided for the doing of any act or the taking of any proceeding is not affected or limited by the continued existence or expiration of a session of court. The continued existence or expiration of a session of court in no way affects the power of a court to do any act or take any proceeding, but no issue of fact shall be submitted to a jury out of session.

(d)   For motions, affidavits. – A written motion, other than one which may be heard ex parte, and notice of the hearing thereof shall be served not later than five days before the time specified for the hearing, unless a different period is fixed by these rules or by order of the court. Such an order may for cause shown be made on ex parte application. When a motion is supported by affidavit, the affidavit shall be served with the motion; and except as otherwise provided in Rule 59(c), opposing affidavits shall be served at least two days before the hearing. If the opposing affidavit is not served on the other parties at least two days before the hearing on the motion, the court may continue the matter for a reasonable period to allow the responding party to prepare a response, proceed with the matter without considering the untimely served affidavit, or take such other action as the ends of justice require. For the purpose of this two-day requirement only, service shall mean personal delivery, facsimile transmission, or other means such that the party actually receives the affidavit within the required time.

(e) Additional time after service by mail. – Whenever a party has the right to do some act or take some proceedings within a prescribed period after the service of a notice or other paper upon him and the notice or paper is served upon him by mail, three days shall be added to the prescribed period.

(f) Additional time for Address Confidentiality Program participants. – Whenever a person participating in the Address Confidentiality Program established by Chapter 15C of the General Statutes has a legal right to act within a prescribed period of 10 days or less after the service of a notice or other paper upon the program participant, and the notice or paper is served upon the program participant by mail, five days shall be added to the prescribed period. (1967, c. 954, s. 1; 2000-127, s. 5; 2002-171, s. 2; 2003-337, s. 2.)

Article 3

Pleadings and Motions.

Rule 7. Pleadings allowed; motions

(a) Pleadings. – There shall be a complaint and an answer; a reply to a counterclaim denominated as such; an answer to a crossclaim, if the answer contains a crossclaim; a third-party complaint if a person who was not an original party is summoned under the provisions of Rule 14; and a third-party answer, if a third-party complaint is served. If the answer alleges contributory negligence, a party may serve a reply alleging last clear chance. No other pleading shall be allowed except that the court may order a reply to an answer or a third-party answer.

(b) Motions and other papers. –

(1) An application to the court for an order shall be by motion which, unless made during a hearing or trial or at a session at which a cause is on the calendar for that session, shall be made in writing, shall state with particularity the grounds therefor, and shall set forth the relief or order sought. The

requirement of writing is fulfilled if the motion is stated in a written notice of the hearing of the motion.

(2) The rules applicable to captions, signing, and other matters of form of pleadings apply to all motions and other papers provided for by these rules.

(3) A motion to transfer under G.S. 7A-258 shall comply with the directives therein specified but the relief thereby obtainable may also be sought in a responsive pleading pursuant to Rule 12(b).

(4) A motion in a civil action in a county that is part of a multicounty judicial district may be heard in another county which is part of that same judicial district with the permission of the senior resident superior court judge of that district or of that judge's designee. Except for emergencies as determined by the senior resident superior court judge or that judge's designee, a motion in a civil action to be heard outside the county in which the case is filed shall be heard at a civil session of court.

(c) Demurrers, pleas, etc., abolished. – Demurrers, pleas, and exceptions for insufficiency shall not be used.

(d) Pleadings not read to jury. – Unless otherwise ordered by the judge, pleadings shall not be read to the jury. (1967, c. 954, s. 1; 1971, c. 1156, s. 1; 2000-127, s. 2; 2005-163, s. 1; 2011-317, s. 1.)

Rule 8. General rules of pleadings

(a) Claims for relief. – A pleading which sets forth a claim for relief, whether an original claim, counterclaim, crossclaim, or third-party claim shall contain

(1) A short and plain statement of the claim sufficiently particular to give the court and the parties notice of the transactions, occurrences, or series of transactions or occurrences, intended to be proved showing that the pleader is entitled to relief, and

(2) A demand for judgment for the relief to which he deems himself entitled. Relief in the alternative or of several different types may be demanded. In all negligence actions, and in all claims for punitive damages in any civil action, wherein the matter in controversy exceeds the sum or value of ten thousand dollars ($10,000), the pleading shall not state the demand for monetary relief,

but shall state that the relief demanded is for damages incurred or to be incurred in excess of ten thousand dollars ($10,000). However, at any time after service of the claim for relief, any party may request of the claimant a written statement of the monetary relief sought, and the claimant shall, within 30 days after such service, provide such statement, which shall not be filed with the clerk until the action has been called for trial or entry of default entered. Such statement may be amended in the manner and at times as provided by Rule 15.

(b) Defenses; form of denials. – A party shall state in short and plain terms his defenses to each claim asserted and shall admit or deny the averments upon which the adverse party relies. If he is without knowledge or information sufficient to form a belief as to the truth of an averment, he shall so state and this has the effect of a denial. Denials shall fairly meet the substance of the averments denied. When a pleader intends in good faith to deny only a part of or a qualification of an averment, he shall specify so much of it as is true and material and shall deny only the remainder. Unless the pleader intends in good faith to controvert all the averments of the preceding pleading, he may make his denials as specific denials of designated averments or paragraphs, or he may generally deny all the averments except such designated averments or paragraphs as he expressly admits; but, when he does so intend to controvert all its averments, he may do so by general denial subject to the obligations set forth in Rule 11.

(c) Affirmative defenses. – In pleading to a preceding pleading, a party shall set forth affirmatively accord and satisfaction, arbitration and award, assumption of risk, contributory negligence, discharge in bankruptcy, duress, estoppel, failure of consideration, fraud, illegality, injury by fellow servant, laches, license, payment, release, res judicata, statute of frauds, statute of limitations, truth in actions for defamation, usury, waiver, and any other matter constituting an avoidance or affirmative defense. Such pleading shall contain a short and plain statement of any matter constituting an avoidance or affirmative defense sufficiently particular to give the court and the parties notice of the transactions, occurrences, or series of transactions or occurrences, intended to be proved. When a party has mistakenly designated a defense as a counterclaim or a counterclaim as a defense, the court, on terms, if justice so requires, shall treat the pleading as if there had been a proper designation.

(d) Effect of failure to deny. – Averments in a pleading to which a responsive pleading is required, other than those as to the amount of damage, are admitted when not denied in the responsive pleading. Averments in a pleading to which no responsive pleading is required or permitted shall be taken as denied or avoided.

(e) Pleading to be concise and direct; consistency. –

(1) Each averment of a pleading shall be simple, concise, and direct. No technical forms of pleading or motions are required.

(2) A party may set forth two or more statements of a claim or defense alternatively or hypothetically, either in one count or defense or in separate counts or defenses. When two or more statements are made in the alternative and one of them if made independently would be sufficient, the pleading is not made insufficient by the insufficiency of one or more of the alternative statements. A party may also state as many separate claims or defenses as he has regardless of consistency and whether based on legal or on equitable grounds or on both. All statements shall be made subject to the obligations set forth in Rule 11.

(f) Construction of pleadings. – All pleadings shall be so construed as to do substantial justice. (1967, c. 954, s. 1; 1975, 2nd Sess., c. 977, s. 5; 1979, ch. 654, s. 4; 1985 (Reg. Sess., 1986), c. 1027, s. 56; 1989 (Reg. Sess., 1990), c. 995, s. 1.)
Rule 9. Pleading special matters

(a) Capacity. – Any party not a natural person shall make an affirmative averment showing its legal existence and capacity to sue. Any party suing in any representative capacity shall make an affirmative averment showing his capacity and authority to sue. When a party desires to raise an issue as to the legal existence of any party or the capacity of any party to sue or be sued or the authority of a party to sue or be sued in a representative capacity, he shall do so by specific negative averment, which shall include such supporting particulars as are peculiarly within the pleader's knowledge.

(b) Fraud, duress, mistake, condition of the mind. – In all averments of fraud, duress or mistake, the circumstances constituting fraud or mistake shall be stated with particularity. Malice, intent, knowledge, and other condition of mind of a person may be averred generally.

(c) Conditions precedent. – In pleading the performance or occurrence of conditions precedent, it is sufficient to aver generally that all conditions precedent have been performed or have occurred. A denial of performance or occurrence shall be made specifically and with particularity.

(d) Official document or act. – In pleading an official document or official act it is sufficient to aver that the document was issued or the act done in compliance with law.

(e) Judgment. – In pleading a judgment, decision or ruling of a domestic or foreign court, judicial or quasi-judicial tribunal, or of a board or officer, it is sufficient to aver the judgment, decision or ruling without setting forth matter showing jurisdiction to render it.

(f) Time and place. – For the purpose of testing the sufficiency of a pleading, averments of time and place are material and shall be considered like all other averments of material matter.

(g) Special damage. – When items of special damage are claimed each shall be averred.

(h) Private statutes. – In pleading a private statute or right derived therefrom it is sufficient to refer to the statute by its title or the day of its ratification if ratified before January 1, 1996, or the date it becomes law if it becomes law on or after January 1, 1996, and the court shall thereupon take judicial notice of it.

(i) Libel and slander. –

(1) In an action for libel or slander it is not necessary to state in the complaint any extrinsic facts for the purpose of showing the application to the plaintiff of the defamatory matter out of which the claim for relief arose, but it is sufficient to state generally that the same was published or spoken concerning the plaintiff, and if such allegation is controverted, the plaintiff is bound to establish on trial that it was so published or spoken.

(2) The defendant may in his answer allege both the truth of the matter charged as defamatory, and any mitigating circumstances to reduce the amount of damages; and whether he proves the justification or not, he may give in evidence the mitigating circumstances.

(j) Medical malpractice. – Any complaint alleging medical malpractice by a health care provider pursuant to G.S. 90-21.11(2)a. in failing to comply with the applicable standard of care under G.S. 90-21.12 shall be dismissed unless:

(1) The pleading specifically asserts that the medical care and all medical records pertaining to the alleged negligence that are available to the plaintiff after reasonable inquiry have been reviewed by a person who is reasonably

expected to qualify as an expert witness under Rule 702 of the Rules of Evidence and who is willing to testify that the medical care did not comply with the applicable standard of care;

(2)   The pleading specifically asserts that the medical care and all medical records pertaining to the alleged negligence that are available to the plaintiff after reasonable inquiry have been reviewed by a person that the complainant will seek to have qualified as an expert witness by motion under Rule 702(e) of the Rules of Evidence and who is willing to testify that the medical care did not comply with the applicable standard of care, and the motion is filed with the complaint; or

(3)   The pleading alleges facts establishing negligence under the existing common-law doctrine of res ipsa loquitur.

Upon motion by the complainant prior to the expiration of the applicable statute of limitations, a resident judge of the superior court for a judicial district in which venue for the cause of action is appropriate under G.S. 1-82 or, if no resident judge for that judicial district is physically present in that judicial district, otherwise available, or able or willing to consider the motion, then any presiding judge of the superior court for that judicial district may allow a motion to extend the statute of limitations for a period not to exceed 120 days to file a complaint in a medical malpractice action in order to comply with this Rule, upon a determination that good cause exists for the granting of the motion and that the ends of justice would be served by an extension. The plaintiff shall provide, at the request of the defendant, proof of compliance with this subsection through up to ten written interrogatories, the answers to which shall be verified by the expert required under this subsection. These interrogatories do not count against the interrogatory limit under Rule 33.

(k)   Punitive damages. – A demand for punitive damages shall be specifically stated, except for the amount, and the aggravating factor that supports the award of punitive damages shall be averred with particularity. The amount of damages shall be pled in accordance with Rule 8. (1967, c. 954, s. 1; 1995, c. 20, s. 10; c. 309, s. 2; c. 514, s. 3; 1998-217, s. 61; 2001-121, s. 1; 2011-400, s. 3.)

Rule 10. Form of pleadings

(a) Caption; names of parties. – Every pleading shall contain a caption setting forth the division of the court in which the action is filed, the title of the action, and a designation as in Rule 7(a). In the complaint the title of the action shall include the names of all the parties, but in other pleadings it is sufficient to state the name of the first party on each side with an appropriate indication of other parties.

(b) Paragraphs; separate statement. – All averments of claim or defense shall be made in numbered paragraphs, the contents of each of which be limited as far as practicable to a statement of a single set of circumstances; and a paragraph may be referred to by number in all succeeding pleadings. Each claim founded upon a separate transaction or occurrence and each defense other than denials shall be stated in a separate count or defense whenever a separation facilitates the clear presentation of the matters set forth.

(c) Adoption by reference; exhibits. – Statements in a pleading may be adopted by reference in a different part of the same pleading or in another pleading or in any motion in the action. A copy of any written instrument which is an exhibit to a pleading is a part thereof for all purposes. (1967, c. 954, s. 1.)

Rule 11. Signing and verification of pleadings

(a) Signing by Attorney. – Every pleading, motion, and other paper of a party represented by an attorney shall be signed by at least one attorney of record in his individual name, whose address shall be stated. A party who is not represented by an attorney shall sign his pleading, motion, or other paper and state his address. Except when otherwise specifically provided by rule or statute, pleadings need not be verified or accompanied by affidavit. The signature of an attorney or party constitutes a certificate by him that he has read the pleading, motion, or other paper; that to the best of his knowledge, information, and belief formed after reasonable inquiry it is well grounded in fact and is warranted by existing law or a good faith argument for the extension, modification, or reversal of existing law, and that it is not interposed for any improper purpose, such as to harass or to cause unnecessary delay or needless increase in the cost of litigation. If a pleading, motion, or other paper is not signed, it shall be stricken unless it is signed promptly after the omission is called to the attention of the pleader or movant. If a pleading, motion, or other paper is signed in violation of this rule, the court, upon motion or upon its own initiative, shall impose upon the person who signed it, a represented party, or both, an appropriate sanction, which may include an order to pay to the other party or parties the amount of the reasonable expenses incurred because of the filing of the pleading, motion, or other paper, including a reasonable attorney's fee.

(b) Verification of pleadings by a party. – In any case in which verification of a pleading shall be required by these rules or by statute, it shall state in substance that the contents of the pleading verified are true to the knowledge of the person making the verification, except as to those matters stated on information and belief, and as to those matters he believes them to be true. Such verification shall be by affidavit of the party, or if there are several parties united in interest and pleading together, by at least one of such parties acquainted with the facts and capable of making the affidavit. Such affidavit may be made by the agent or attorney of a party in the cases and in the manner provided in section (c) of this rule.

(c) Verification of pleadings by an agent or attorney. – Such verification may be made by the agent or attorney of a party for whom the pleading is filed, if the action or defense is founded upon a written instrument for the payment of money only and the instrument or a true copy thereof is in the possession of the agent or attorney, or if all the material allegations of the pleadings are within the personal knowledge of the agent or attorney. When the pleading is verified by such agent or attorney, he shall set forth in the affidavit:

(1) That the action or defense is founded upon a written instrument for the payment of money only and the instrument or a true copy thereof is in his possession, or

(2) a. That all the material allegations of the pleadings are true to his personal knowledge and

b. The reasons why the affidavit is not made by the party.
(d) Verification by corporation or the State. – When a corporation is a party the verification may be made by any officer, or managing or local agent thereof upon whom summons might be served; and when the State or any officer thereof in its behalf is a party, the verification may be made by any person acquainted with the facts. (1967, c. 954, s. 1; 1985 (Reg. Sess., 1986), c. 1027, s. 55.)

Rule 12. Defenses and objections; When and how presented; by pleading or motion; motion for judgment on pleading

(a) (1) When Presented. – A defendant shall serve his answer within 30 days after service of the summons and complaint upon him. A party served with a pleading stating a crossclaim against him shall serve an answer thereto within 30 days after service upon him. The plaintiff shall serve his reply to a counterclaim in the answer within 30 days after service of the answer or, if a reply is ordered by the court, within 30 days after service of the order, unless the order otherwise directs. Service of a motion permitted under this rule alters these periods of time as follows, unless a different time is fixed by order of the court:

a. The responsive pleading shall be served within 20 days after notice of the court's action in ruling on the motion or postponing its disposition until the trial on the merits;

b. If the court grants a motion for a more definite statement, the responsive pleading shall be served within 20 days after service of the more definite statement.

(2) Cases Removed to United States District Court. – Upon the filing in a district court of the United States of a petition for the removal of a civil action or proceeding from a court in this State and the filing of a copy of the petition in the State court, the State court shall proceed no further therein unless and until the case is remanded. If it shall be finally determined in the United States courts that the action or proceeding was not removable or was improperly removed, or for other reason should be remanded, and a final order is entered remanding the action or proceeding to the State court, the defendant or defendants, or any other party who would have been permitted or required to file a pleading had the proceedings to remove not been instituted, shall have 30 days after the filing in such State court of a certified copy of the order of remand to file motions and to answer or otherwise plead.

(b) How Presented. – Every defense, in law or fact, to a claim for relief in any pleading, whether a claim, counterclaim, crossclaim, or third-party claim, shall be asserted in the responsive pleading thereto if one is required, except that the following defenses may at the option of the pleader be made by motion:

(1) Lack of jurisdiction over the subject matter,

(2) Lack of jurisdiction over the person,

(3) Improper venue or division,

(4) Insufficiency of process,

(5) Insufficiency of service of process,

(6) Failure to state a claim upon which relief can be granted,

(7) Failure to join a necessary party.

A motion making any of these defenses shall be made before pleading if a further pleading is permitted. The consequences of failure to make such a motion shall be as provided in sections (g) and (h). No defense or objection is waived by being joined with one or more other defenses or objections in a responsive pleading or motion. Obtaining an extension of time within which to answer or otherwise plead shall not constitute a waiver of any defense herein set forth. If a pleading sets forth a claim for relief to which the adverse party is not required to serve a responsive pleading, he may assert at the trial any defense in law or fact to that claim for relief. If, on a motion asserting the defense numbered (6), to dismiss for failure of the pleading to state a claim upon which relief can be granted, matters outside the pleading are presented to and not excluded by the court, the motion shall be treated as one for summary judgment and disposed of as provided in Rule 56, and all parties shall be given reasonable opportunity to present all material made pertinent to such a motion by Rule 56.

(c) Motion for judgment on the pleadings. – After the pleadings are closed but within such time as not to delay the trial, any party may move for judgment on the pleadings. If, on a motion for judgment on the pleadings, matters outside the pleadings are presented to and not excluded by the court, the motion shall be treated as one for summary judgment and disposed of as provided in Rule 56, and all parties shall be given reasonable opportunity to present all material made pertinent to such a motion by Rule 56.

(d) Preliminary hearings. – The defenses specifically enumerated (1) through (7) in section (b) of this rule, whether made in a pleading or by motion, and the motion for judgment on the pleadings mentioned in section (c) of this rule shall be heard and determined before trial on application of any party, unless the judge orders that the hearing and determination thereof be deferred until the trial.

(e) Motion for more definite statement. – If a pleading to which a responsive pleading is permitted is so vague or ambiguous that a party cannot reasonably be required to frame a responsive pleading, he may move for a more definite statement before interposing his responsive pleading. The motion shall point out the defects complained of and the details desired. If the motion is granted and the order of the judge is not obeyed within 20 days after notice of the order or within such other time as the judge may fix, the judge may strike the pleading to which the motion was directed or make such orders as he deems just.

(f) Motion to strike. – Upon motion made by a party before responding to a pleading or, if no responsive pleading is permitted by these rules, upon motion made by a party within 30 days after the service of the pleading upon him or upon the judge's own initiative at any time, the judge may order stricken from any pleading any insufficient defense or any redundant, irrelevant, immaterial, impertinent, or scandalous matter.

(g) Consolidation of defenses in motion. – A party who makes a motion under this rule may join with it any other motions herein provided for and then available to him. If a party makes a motion under this rule but omits therefrom any defense or objection then available to him which this rule permits to be raised by motion, he shall not thereafter make a motion based on the defense or objection so omitted, except a motion as provided in section (h)(2) hereof on any of the grounds there stated.

(h) Waiver or preservation of certain defenses. –

(1) A defense of lack of jurisdiction over the person, improper venue, insufficiency of process, or insufficiency of service of process is waived (i) if omitted from a motion in the circumstances described in section (g), or (ii) if it is neither made by motion under this rule nor included in a responsive pleading or an amendment thereof permitted by Rule 15(a) to be made as a matter of course.

(2) A defense of failure to state a claim upon which relief can be granted, a defense of failure to join a necessary party, and an objection of failure to state a legal defense to a claim may be made in any pleading permitted or ordered under Rule 7(a), or by motion for judgment on the pleadings, or at the trial on the merits.

(3)   Whenever it appears by suggestion of the parties or otherwise that the court lacks jurisdiction of the subject matter, the court shall dismiss the action. (1967, c. 954, s. 1; 1971, c. 1236; 1975, c. 76, s. 2.)

Rule 13. Counterclaim and crossclaim

(a)   Compulsory counterclaims. – A pleading shall state as a counterclaim any claim which at the time of serving the pleading the pleader has against any opposing party, if it arises out of the transaction or occurrence that is the subject matter of the opposing party's claim and does not require for its adjudication the presence of third parties of whom the court cannot acquire jurisdiction. But the pleader need not state the claim if

(1) At the time the action was commenced the claim was the subject of another pending action, or

(2) The opposing party brought suit upon his claim by attachment or other process by which the court did not acquire jurisdiction to render a personal judgment on that claim, and the pleader is not stating any counterclaim under this rule.

(b)   Permissive counterclaim. – A pleading may state as a counterclaim any claim against an opposing party not arising out of the transaction or occurrence that is the subject matter of the opposing party's claim.

(c)   Counterclaim exceeding opposing claim. – A counterclaim may or may not diminish or defeat the recovery sought by the opposing party. It may claim relief exceeding in amount or different in kind from that sought in the pleading of the opposing party.

(d)   Counterclaim against the State of North Carolina. – These rules shall not be construed to enlarge beyond the limits fixed by law the right to assert counterclaims or to claim credit against the State of North Carolina or an officer or agency thereof.

(e)   Counterclaim maturing or acquired after pleading. – A claim which either matured or was acquired by the pleader after serving his pleading may, with the permission of the court, be presented as a counterclaim by supplemental pleading.

(f) Omitted counterclaim. – When a pleader fails to set up a counterclaim through oversight, inadvertence, or excusable neglect, or when justice requires, he may by leave of court set up the counterclaim by amendment.

(g) Crossclaim against coparty. – A pleading may state as a crossclaim any claim by one party against a coparty arising out of the transaction or occurrence that is the subject matter either of the original action or of a counterclaim therein or relating to any property that is the subject matter of the original action. Such crossclaim may include a claim that the party against whom it is asserted is or may be liable to the crossclaimant for all or part of a claim asserted in the action against the crossclaimant.

(h) Additional parties may be brought in. – When the presence of parties other than those to the original action is required for the granting of complete relief in the determination of a counterclaim or crossclaim, the court shall order them to be brought in as defendants as provided in these rules, if jurisdiction of them can be obtained.

(i) Separate trial; separate judgment. – If the court orders separate trials as provided in Rule 42(b), judgment on a counterclaim or crossclaim may be rendered in accordance with the terms of Rule 54(b) when the court has jurisdiction so to do, even if the claims of the opposing party have been dismissed or otherwise disposed of. (1967, c. 954, s. 1.)

Rule 14. Third-party practice

(a) When defendant may bring in third party. – At any time after commencement of the action a defendant, as a third-party plaintiff, may cause a summons and complaint to be served upon a person not a party to the action who is or may be liable to him for all or part of the plaintiff's claim against him. Leave to make the service need not be obtained if the third-party complaint is filed not later than 45 days after the answer to the complaint is served. Otherwise leave must be obtained on motion upon notice to all parties to the action. The person served with the summons and third-party complaint, hereinafter called the third-party defendant, shall make his defense to the third-party plaintiff's claim as provided in Rule 12 and his counterclaims against the third-party plaintiff and crossclaim against other third-party defendants as provided in Rule 13. The third-party defendant may assert against the plaintiff any defenses which the third-party plaintiff has to the plaintiff's claim. The third-party defendant may also assert any claim against the plaintiff arising out of the transaction or occurrence that is the subject matter of the plaintiff's claim against the third-party plaintiff. The plaintiff may assert any claim against the third-party defendant arising out of the transaction or occurrence that is the subject matter of the plaintiff's claim against the third-party plaintiff, and the third-party defendant thereupon shall assert his defenses as provided in Rule 12 and his counterclaims and crossclaims as provided in Rule 13. Any party may move for severance, separate trial, or dismissal of the third-party claim. A third-party defendant may proceed under this rule against any person not a party to the action who is or may be liable to him for all or part of the claim made in the action against the third-party defendant.

Where the normal statute of limitations period in an action arising on a contract is extended as provided in G.S. 1-47(2) or in any action arising on a contract or promissory note, upon motion of the defendant the court may order to be made parties additional defendants, including any party of whom the plaintiff is a subrogee, assignee, third-party beneficiary, endorsee, agent or transferee, or such other person as has received the benefit of the contract by transfer of interest.

(b) When plaintiff may bring in third party. – When a counterclaim is asserted against a plaintiff, he may cause a third party to be brought in under circumstances which under this rule would entitle a defendant to do so.

(c) Rule applicable to State of North Carolina. – Notwithstanding the provisions of the Tort Claims Act, the State of North Carolina may be made a third party under subsection (a) or a third-party defendant under subsection (b) in any tort action. In such cases, the same rules governing liability and the limits of liability of the State and its agencies shall apply as is provided for in the Tort Claims Act. (1967, c. 954, s. 1; 1969, c. 810, s. 2; 1975, c. 587, s. 1; 1981, c. 92; c. 810.)

Rule 15. Amended and supplemental pleadings

(a) Amendments. – A party may amend his pleading once as a matter of course at any time before a responsive pleading is served or, if the pleading is one to which no responsive pleading is permitted and the action has not been placed upon the trial calendar, he may so amend it at any time within 30 days after it is served. Otherwise a party may amend his pleading only by leave of court or by written consent of the adverse party; and leave shall be freely given when justice so requires. A party shall plead in response to an amended pleading within 30 days after service of the amended pleading, unless the court otherwise orders.

(b) Amendments to conform to the evidence. – When issues not raised by the pleadings are tried by the express or implied consent of the parties, they shall be treated in all respects as if they had been raised in the pleadings. Such amendment of the pleadings as may be necessary to cause them to conform to the evidence and to raise these issues may be made upon motion of any party at any time, either before or after judgment, but failure so to amend does not affect the result of the trial of these issues. If evidence is objected to at the trial on the ground that it is not within the issues raised by the pleadings, the court may allow the pleadings to be amended and shall do so freely when the presentation of the merits of the action will be served thereby and the objecting party fails to satisfy the court that the admission of such evidence would prejudice him in maintaining his action or defense upon the merits. The court may grant a continuance to enable the objecting party to meet such evidence.

(c) Relation back of amendments. – A claim asserted in an amended pleading is deemed to have been interposed at the time the claim in the original pleading was interposed, unless the original pleading does not give notice of the transactions, occurrences, or series of transactions or occurrences, to be proved pursuant to the amended pleading.

(d) Supplemental pleadings. – Upon motion of a party the court may, upon reasonable notice and upon such terms as are just, permit him to serve a supplemental pleading setting forth transactions or occurrences or events which may have happened since the date of the pleading sought to be supplemented, whether or not the original pleading is defective in its statement of a claim for relief or defense. If the court deems it advisable that the adverse party plead thereto, it shall so order, specifying the time therefor. (1967, c. 954, s. 1.)

Rule 16. Pre-trial procedure; formulating issues

(a) In any action, the court may in its discretion direct the attorneys for the parties to appear before the court for a conference to consider

(1) The simplification and formulation of the issues;

(2) The necessity or desirability of amendments to the pleadings;

(3)   The possibility of obtaining admissions of fact and of documents which will avoid unnecessary proof;

(4)   The limitation of the number of expert witnesses;

(5)   The advisability or necessity of a reference of the case, either in whole or in part;

(6)   Matters of which the court is to be asked to take judicial notice;

(7)   Such other matters as may aid in the disposition of the action.

If a conference is held, the judge shall make an order which recites the action taken at the conference, any amendments allowed to the pleadings, and any agreements made by the parties as to any of the matters considered, and which may limit the issues for trial to those not disposed of by admissions or agreements of counsel; and such order when entered controls the subsequent course of the action, unless modified at the trial to prevent manifest injustice. If any issue for trial as stated in the order is not raised by the pleadings in accordance with the provisions of Rule 8, upon motion of any party, the order shall require amendment of the pleadings.

(b)   In a medical malpractice action as defined in G.S. 90-21.11, at the close of the discovery period scheduled pursuant to Rule 26(g), the judge shall schedule a final conference. After the conference, the judge shall refer any consent order calendaring the case for trial to the senior resident superior court judge or the chief district court judge, who shall approve the consent order unless the judge finds that:

(1)   The date specified in the order is unavailable,

(2)   The terms of the order unreasonably delay the trial, or
(3)   The ends of justice would not be served by approving the order.

If the senior resident superior court judge or the chief district court judge does not approve the consent order, the judge shall calendar the case for trial.

In calendaring the case, the court shall take into consideration the nature and complexity of the case, the proximity and convenience of witnesses, the needs of counsel for both parties concerning their respective calendars, the benefits of an early disposition and such other matters as the court may deem proper. (1967, c. 954, s. 1; 1987, c. 859, s. 4; 2011-199, s. 1.)

Article 4.

Parties.

Rule 17. Parties plaintiff and defendant; capacity

(a) Real party in interest. – Every claim shall be prosecuted in the name of the real party in interest; but an executor, administrator, guardian, trustee of an express trust, a party with whom or in whose name a contract has been made for the benefit of another, or a party authorized by statute may sue in his own name without joining with him the party for whose benefit the action is brought; and when a statute of the State so provides, an action for the use or benefit of another shall be brought in the name of the State of North Carolina. No action shall be dismissed on the ground that it is not prosecuted in the name of the real party in interest until a reasonable time has been allowed after objection for ratification of commencement of the action by, or joinder or substitution of, the real party in interest; and such ratification, joinder, or substitution shall have the same effect as if the action had been commenced in the name of the real party in interest.

(b) Infants, incompetents, etc. –

(1) Infants, etc., Sue by Guardian or Guardian Ad Litem. – In actions or special proceedings when any of the parties plaintiff are infants or incompetent persons, whether residents or nonresidents of this State, they must appear by general or testamentary guardian, if they have any within the State or by guardian ad litem appointed as hereinafter provided; but if the action or proceeding is against such guardian, or if there is no such known guardian, then such persons may appear by guardian ad litem.

(2) Infants, etc., Defend by Guardian Ad Litem. – In actions or special proceedings when any of the defendants are infants or incompetent persons, whether residents or nonresidents of this State, they must defend by general or testamentary guardian, if they have any within this State or by guardian ad litem appointed as hereinafter provided; and if they have no known general or testamentary guardian in the State, and any of them have been summoned, the court in which said action or special proceeding is pending, upon motion of any

of the parties, may appoint some discreet person to act as guardian ad litem, to defend in behalf of such infants, or incompetent persons, and fix and tax his fee as part of the costs. The guardian so appointed shall, if the cause is a civil action, file his answer to the complaint within the time required for other defendants, unless the time is extended by the court; and if the cause is a special proceeding, a copy of the complaint, with the summons, must be served on him. After 20 days' notice of the summons and complaint in the special proceeding, and after answer filed as above prescribed in the civil action, the court may proceed to final judgment as effectually and in the same manner as if there had been personal service upon the said infant or incompetent persons or defendants.

All orders or final judgments duly entered in any action or special proceeding prior to April 8, 1974, when any of the defendants were infants or incompetent persons, whether residents or nonresidents of this State, and were defended therein by a general or testamentary guardian or guardian ad litem, and summons and complaint or petition in said action or special proceeding were duly served upon the guardian or guardian ad litem and answer duly filed by said guardian or guardian ad litem, shall be good and valid notwithstanding that said order or final judgment was entered less than 20 days after notice of the summons and complaint served upon said guardian or guardian ad litem.

(3) Appointment of Guardian Ad Litem Notwithstanding the Existence of a General or Testamentary Guardian. – Notwithstanding the provisions of subsections (b)(1) and (b)(2), a guardian ad litem for an infant or incompetent person may be appointed in any case when it is deemed by the court in which the action is pending expedient to have the infant, or insane or incompetent person so represented, notwithstanding such person may have a general or testamentary guardian.

(4) Appointment of Guardian Ad Litem for Unborn Persons. – In all actions in rem and quasi in rem and in all actions and special proceedings which involve the construction of wills, trusts and contracts or any instrument in writing, or which involve the determination of the ownership of property or the distribution of property, if there is a possibility that some person may thereafter be born who, if then living, would be a necessary or proper party to such action or special proceeding, the court in which said action or special proceeding is pending, upon motion of any of the parties or upon its own motion, may appoint some discreet person guardian ad litem to defend on behalf of such unborn person. Service upon the guardian ad litem appointed for such unborn person shall have the same force and effect as service upon such unborn person would

have had if such person had been living. All proceedings by and against the said guardian ad litem after appointment shall be governed by all provisions of the law applicable to guardians ad litem for living persons.

(5) Appointment of Guardian Ad Litem for Corporations, Trusts, or Other Entities Not in Existence. – In all actions which involve the construction of wills, trusts, contracts or written instruments, or the determination of the ownership of property or the disposition or distribution of property pursuant to the provisions of a will, trust, contract or written instrument, if such will, trust, contract or written instrument provides benefits for disposition or distribution of property to a corporation, a trust, or an entity thereafter to be formed for the purpose of carrying into effect some provision of the said will, trust, contract or written instrument, the court in which said action or special proceeding is pending, upon motion of any of the parties or upon its own motion, may appoint some discreet person guardian ad litem for such corporation, trust or other entity. Service upon the guardian ad litem appointed for such corporation, trust or other entity shall have the same force and effect as service upon such corporation, trust or entity would have had if such corporation, trust or other entity had been in existence. All proceedings by and against the said guardian ad litem after appointment shall be governed by all provisions of the law applicable to guardians ad litem for living persons.
(6) Repealed by Session Laws 1981, c. 599, s. 1.

(7) Miscellaneous Provisions. – The provisions of this rule are in addition to any other remedies or procedures authorized or permitted by law, and it shall not be construed to repeal or to limit the doctrine of virtual representation or any other law or rule of law by which unborn persons or nonexistent corporations, trusts or other entities may be represented in or bound by any judgment or order entered in any action or special proceeding. This rule shall apply to all pending actions and special proceedings to which it may be constitutionally applicable. All judgments and orders heretofore entered in any action in which a guardian or guardians ad litem have been appointed for any unborn person or persons or any nonexistent corporations, trusts or other entities, are hereby validated as of the several dates of entry thereof in the same manner and to the full extent that they would have been valid if this rule had been in effect at the time of the appointment of such guardians ad litem; provided, however, that the provisions of this sentence shall be applicable only in such cases and to the extent to which the application thereof shall not be prevented by any constitutional limitation.

(c) Guardian ad litem for infants, insane or incompetent persons; appointment procedure. – When a guardian ad litem is appointed to represent an infant or insane or incompetent person, he must be appointed as follows:

(1) When an infant or insane or incompetent person is plaintiff, the appointment shall be made at any time prior to or at the time of the commencement of the action, upon the written application of any relative or friend of said infant or insane or incompetent person or by the court on its own motion.

(2) When an infant is defendant and service under Rule 4(j)(1)a is made upon him the appointment may be made upon the written application of any relative or friend of said infant, or, if no such application is made within 10 days after service of summons, upon the written application of any other party to the action or, at any time by the court on its own motion.

(3) When an infant or insane or incompetent person is defendant and service can be made upon him only by publication, the appointment may be made upon the written application of any relative or friend of said infant, or upon the written application of any other party to the action, or by the court on its own motion, before completion of publication, whereupon service of the summons with copy of the complaint shall be made forthwith upon said guardian so appointed requiring him to make defense at the same time that the defendant is required to make defense in the notice of publication.

(4) When an insane or incompetent person is defendant and service by publication is not required, the appointment may be made upon the written application of any relative or friend of said defendant, or upon the written application of any other party to the action, or by the court on its own motion, prior to or at the time of the commencement of the action, and service upon the insane or incompetent defendant may thereupon be dispensed with by order of the court making such appointment.

(d) Guardian ad litem for persons not ascertained or for persons, trusts or corporations not in being. – When under the terms of a written instrument, or for any other reason, a person or persons who are not in being, or any corporation, trust, or other legal entity which is not in being, may be or may become legally or equitably interested in any property, real or personal, the court in which an action or proceeding of any kind relative to or affecting such property is pending, may, upon the written application of any party to such action or proceeding or of other person interested, appoint a guardian ad litem to represent such person or persons not ascertained or such persons, trusts or corporations not in being.

(e) Duty of guardian ad litem; effect of judgment or decree where party represented by guardian ad litem. – Any guardian ad litem appointed for any party pursuant to any of the provisions of this rule shall file and serve such pleadings as may be required within the times specified by these rules, unless extension of time is obtained. After the appointment of a guardian ad litem under any provision of this rule and after the service and filing of such pleadings as may be required by such guardian ad litem, the court may proceed to final judgment, order or decree against any party so represented as effectually and in the same manner as if said party had been under no legal disability, had been ascertained and in being, and had been present in court after legal notice in the action in which such final judgment, order or decree is entered. (1967, c. 954, s. 1; 1969, c. 895, ss. 5, 6; 1971, c. 1156, ss. 3, 4; 1973, c. 1199; 1981, c. 599, s. 1; 1987, c. 550, s. 13.)

Rule 18. Joinder of claims and remedies

(a) Joinder of claims. – A party asserting a claim for relief as an original claim, counterclaim, cross claim, or third-party claim, may join, either as independent or as alternate claims, as many claims, legal or equitable, as he has against an opposing party.

(b) Joinder of remedies; fraudulent conveyances. – Whenever a claim is one heretofore cognizable only after another claim has been prosecuted to a conclusion, the two claims may be joined in a single action; but the court shall grant relief in that action only in accordance with the relative substantive rights of the parties. In particular, a plaintiff may state a claim for money and a claim to have set aside a conveyance fraudulent as to him, without first having obtained a judgment establishing the claim for money. (1967, c. 954, s. 1; 1969, c. 895, s. 7.)

Rule 19. Necessary joinder of parties.

(a) Necessary joinder. – Subject to the provisions of Rule 23, those who are united in interest must be joined as plaintiffs or defendants; but if the consent of anyone who should have been joined as plaintiff cannot be obtained he may be made a defendant, the reason therefor being stated in the complaint; provided, however, in all cases of joint contracts, a claim may be asserted against all or any number of the persons making such contracts.

(b) Joinder of parties not united in interest. – The court may determine any claim before it when it can do so without prejudice to the rights of any party or to the rights of others not before the court; but when a complete determination of such claim cannot be made without the presence of other parties, the court shall order such other parties summoned to appear in the action.

(c) Joinder of parties not united in interest – Names of omitted persons and reasons for nonjoinder to be pleaded. – In any pleading in which relief is asked, the pleader shall set forth the names, if known to him, of persons who ought to be parties if complete relief is to be accorded between those already parties, but who are not joined, and shall state why they are omitted. (1967, c. 954, s. 1.)

Rule 20. Permissive joinder of parties

(a) Permissive joinder. – All persons may join in one action as plaintiffs if they assert any right to relief jointly, severally, or in the alternative in respect of or arising out of the same transaction, occurrence, or series of transactions or occurrences and if any question of law or fact common to all parties will arise in the action. All persons may be joined in one action as defendants if there is asserted against them jointly, severally, or in the alternative, any right to relief in respect of or arising out of the same transaction, occurrence, or series of transactions or occurrences and if any question of law or fact common to all parties will arise in the action. A plaintiff or defendant need not be interested in obtaining or defending against all the relief demanded. Judgment may be given for one or more of the plaintiffs according to their respective rights to relief, and against one or more defendants according to their respective liabilities.

(b) Separate trial. – The court shall make such orders as will prevent a party from being embarrassed, delayed, or put to expense by the inclusion of a party against whom he asserts no claim and who asserts no claim against him, and shall order separate trials or make other orders to prevent delay or prejudice. (1967, c. 954, s. 1; 1973, c. 75.)

Rule 21. Procedure upon misjoinder and nonjoinder

Neither misjoinder of parties nor misjoinder of parties and claims is ground for dismissal of an action; but on such terms as are just parties may be dropped or added by order of the court on motion of any party or on its own initiative at any stage of the action. Any claim against a party may be severed and proceeded with separately. (1967, c. 954, s. 1.)

Rule 22. Interpleader

(a)   Persons having claims against the plaintiff may be joined as defendants and required to interplead when their claims expose or may expose the plaintiff to double or multiple liability. It is not ground for objection to the joinder that the claims of the several claimants or the titles on which their claims depend do not have a common origin or are not identical but are adverse to and independent of one another, or that the plaintiff avers that he is not liable in whole or in part to any or all of the claimants. A defendant exposed to similar liability may obtain such interpleader by way of crossclaim or counterclaim. The provisions of this rule supplement and do not in any way limit the joinder of parties permitted in Rule 20.

(b)   Where funds are subject to competing claims by parties to the action, the court may order the party in possession of the funds either to deposit the funds in an interest bearing account in a bank, savings and loan, or trust company licensed to do business in this State or to deposit the funds with the clerk. If the funds are deposited in a bank, savings and loan, or trust company, the court shall specify the type of interest bearing account to be used. Funds deposited with the clerk shall be invested or deposited as provided in G.S. 7A-112 and G.S. 7A-112.1. Upon determination of the action, the judgment shall provide for disbursement of the principal and interest earned on the funds while so deposited. (1967, c. 954, s. 1; 1989, c. 668.)

Rule 23. Class actions

(a)   Representation. – If persons constituting a class are so numerous as to make it impracticable to bring them all before the court, such of them, one or more, as will fairly insure the adequate representation of all may, on behalf of all, sue or be sued.

(b)   Secondary action by shareholders. – In an action brought to enforce a secondary right on the part of one or more shareholders or members of a corporation or an unincorporated association because the corporation or association refuses to enforce rights which may properly be asserted by it, the complaint shall be verified by oath.

(c) Dismissal or compromise. – A class action shall not be dismissed or compromised without the approval of the judge. In an action under this rule, notice of a proposed dismissal or compromise shall be given to all members of the class in such manner as the judge directs.

(d) Tax Class Actions. – In addition to all of the requirements set out in this rule, a class action seeking the refund of a State tax paid due to an alleged unconstitutional statute may be brought and maintained only as provided in G.S. 105-241.18. (1967, c. 954, s. 1; 2008-107, s. 28.28(a).)

Rule 24. Intervention

(a) Intervention of right. – Upon timely application anyone shall be permitted to intervene in an action:

(1) When a statute confers an unconditional right to intervene; or

(2) When the applicant claims an interest relating to the property or transaction which is the subject of the action and he is so situated that the disposition of the action may as a practical matter impair or impede his ability to protect that interest, unless the applicant's interest is adequately represented by existing parties.

(b) Permissive intervention. – Upon timely application anyone may be permitted to intervene in an action.

(1) When a statute confers a conditional right to intervene; or
(2) When an applicant's claim or defense and the main action have a question of law or fact in common. When a party to an action relies for ground of claim or defense upon any statute or executive order administered by a federal or State governmental officer or agency or upon any regulation, order, requirement, or agreement issued or made pursuant to the statute or executive order, such officer or agency upon timely application may be permitted to intervene in the action. In exercising its discretion the court shall consider whether the intervention will unduly delay or prejudice the adjudication of the rights of the original parties.

(c) Procedure. – A person desiring to intervene shall serve a motion to intervene upon all parties affected thereby. The motion shall state the grounds therefor and shall be accompanied by a pleading setting forth the claim or defense for which intervention is sought. The same procedure shall be followed when a statute gives a right to intervene, except when the statute prescribes a different procedure. (1967, c. 954, s. 1.)

Rule 25. Substitution of parties upon death, incompetency or transfer of interest; abatement

(a) Death. – No action abates by reason of the death of a party if the cause of action survives. In such case, the court, on motion at any time within the time specified for the presentation of claims in G.S. 28A-19-3, may order the substitution of said party's personal representative or collector and allow the action to be continued by or against the substituted party.

(b) Insanity or incompetency. – No action abates by reason of the incompetency or insanity of a party. If such incompetency or insanity is adjudicated, the court, on motion at any time within one year after such adjudication, or afterwards on a supplemental complaint, may order that said party be represented by his general guardian or trustee or a guardian ad litem, and, allow the action to be continued. If there is no adjudication, any party may suggest such incompetency or insanity to the court and it shall enter such order in respect thereto as justice may require.

(c) Abatement ordered unless action continued. – At any time after the death, insanity or incompetency of a party, the court in which an action is pending, upon notice to such person as it directs and upon motion of any party aggrieved, may order that the action be abated, unless it is continued by the proper parties, within a time to be fixed by the court, not less than six nor more than 12 months from the granting of the order.

(d) Transfer of interest. – In case of any transfer of interest other than by death, the action shall be continued in the name of the original party; but, upon motion of any party, the court may allow the person to whom the transfer is made to be joined with the original party.

(e) Death of receiver of corporation. – No action against a receiver of a corporation abates by reason of his death, but, upon suggestion of the facts on the record, it continues against his successor or against the corporation in case a new receiver is not appointed and such successor or the corporation is automatically substituted as a party.

(f) Public officers; death or separation from office. –

(1) When a public officer is a party to an action in his official capacity and during its pendency dies, resigns or otherwise ceases to hold office, the action does not abate and his successor is automatically substituted as a party. Proceedings following the substitution shall be in the name of the substituted party, but any misnomer not affecting substantial rights of the parties shall be disregarded. An order of substitution may be entered at any time, but the omission to enter such an order shall not affect the substitution.

(2) When a public officer sues or is sued in his official capacity, he may be described as a party by his official title rather than by name; but the court may require his name to be added.

(g) No abatement after verdict. – After a verdict is rendered in any action, the action does not abate by reason of the death of a party, whether or not the cause of action upon which it is based is a type which survives. (1967, c. 954, s. 1; 1977, c. 446, s. 3.)

Article 5

Depositions and Discovery.

Rule 26. General provisions governing discovery

(a) Discovery methods. – Parties may obtain discovery by one or more of the following methods: depositions upon oral examination or written questions; written interrogatories; production of documents or things or permission to enter upon land or other property, for inspection and other purposes; physical and mental examinations; and requests for admission.

(b) Discovery scope and limits. – Unless otherwise limited by order of the court in accordance with these rules, the scope of discovery is as follows:

(1) In General. – Parties may obtain discovery regarding any matter, not privileged, which is relevant to the subject matter involved in the pending action, whether it relates to the claim or defense of the party seeking discovery or to the claim or defense of any other party, including the existence, description, nature,

custody, condition and location of any books, documents, electronically stored information, or other tangible things and the identity and location of persons having knowledge of any discoverable matter. It is not ground for objection that the information sought will be inadmissible at the trial if the information sought appears reasonably calculated to lead to the discovery of admissible evidence nor is it grounds for objection that the examining party has knowledge of the information as to which discovery is sought. For the purposes of these rules regarding discovery, the phrase "electronically stored information" includes reasonably accessible metadata that will enable the discovering party to have the ability to access such information as the date sent, date received, author, and recipients. The phrase does not include other metadata unless the parties agree otherwise or the court orders otherwise upon motion of a party and a showing of good cause for the production of certain metadata.

(1a) Limitations on Frequency and Extent. – The frequency or extent of use of the discovery methods set forth in section (a) shall be limited by the court if it determines that: (i) the discovery sought is unreasonably cumulative or duplicative, or is obtainable from some other source that is more convenient, less burdensome, or less expensive; (ii) the party seeking discovery has had ample opportunity by discovery in the action to obtain the information sought; or (iii) the discovery is unduly burdensome or expensive, taking into account the needs of the case, the amount in controversy, limitations on the parties' resources, and the importance of the issues at stake in the litigation. The court may act upon its own initiative after reasonable notice or pursuant to a motion under section (c).

(1b) Specific Limitations on Electronically Stored Information. – In addition to any limitations imposed by subdivision (b)(1a) of this rule, discovery of electronically stored information is subject to the limitations set forth in Rule 34(b). The court may specify conditions for the discovery, including allocation of discovery costs.

(2) Insurance Agreements. – A party may obtain discovery of the existence and contents of any insurance agreement under which any person carrying on an insurance business may be liable to satisfy part or all of a judgment which may be entered in the action or to indemnify or reimburse for payments made to satisfy the judgment. Information concerning the insurance agreement is not by reason of disclosure admissible in evidence at trial. For purposes of this subsection, an application for insurance shall not be treated as part of an insurance agreement.

(3) Trial Preparation; Materials. – Subject to the provisions of subsection (b)(4) of this rule, a party may obtain discovery of documents and tangible things otherwise discoverable under subsection (b)(1) of this rule and prepared in anticipation of litigation or for trial by or for another party or by or for that other party's consultant, surety, indemnitor, insurer, or agent only upon a showing that the party seeking discovery has substantial need of the materials in the preparation of the case and that the party is unable without undue hardship to obtain the substantial equivalent of the materials by other means. In ordering discovery of such materials when the required showing has been made, the court may not permit disclosure of the mental impressions, conclusions, opinions, or legal theories of an attorney or other representative of a party concerning the litigation in which the material is sought or work product of the attorney or attorneys of record in the particular action.

A party may obtain without the required showing a statement concerning the action or its subject matter previously made by that party. Upon request, a person not a party may obtain without the required showing a statement concerning the action or its subject matter previously made by that person. If the request is refused, the person may move for a court order. The provisions of Rule 37(a)(4) apply to the award of expenses incurred in relation to the motion. For purposes of this paragraph, a statement previously made is (i) a written statement signed or otherwise adopted or approved by the person making it, or (ii) a stenographic, mechanical, electrical, or other recording, or a transcription thereof, which is a substantially verbatim recital of an oral statement by the person making it and contemporaneously recorded.

(4) Trial Preparation; Experts. – Discovery of facts known and opinions held by experts, otherwise discoverable under the provisions of subsection (b)(1) of this rule and acquired or developed in anticipation of litigation or for trial, may be obtained only as follows:

a. 1. A party may through interrogatories require any other party to identify each person whom the other party expects to call as an expert witness at trial, to state the subject matter on which the expert is expected to testify, and to state the substance of the facts and opinions to which the expert is expected to testify and a summary of the grounds for each opinion.

2. Upon motion, the court may order further discovery by other means, subject to such restrictions as to scope and such provisions, pursuant to sub-subdivision (b)(4)b. of this rule, concerning fees and expenses as the court may deem appropriate.

b. Unless manifest injustice would result, (i) the court shall require that the party seeking discovery pay the expert a reasonable fee for time spent in responding to discovery under subdivision (b)(4)a.2. of this rule; and (ii) with respect to discovery obtained under subdivision (b)(4)a.2. of this rule the court may require the party seeking discovery to pay the other party a fair portion of the fees and expenses reasonably incurred by the latter party in obtaining facts and opinions from the expert.

(5) Claiming Privilege or Protecting Trial-Preparation Materials.

a. Information withheld. – When a party withholds information otherwise discoverable by claiming that the information is privileged or subject to protection as trial-preparation material, the party must (i) expressly make the claim and (ii) describe the nature of the documents, communications, or tangible things not produced or disclosed, and do so in a manner that, without revealing information itself privileged or protected, will enable other parties to assess the claim.

b. Information produced. – If information subject to a claim of privilege or protection as trial-preparation material is inadvertently produced in response to a discovery request, the party that produced the material may assert the claim by notifying any party that received the information of the claim and basis for it. After being notified, a party (i) must promptly return, sequester, or destroy the specified information and any copies it has, (ii) must not use or disclose the information until the claim is resolved, (iii) must take reasonable steps to retrieve the information if the party disclosed it before being notified, and (iv) may promptly present the information to the court under seal for determination of the claim. The producing party must preserve the information until the claim is resolved.

(c) Protective orders. – Upon motion by a party or by the person from whom discovery is sought, and for good cause shown, the judge of the court in which the action is pending may make any order which justice requires to protect a party or person from unreasonable annoyance, embarrassment, oppression, or undue burden or expense, including one or more of the following: (i) that the discovery not be had; (ii) that the discovery may be had only on specified terms and conditions, including a designation of the time or place; (iii) that the discovery may be had only by a method of discovery other than that selected by the party seeking discovery; (iv) that certain matters not be inquired into, or that the scope of the discovery be limited to certain matters; (v) that discovery be conducted with no one present except persons designated by the court; (vi) that a deposition after being sealed be opened only by order of the court; (vii) that a trade secret or other confidential research, development, or commercial information not be disclosed or be disclosed only in a designated way; (viii) that the parties simultaneously file specified documents or information enclosed in sealed envelopes to be opened as directed by the court.

A party seeking a protective order on the basis that electronically stored information sought is from a source identified as not reasonably accessible because of undue burden or cost has the burden of showing that the basis exists. If the showing is made, the court may nonetheless order discovery from the source if the requesting party shows good cause, but only after considering the limitations of subsection [subdivision] (b)(1a) of this rule.

If the motion for a protective order is denied in whole or in part, the court may, on such terms and conditions as are just, order that any party or person provide or permit discovery. The provisions of Rule 37(a)(4) apply to the award of expenses incurred in relation to the motion.

(d) Sequence and timing of discovery. – Unless the court upon motion, for the convenience of parties and witnesses and in the interests of justice, orders otherwise, methods of discovery may be used in any sequence and the fact that a party is conducting discovery, whether by deposition or otherwise, shall not operate to delay any other party's discovery. Any order or rule of court setting the time within which discovery must be completed shall be construed to fix the date after which the pendency of discovery will not be allowed to delay trial or any other proceeding before the court, but shall not be construed to prevent any party from utilizing any procedures afforded under Rules 26 through 36, so long as trial or any hearing before the court is not thereby delayed.

(e) Supplementation of responses. – A party who has responded to a request for discovery with a response that was complete when made is under no duty to supplement the party's response to include information thereafter acquired, except as follows:

(1) A party is under a duty seasonably to supplement the party's response with respect to any question directly addressed to (i) the identity and location of persons having knowledge of discoverable matters, and (ii) the identity of each person expected to be called as an expert witness at trial, the subject matter on which the person is expected to testify, and the substance of the testimony.

(2)   A party is under a duty seasonably to amend a prior response if the party obtains information upon the basis of which (i) the party knows that the response was incorrect when made, or (ii) the party knows that the response though correct when made is no longer true and the circumstances are such that a failure to amend the response is in substance a knowing concealment.

(3)   A duty to supplement responses may be imposed by order of the court, agreement of the parties, or at any time prior to trial through new requests for supplementation of prior responses.

(f)   Discovery meeting, discovery conference, discovery plan. –

(1)   No earlier than 40 days after the complaint is filed in an action, any party's attorney or an unrepresented party may request a meeting on the subject of discovery, including the discovery of electronically stored information. If such a request is filed, the parties shall meet in the county in which the action is pending not less than 21 days after the initial request for a meeting is filed and served upon the parties, unless agreed otherwise by the parties or their attorneys and unless an earlier time for the meeting is ordered by the court or agreed by the parties. Even if the parties or their attorneys do not seek to have a discovery meeting, at any time after commencement of an action the court may direct the parties or their attorneys to appear before it for a discovery conference.

(2)   During a discovery meeting held pursuant to subdivision (f)(1) of this rule, the attorneys and any unrepresented parties shall (i) consider the nature and basis of the parties' claims and defenses and the possibilities for promptly settling or resolving the case and (ii) discuss the preparation of a discovery plan as set forth in subdivision (f)(3) of this rule. Attorneys for the parties, and any unrepresented parties, that have appeared in the case are jointly responsible for arranging the meeting, for being prepared to discuss a discovery plan, and for attempting in good faith to agree on a discovery plan. The meeting may be held by telephone, by videoconference, or in person, or a combination thereof, unless the court, on motion, orders the attorneys and the unrepresented parties to attend in person. If a discovery plan is agreed upon, the plan shall be submitted to the court within 14 days after the meeting, and the parties may request a conference with the court regarding the plan. If the parties do not agree upon a discovery plan, they shall submit to the court within 14 days after the meeting a joint report containing those parts of a discovery plan upon which they agree and the position of each of the parties on the parts upon which they disagree. Unless the parties agree otherwise, the attorney for the first plaintiff

listed on the complaint shall be responsible for submitting the discovery plan or joint report.

(3) A discovery plan shall contain the following: (i) a statement of the issues as they then appear; (ii) a proposed plan and schedule of discovery, including the discovery of electronically stored information; (iii) with respect to electronically stored information, and if appropriate under the circumstances of the case, a reference to the preservation of such information, the media form, format, or procedures by which such information will be produced, the allocation of the costs of preservation, production, and, if necessary, restoration, of such information, the method for asserting or preserving claims of privilege or of protection of the information as trial-preparation materials if different from that provided in subdivision (b)(5) of this rule, the method for asserting or preserving confidentiality and proprietary status, and any other matters addressed by the parties; (iv) any limitations proposed to be placed on discovery, including, if appropriate under the circumstances of the case, that discovery be conducted in phases or be limited to or focused on particular issues; (v) when discovery should be completed; and (vi) if appropriate under the circumstances of the case, any limitations or conditions pursuant to subsection (c) of this rule regarding protective orders.

(4) If the parties are unable to agree to a discovery plan at a meeting held pursuant to subdivision (f)(1) of this rule, they shall, upon motion of any party, appear before the court for a discovery conference at which the court shall order the entry of a discovery plan after consideration of the report required to be submitted under subdivision (f)(2) of this rule and the position of the parties. The order may address other matters, including the allocation of discovery costs, as are necessary for the proper management of discovery in the action. An order may be altered or amended as justice may require.

The court may combine the discovery conference with a pretrial conference authorized by Rule 16. A discovery conference in a medical malpractice action shall be governed by subsection (f1) of this rule.

(f1) Medical malpractice discovery conference. – In a medical malpractice action as defined in G.S. 90-21.11, upon the case coming at issue or the filing of a responsive pleading or motion requiring a determination by the court, the judge shall, within 30 days, direct the attorneys for the parties to appear for a discovery conference. At the conference the court may consider the matters set out in Rule 16 and subdivision (f)(3) of this rule and shall:

(1) Rule on all motions;

(2) Establish an appropriate schedule for designating expert witnesses, consistent with a discovery schedule pursuant to subdivision (3), to be complied with by all parties to the action such that there is a deadline for designating all expert witnesses within an appropriate time for all parties to implement discovery mechanisms with regard to the designated expert witnesses;

(3) Establish by order an appropriate discovery schedule designated so that, unless good cause is shown at the conference for a longer time, and subject to further orders of the court, discovery shall be completed within 150 days after the order is issued; nothing herein shall be construed to prevent any party from utilizing any procedures afforded under Rules 26 through 36, so long as trial or any hearing before the court is not thereby delayed; and

(4) Approve any consent order which may be presented by counsel for the parties relating to subdivisions (2) and (3) of this subsection, unless the court finds that the terms of the consent order are unreasonable.

If a party fails to identify an expert witness as ordered, the court shall, upon motion by the moving party, impose an appropriate sanction, which may include dismissal of the action, entry of default against the defendant, or exclusion of the testimony of the expert witness at trial.

(g) Signing of discovery requests, responses, and objections. – Every request for discovery or response or objection thereto made by a party represented by an attorney shall be signed by at least one attorney of record in that attorney's name, whose address shall be stated. A party who is not represented by an attorney shall sign the request, response, or objection and state that party's address. The signature of the attorney or party constitutes a certification that the attorney or party has read the request, response, or objection and that to the best of the knowledge, information, and belief of that attorney or party formed after a reasonable inquiry it is: (1) consistent with the rules and warranted by existing law or a good faith argument for the extension, modification, or reversal of existing law; (2) not interposed for any improper purpose, such as to harass or cause unnecessary delay or needless increase in the cost of litigation; and (3) not unreasonable or unduly burdensome or expensive, given the needs of the case, the discovery already had in the case, the amount in controversy, and the importance of the issues at stake in the litigation. If a request, response, or objection is not signed, it shall be stricken unless it is signed promptly after the omission is called to the attention of the party making the request, response, or objection and a party shall not be obligated to take any action with respect to it until it is signed.

If a certification is made in violation of the rule, the court, upon motion or upon its own initiative, shall impose upon the person who made the certification, the party on whose behalf the request, response, or objection is made, or both, an appropriate sanction, which may include an order to pay the amount of the reasonable expenses incurred because of the violation, including a reasonable attorney's fee. (1967, c. 954, s. 1; 1971, c. 750; 1975, c. 762, s. 2; 1985, c. 603, ss. 1-4; 1987, c. 859, s. 3; 2011-199, s. 2.)

Rule 27. Depositions before action or pending appeal

(a)   Before action. –

(1)   Petition. – A person who desires to perpetuate that person's own testimony or the testimony of another person regarding any matter may file a verified petition in the appropriate court in a county where any expected adverse party resides. The petition shall be entitled in the name of the petitioner and shall show: (i) that the petitioner expects that the petitioner, or the petitioner's personal representative, heirs or devisees, will be a party to an action cognizable in any court, but that the petitioner is presently unable to bring it or cause it to be brought, (ii) the subject matter of the expected action and the petitioner's reasons for desiring to perpetuate it, (iii) the facts which the petitioner desires to establish by the proposed testimony and the petitioner's reasons for desiring to perpetuate it, (iv) the names or a description of the persons the petitioner expects will be adverse parties and their addresses so far as known, and (v) the names and addresses of the persons to be examined and the substance of the testimony which the petitioner expects to elicit from each, and shall ask for an order authorizing the petitioner to take the depositions of the persons to be examined named in the petition, for the purpose of perpetuating their testimony.

(2)   Notice and Service. – The petitioner shall thereafter serve a notice upon each person named in the petition as an expected adverse party, together with a copy of the petition, stating that the petitioner will apply to the court, at a time and place named therein, for the order described in the petition. At least 20 days before the date of hearing (or within such time as the court may direct) the notice shall be served in the manner provided in Rule 4(j)(1) or (2) for service of summons; but if such service cannot with due diligence be made upon any

expected adverse party named in the petition, the court may make such order as is just for service by publication or otherwise, and shall appoint, for persons not served in the manner provided in Rule 4(j)(1) or (2), an attorney who shall represent them, in case they are not otherwise represented. If any expected adverse party is a minor or incompetent the provisions of Rule 17(c) apply.

(3) Order and Examination. – If the court is satisfied that the perpetuation of the testimony may prevent a failure or delay of justice, it shall make an order designating or describing the persons whose depositions may be taken and specifying the subject matter of the examination and whether the depositions shall be taken upon oral examination or written questions. The depositions may then be taken in accordance with these rules; and the court may make orders of the character provided for by Rules 34 and 35. For the purpose of applying these rules to depositions for perpetuating testimony, each reference therein to the court in which the action is pending shall be deemed to refer to the court in which the petition for such deposition was filed.

(4) Use of Deposition. – If a deposition to perpetuate testimony is taken under these rules or if, although not so taken, it would be admissible in evidence in the courts of the United States or the state in which it is taken, it may be used in any action involving the same subject matter subsequently brought in a court of this State in accordance with the provisions of Rule 32(a), or in any other court under whose rules it is admissible.

(b) Pending appeal. – If an appeal has been taken from the determination of any court or if petition for review or certiorari has been served and filed, or before the taking of an appeal or the filing of a petition for review or certiorari if the time therefor has not expired, the court in which the determination was made may allow the taking of the depositions of witnesses to perpetuate their testimony for use in the event of further proceedings in the trial court. In such case the party who desires to perpetuate the testimony may make a motion in the trial court for leave to take the depositions, upon the same notice and service thereof as if the action was pending in the trial court. The motion shall show (i) the names and addresses of the persons to be examined and the substance of the testimony which the party expects to elicit from each; (ii) the reasons for perpetuating their testimony. If the court finds that the perpetuation of the testimony is proper to avoid a failure or delay of justice, it may make an order allowing the depositions to be taken and may make orders of the character provided for by Rules 34 and 35, and thereupon the depositions may be taken and used in the same manner and under the same conditions as are prescribed in these rules for depositions taken in actions pending in the trial court.

(c)   Perpetuation by action. – This rule does not limit the power of a court to entertain an action to perpetuate testimony. (1967, c. 954, s. 1; 1975, c. 762, s. 2; 2011-284, s. 5.)

Rule 28. Persons before whom depositions may be taken

(a)   Within the United States. – Within the United States or within a territory or insular possession subject to the dominion of the United States, depositions shall be taken before a person authorized to administer oaths by the laws of this State, of the United States or of the place where the examination is held, or before a person appointed by the court in which the action is pending. A person so appointed has power to administer oaths and take testimony.

(b)   In foreign countries. – Depositions may be taken in a foreign country:

(1)   Pursuant to any applicable treaty or convention;

(2)   Pursuant to a letter of request, whether or not captioned a letter rogatory;

(3)   On notice before a person authorized to administer oaths in the place where the examination is held, either by the law thereof or by the law of the United States; or

(4)   Before a person commissioned by the court, and a person so commissioned shall have the power by virtue of his commission to administer any necessary oath and take testimony. A commission or a letter of request shall be issued on application and notice and on terms that are just and appropriate. It is not requisite to the issuance of a commission or a letter of request that the taking of the deposition in any other manner is impracticable or inconvenient; and both a commission and a letter of request may be issued in proper cases. A notice or commission may designate the person before whom the deposition is to be taken either by name or descriptive title. A letter of request may be addressed "To the Appropriate Authority in (here name the country)." When a letter of request or any other device is used pursuant to any applicable treaty or convention, it shall be captioned in the form prescribed by that treaty or convention. Evidence obtained in response to a letter of request

need not be excluded merely because the testimony was not taken under oath, or any similar departure from the requirements for depositions taken within the United States under these rules.

(c)   Disqualification for interest. – Unless the parties agree otherwise by stipulation as provided in Rule 29, no deposition shall be taken before a person who is any of the following:

(1)   A relative, employee, or attorney of any of the parties;

(2)   A relative or employee of an attorney of the parties;

(3)   Financially interested in the action; or

(4)   An independent contractor if the contractor or the contractor's principal is under a blanket contract for the court reporting services with an attorney of the parties, party to the action, or party having a financial interest in the action. Notwithstanding the disqualification under this rule, the party desiring to take the deposition under a stipulation shall disclose the disqualification in writing in a Rule 30(b) notice of deposition and shall inform all parties to the litigation on the record of the existence of the disqualification under this rule and of the proposed stipulation waiving the disqualification. Any party opposing the proposed stipulation as provided in the notice of deposition shall give timely written notice of his or her opposition to all parties.

For the purposes of this rule, a blanket contract means a contract to perform court reporting services over a fixed period of time or an indefinite period of time, rather than on a case by case basis, or any other contractual arrangement which compels, guarantees, regulates, or controls the use of particular court reporting services in future cases.

Notwithstanding any other provision of law, a person is prohibited from taking a deposition under any contractual agreement that requires transmission of the original transcript without the transcript having been certified as provided in Rule 30(f) by the person before whom the deposition was taken.

Notwithstanding the provisions of this subsection, a person otherwise disqualified from taking a deposition under this subsection may take a deposition provided that the deposition is taken by videotape in compliance with Rule 30(b)(4) and Rule 30(f), and the notice for the taking of the deposition states the name of the person before whom the deposition will be taken and that person's relationship, if any, to a party or a party's attorney, provided that the deposition is also recorded by stenographic means by a nondisqualified person.

(d) Depositions to be used in foreign countries.

(1) A person desiring to take depositions in this State to be used in proceedings pending in the courts of any other country may present to a judge of the superior or district court a commission, order, notice, consent, or other authority under which the deposition is to be taken, whereupon it shall be the duty of the judge to issue the necessary subpoenas pursuant to Rule 45. Orders of the character provided in Rules 30(b), 30(d), and 45(b) may be made upon proper application therefor by the person to whom such subpoena is directed. Failure by any person without adequate excuse to obey a subpoena served upon him pursuant to this rule may be deemed a contempt of the court from which the subpoena issued.

(2) The commissioner herein provided for shall not proceed to act under and by virtue of his appointment until the party seeking to obtain such deposition has deposited with him a sufficient sum of money to cover all costs and charges incident to the taking of the deposition, including such witness fees as are allowed to witnesses in this State for attendance upon the superior court. From such deposit the commissioner shall retain whatever amount may be due him for services, pay the witness fees and other costs that may have been incurred by reason of taking such deposition, and if any balance remains in his hands, he shall pay the same to the party by whom it was advanced. (1967, c. 954, s. 1; 1975, c. 762, s. 2; 1995, c. 389, s. 4; 1999-264, s. 1; 2001-379, s. 4; 2011-247, s. 2.)

Rule 29. Stipulations regarding discovery procedure

Unless the court orders otherwise, the parties may by written stipulation (i) provide that depositions may be taken before any person, at any time or place, upon any notice, and in any manner and when so taken may be used like other depositions, and (ii) modify the procedures provided by these rules for other methods of discovery. (1967, c. 954, s. 1; 1975, c. 762, s. 1.)

Rule 30. Depositions upon oral examination

(a) When depositions may be taken. – After commencement of the action, any party may take the testimony of any person, including a party, by deposition upon oral examination. Leave of court, granted with or without notice, must be obtained only if the plaintiff seeks to take a deposition prior to the expiration of 30 days after service of the summons and complaint upon any defendant or service made under Rule 4(e), except that leave is not required (i) if a defendant has served a notice of taking deposition or otherwise sought discovery, or (ii) if special notice is given as provided in subsection (b)(2) of this rule. The attendance of witnesses may be compelled by subpoena as provided in Rule 45, provided that no subpoena need be served on a deponent who is a party or an officer, director or managing agent of a party, provided the party has been served with notice pursuant to subsection (b)(1) of this rule. The deposition of a person confined in prison or of a patient receiving in-patient care in or confined to an institution or hospital for the mentally ill or mentally handicapped may be taken only by leave of court on such terms as the court prescribes.

(b)   Notice of examination; general requirements; place of examination; special notice; nonstenographic recording; production of documents and things; deposition of organization. –

(1)   A party desiring to take the deposition of any person upon oral examination shall give notice in writing to every other party to the action. The notice shall state the time and place for taking the deposition and the name and address of each person to be examined, if known, and, if the name is not known, a general description sufficient to identify him or the particular class or group to which he belongs. If a subpoena duces tecum is to be served on the person to be examined, the designation of the materials to be produced as set forth in the subpoena shall be attached to or included in the notice. The notice shall be served on all parties at least 15 days prior to the taking of the deposition when any party required to be served resides without the State and shall be served on all parties at least 10 days prior to the taking of the deposition when all of the parties required to be served reside within the State. Depositions of parties, officers, directors or managing agents of parties or of other persons designated pursuant to subsection (b)(6) hereof to testify on behalf of a party may be taken only at the following places:

A resident of the State may be required to attend for examination by deposition only in the county wherein he resides or is employed or transacts his business in person. A nonresident of the State may be required to attend for such examination only in the county wherein he resides or within 50 miles of the place of service except that a judge, as defined by subdivision (h) of this rule, may, upon motion showing good cause, require that a party who selected the county where the action is pending as the forum for the action or an officer, director or managing agent of such a party, or a person designated pursuant to subsection (b)(6) hereof to testify on behalf of such a party present himself for the taking of his deposition in the county where the action is pending. The judge upon granting the motion may make any other orders allowed by Rule 26(c) with respect thereto, including orders with respect to the expenses of the deponent.

(2) Leave of court is not required for the taking of a deposition by plaintiff if the notice (i) states that the person to be examined is about to go out of the county where the action is pending and more than 100 miles from the place of trial, or is about to go out of the United States, or is bound on a voyage to sea, and will be unavailable for examination unless his deposition is taken before expiration of the 30-day period, and (ii) sets forth facts to support the statement. The plaintiff's attorney shall sign the notice, and his signature constitutes a certification by him that to the best of his knowledge, information, and belief the statement and supporting facts are true. The sanctions provided by Rule 11 are applicable to the certification.

If a party shows that when he was served with notice under this subsection (b)(2) he was unable through the exercise of diligence to obtain counsel to represent him at the taking of the deposition, the deposition may not be used against him.

(3) The court may for cause shown enlarge or shorten the time for taking the deposition.

(4) Unless the court orders otherwise, testimony at a deposition may be recorded by sound recording, sound-and-visual, or stenographic means. If the testimony is to be taken by other means in addition to or in lieu of stenographic means, the notice shall state the methods by which it shall be taken and shall state whether a stenographer will be present at the deposition. In the case of a deposition taken by stenographic means, the party that provides for the stenographer shall provide for the transcribing of the testimony taken. If the deposition is by sound recording only, the party noticing the deposition shall provide for the transcribing of the testimony taken. If the deposition is by sound-and-visual means, the appearance or demeanor of deponents or attorneys shall not be distorted through camera techniques. Regardless of the method stated in the notice, any party or the deponent may have the testimony recorded by stenographic means.

(5) A party deponent, deponents who are officers, directors or managing agents of parties and other persons designated pursuant to subsection (b)(6)

hereof to testify on behalf of a party may not be served with a subpoena duces tecum, but the notice to a party for the deposition of such a deponent may be accompanied by a request made in compliance with Rule 34 for the production of documents and tangible things at the taking of the deposition. The procedure of Rule 34, except as to time for response, shall apply to the request. When a notice to take such a deposition is accompanied by a request made in compliance with Rule 34 the notice and the request must be served at least 15 days earlier than would otherwise be required by Rule 30(b)(1), and any objections to such a request must be served at least seven days prior to the taking of the deposition.

(6)   A party may in his notice and in a subpoena name as the deponent a public or private corporation or a partnership or association or governmental agency and describe with reasonable particularity the matters on which examination is requested. In that event, the organization so named shall designate one or more officers, directors, or managing agents, or other persons who consent to testify on its behalf, and may set forth, for each person designated, the matters on which he will testify. A subpoena shall advise a nonparty organization of its duty to make such a designation. It shall not be necessary to serve a subpoena on an organization which is a party, but the notice, served on a party without an accompanying subpoena shall clearly advise such of its duty to make the required designation. The persons so designated shall testify as to matters known or reasonably available to the organization. This subsection (b)(6) does not preclude taking a deposition by any other procedure authorized in these rules.

(7)   The parties may stipulate in writing or the court may upon motion order that a deposition be taken by telephone. For the purposes of this rule and Rules 28(a), 37(a)(1) and 45(d), a deposition taken by telephone is taken in the district and the place where the deponent is to answer questions propounded to him.

(c)   Examination and cross-examination; record of examination; oath; objections. – Examination and cross-examination of witnesses may proceed as permitted at the trial under the provisions of Rule 43(b). The person before whom the deposition is to be taken shall put the deponent on oath and shall personally, or by someone acting under his direction and in his presence, record the testimony of the deponent. The testimony shall be taken stenographically or recorded by any other means ordered in accordance with subsection (b)(4) of this rule. If requested by one of the parties, the testimony shall be transcribed.

All objections made at the time of the examination to the qualifications of the person before whom the deposition is taken, or to the manner of taking it, or to the evidence presented, or to the conduct of any party, and any other objection to the proceedings, shall be noted upon the deposition by the person before whom the deposition is taken. Subject to any limitations imposed by orders entered pursuant to Rule 26(c) or 30(d), evidence objected to shall be taken subject to the objections. In lieu of participating in the oral examination, parties may serve written questions in a sealed envelope on the party who served the notice of taking the deposition, and he shall transmit them to the person before whom the deposition is to be taken who shall open them at the deposition, propound them to the witness and record the answers verbatim.

(d) Motion to terminate or limit examination. – At any time during the taking of the deposition, on motion of a party or of the deponent and upon a showing that the examination is being conducted in bad faith or in such manner as unreasonably to annoy, embarrass, or oppress the deponent or party, a judge of the court in which the action is pending or any judge in the county where the deposition is being taken may order before whom the examination is being taken to cease forthwith from taking the deposition, or may limit the scope and manner of the taking of the deposition as provided in Rule 26(c). If the order made terminates the examination, it shall be resumed thereafter only upon the order of a judge of the court in which the action is pending. Upon demand of the objecting party or deponent, the taking of the deposition shall be suspended for the time necessary to make a motion for an order. The provisions of Rule 37(a)(4) apply to the award of expenses incurred in relation to the motion.

(e) Submission to deponent; changes; signing. – The sound-and-visual recording, or the transcript of it, if any, the transcript of the sound recording, or the transcript of a deposition taken by stenographic means, shall be submitted to the deponent for examination and shall be reviewed by the deponent, unless such examination and review are waived by the deponent and by the parties. If there are changes in form or substance, the deponent shall sign a statement reciting such changes and the reasons given by the deponent for making them. The person administering the oath shall indicate in the certificate prescribed by subdivision (f)(1) whether any review was requested and, if so, shall append any changes made by the deponent. The certificate shall then be signed by the deponent, unless the parties by stipulation waive the signing or the deponent is ill or cannot be found or refuses to sign. If the certificate is not signed by the deponent within 30 days of its submission to him, the person before whom the deposition was taken shall sign the certificate and state on the certificate the fact of the waiver or of the illness or absence of the deponent or the fact of the refusal or failure to sign together with the reason, if any, given therefor; and the deposition may then be used as fully as though the certificate were signed unless on a motion to suppress under Rule 32(d)(4) the court holds that the reasons given for the refusal to sign require rejection of the deposition in whole or in part.

(f) Certification by person administering the oath; exhibits; copies. –

(1) The person administering the oath shall certify that the deponent was duly sworn by him and that the deposition is a true record of the testimony given by the deponent. This certificate shall be in writing and accompany the sound-and-visual or sound recording or transcript of the deposition. He shall then place the deposition in an envelope or package endorsed with the title of the action and marked "Deposition of (here insert name of witness)" and shall personally deliver it or mail it by first class mail to the party taking the deposition or his attorney who shall preserve it as the court's copy.

Documents and things produced for inspection during the examination of the deponent shall, upon the request of a party, be marked for identification and annexed to and returned with the deposition, and may be inspected and copied by any party, except that (i) the person producing the materials may substitute copies to be marked for identification, if he affords to all parties fair opportunity to verify the copies by comparison with the originals, and (ii) if the person producing the materials requests their return, the person before whom the deposition is taken shall mark them, give each party an opportunity to inspect and copy them, and return them to the person producing them, and the materials may then be used in the manner as if annexed to and returned with the deposition. Any party may move for an order that the original be annexed to and returned with the deposition to the court, pending final disposition of the case.

(2) Upon payment of reasonable charges therefor, the person administering the oath shall furnish a copy of the deposition to any party or to the deponent.

(3) Repealed by Session Laws 2005-138, s. 3, effective October 1, 2005.

(g) Failure to attend or to serve subpoena; expenses. –

(1) If the party giving the notice of the taking of a deposition fails to attend and proceed therewith and another party attends in person or by attorney pursuant to the notice, the judge may order the party giving the notice to pay to

such other party the reasonable expenses incurred by him and his attorney in attending, including reasonable attorney's fees.

(2)   If the party giving the notice of the taking of a deposition of a witness fails to serve a subpoena upon him and the witness because of such failure does not attend, and if another party attends in person or by attorney because he expects the deposition of that witness to be taken, the judge may order the party giving the notice to pay to such other party the reasonable expenses incurred by him and his attorney in attending, including reasonable attorney's fees.

(h)   Judge; definition. –

(1)   In respect to actions in the superior court, a judge of the court in which the action is pending shall, for the purposes of this rule, and Rule 26, Rule 31, Rule 33, Rule 34, Rule 35, Rule 36 and Rule 37, be a superior court judge who has jurisdiction pursuant to G.S. 7A-47.1 or G.S. 7A-48 in that county.

(2)   In respect to actions in the district court, a judge of the court in which the action is pending shall, for the purposes of this rule, Rule 26, Rule 31, Rule 33, Rule 34, Rule 35, Rule 36 and Rule 37, be the chief district judge or any judge designated by him pursuant to G.S. 7A-192.

(3)   In respect to actions in either the superior court or the district court, a judge of the court in the county where the deposition is being taken shall, for the purposes of this rule, be a superior court judge who has jurisdiction pursuant to G.S. 7A-47.1 or G.S. 7A-48 in that county, or the chief judge of the district court or any judge designated by him pursuant to G.S. 7A-192. (1967, c. 954, s. 1; 1973, c. 828, s. 1; c. 1126, ss. 1, 2; 1975, c. 762, s. 2; 1977, c. 769; 1983, c. 201, s. 2; c. 801, ss. 1, 2; 1987 (Reg. Sess., 1988), c. 1037, s. 42; 1995, c. 353, ss. 1-3; 1995 (Reg. Sess., 1996), c. 742, s. 4; 2005-138, s. 3.)

Rule 31. Depositions upon written questions

(a)   Serving questions; notice. – After commencement of the action, any party may take the testimony of any person, including a party, by deposition upon written questions. The attendance of witnesses may be compelled by the use of subpoena as provided in Rule 45 provided that no subpoena need be served on a deponent who is a party or an officer, director or managing agent of a party, provided the party has been served with notice pursuant to this rule. Such a deposition shall be taken in the county where the witness resides or is employed or transacts his business in person unless the witness agrees that it may be taken elsewhere. The deposition of a person confined in prison or of a patient receiving in-patient care in or confined to an institution or hospital for the mentally ill or mentally handicapped may be taken only by leave of court on such terms as the court prescribes.

A party desiring to take a deposition upon written questions shall serve them upon every other party with a notice stating (i) the name and address of the person who is to answer them, if known, and if the name is not known, a general description sufficient to identify him or the particular class or group to which he belongs, and (ii) the name or descriptive title and address of the officer before whom the deposition is to be taken. A deposition upon written questions may be taken of a public or private corporation or a partnership or association or governmental agency in accordance with the provisions of Rule 30(b)(6).

Within 30 days after the notice and written questions are served, a party may serve cross questions upon all other parties. Within 10 days after being served with cross questions, a party may serve redirect questions upon all other parties. Within 10 days after being served with redirect questions, a party may serve recross questions upon all other parties. The court may for cause shown enlarge or shorten the time.

(b)   Person to take responses and prepare record. – A copy of the notice and copies of all questions served shall be delivered by the party taking the deposition to the person designated in the notice to take the deposition, who shall proceed promptly, in the manner provided by Rule 30(c), (e), and (f), to take the testimony of the deponent in response to the questions and to prepare, certify, and mail the deposition, attaching thereto the copy of the notice and the questions received by him.

(c)   Repealed by Session Laws 2005-138, s. 4, effective October 1, 2005. (1967, c. 954, s. 1; 1975, c. 762, s. 2; 2005-138, s. 4.)
Rule 32. Use of depositions in court proceedings

(a)   Use of depositions. – At the trial or upon the hearing of a motion or an interlocutory proceeding or upon a hearing before a referee, any part or all of a deposition, so far as admissible under the rules of evidence applied as though the witness were then present and testifying, may be used against any party who was present or represented at the taking of the deposition or who had reasonable notice thereof, in accordance with any of the following provisions:

(1)   Any deposition may be used by any party for the purpose of contradicting or impeaching the testimony of deponent as a witness.

(2) The deposition of a person called as a witness may also be used as substantive evidence by any party adverse to the party who called the deponent as a witness and it may be used by the party calling deponent as a witness as substantive evidence of such facts stated in the deposition as are in conflict with or inconsistent with the testimony of deponent as a witness.

(3) The deposition of a party or of any one who at the time of taking the deposition was an officer, director, or managing agent, or a person designated under Rule 30(b)(6) or 31(a) to testify on behalf of a public or private corporation, partnership or association or governmental agency which is a party may be used by an adverse party for any purpose, whether or not the deponent testifies at the trial or hearing.

(4) The deposition of a witness, whether or not a party, may be used by any party for any purpose if the court finds: that the witness is dead; or that the witness is at a greater distance than 100 miles from the place of trial or hearing, or is out of the United States, unless it appears that the absence of the witness was procured by the party offering the deposition; or that the witness is unable to attend or testify because of age, illness, infirmity, or imprisonment; or that the party offering the deposition has been unable to procure the attendance of the witness by subpoena; or upon application and notice, that such exceptional circumstances exist as to make it desirable, in the interest of justice and with due regard to the importance of presenting testimony of witnesses orally in open court, to allow the deposition to be used; or the witness is an expert witness whose testimony has been procured by videotape as provided for under Rule 30(b)(4).

(5) If only part of a deposition is offered in evidence by a party, an adverse party may require him to introduce any other part which is relevant to the part introduced, and any party may introduce any other parts.

Substitution of parties pursuant to Rule 25 does not affect the right to use depositions previously taken; and, when an action in any court of the United States or of any state has been dismissed and another action involving the same subject matter is afterward brought between the same parties or their representatives or successors in interest, all depositions lawfully taken in the former action and duly prepared, certified, and delivered in accordance with Rule 30 may be used in the latter as if originally taken therefor.

(b) Objections to admissibility. – Subject to the provisions of Rules 28(b) and subsection (d)(3) of this rule, objection may be made at the trial or hearing to receiving in evidence any deposition or part thereof for any reason which would require the exclusion of the evidence if the witness were then present and testifying.

(c) Effect of taking or using depositions. – A party does not make a person his own witness for any purpose by taking his deposition. The introduction in evidence of the deposition or any part thereof for any purpose other than that of contradicting or impeaching the deponent makes the deponent the witness of the party introducing the deposition, but this shall not apply to the use by an adverse party of a deposition under subsection (a)(2) or (a)(3) of this rule. At the trial or hearing any party may rebut any relevant evidence contained in a deposition whether introduced by him or by any other party.

(d) Effect of errors and irregularities in depositions. –

(1) As to Notice. – All errors and irregularities in the notice for taking a deposition are waived unless written objection is promptly served upon the party giving the notice.

(2) As to Disqualification of Person before Whom Taken. – Objection to taking a deposition because of disqualification of the person before whom it is to be taken is waived unless made before the taking of the deposition begins or as soon thereafter as the disqualification becomes known or could be discovered with reasonable diligence.

(3) As to Taking of Deposition. –

a. Objections to the competency of a witness or to the competency, relevancy, or materiality of testimony are not waived by failure to make them before or during the taking of the deposition, unless the ground of the objection is one which might have been obviated or removed if presented at that time.

b. Errors and irregularities occurring at the oral examination in the manner of taking the deposition, in the form of the questions or answers, in the oath or affirmation, or in the conduct of parties, and errors of any kind which might be obviated, removed, or cured if promptly presented, are waived unless seasonable objection thereto is made at the taking of the deposition.

c. Objections to the form of written questions submitted under Rule 31 are waived unless served in writing upon the party propounding them within the time allowed for serving the succeeding cross or other questions and within five days after service of the last questions authorized.

(4) As to Completion and Return of Deposition. – Errors and irregularities in the manner in which the testimony is transcribed or the deposition is prepared, signed, certified, sealed, indorsed, transmitted, or otherwise dealt with by the person taking the deposition under Rules 30 and 31 are waived unless a motion to suppress the deposition or some part thereof is made with reasonable promptness after such defeat is, or with due diligence might have been, ascertained. (1967, c. 954, s. 1; 1975, c. 762, s. 2; 1977, c. 984; 1981, c. 599, s. 2; 2005-138, ss. 5, 6.)
Rule 33. Interrogatories to parties

(a) Availability; procedures for use. – Any party may serve upon any other party written interrogatories to be answered by the party served or, if the party served is a public or private corporation or a partnership or association or governmental agency, by any officer or agent, who shall furnish such information as is available to the party. Interrogatories may, without leave of court, be served upon the plaintiff after commencement of the action and upon any other party with or after service of the summons and complaint upon that party.

A party may direct no more than 50 interrogatories, in one or more sets, to any other party, except upon leave granted by the Court for good cause shown or by agreement of the other party. Interrogatory parts and subparts shall be counted as separate interrogatories for purposes of this rule.
There shall be sufficient space following each interrogatory in which the respondent may state the response. The respondent shall: (1) state the response in the space provided, using additional pages if necessary; or (2) restate the interrogatory to be followed by the response.

Each interrogatory shall be answered separately and fully in writing under oath, unless it is objected to, in which event the reasons for objection shall be stated in lieu of an answer. An objection to an interrogatory shall be made by stating the objection and the reason therefor either in the space following the interrogatory or following the restated interrogatory. The answers are to be signed by the person making them, and the objections signed by the attorney making them. The party upon whom the interrogatories have been served shall serve a copy of the answers, and objections if any, within 30 days after the service of the interrogatories, except that a defendant may serve answers or objections within 45 days after service of the summons and complaint upon the defendant. The court may allow a shorter or longer time. The party submitting the interrogatories may move for an order under Rule 37(a) with respect to any objection to or other failure to answer an interrogatory.

(b) Scope; use at trial. – Interrogatories may relate to any matters which can be inquired into under Rule 26(b), and the answers may be used to the extent permitted by the rules of evidence.

An interrogatory otherwise proper is not necessarily objectionable merely because an answer to the interrogatory involves an opinion or contention that relates to fact or the application of law to fact, but the court may order that such an interrogatory need not be answered until after designated discovery has been completed or until a pretrial conference or other later time.

(c) Option to produce business records. – Where the answer to an interrogatory may be derived or ascertained from the business records, including electronically stored information, of the party upon whom the interrogatory has been served or from an examination, audit or inspection of such business records, or from a compilation, abstract or summary based thereon, and the burden of deriving or ascertaining the answer is substantially the same for the party serving the interrogatory as for the party served, it is a sufficient answer to such interrogatory to specify the records from which the answer may be derived or ascertained and to afford to the party serving the interrogatory reasonable opportunity to examine, audit or inspect such records and to make copies, compilations, abstracts or summaries. A specification shall be in sufficient detail to permit the interrogating party to locate and to identify, as readily as can the party served, the records from which the answer may be ascertained. (1967, c. 954, s. 1; 1971, c. 1156, s. 4.5; 1975, c. 99; c. 762, s. 2; 1987, c. 73; c. 613, s. 1; 2011-199, s. 3(c).)

Rule 34. Production of documents, electronically stored information, and things; entry upon land for inspection and other purposes

(a) Scope. – Any party may serve on any other party a request (i) to produce and permit the party making the request, or someone acting on that party's behalf, to inspect and copy, test, or sample any designated documents, electronically stored information, or tangible things which constitute or contain matters within the scope of Rule 26(b) and which are in the possession, custody or control of the party upon whom the request is served; or (ii) to permit entry upon designated land or other property in the possession or control of the party upon whom the request is served for the purpose of inspection and measuring, surveying, photographing, testing, or sampling the property or any designated object or operation thereon, within the scope of Rule 26(b).

(b) Procedure. – The request may, without leave of court, be served upon the plaintiff after commencement of the action and upon any other party with or after service of the summons and complaint upon that party. The request shall set forth the items to be inspected either by individual item or by category, and describe each item and category with reasonable particularity. The request shall specify a reasonable time, place, and manner of making the inspection and performing the related acts. The request may specify the form or forms in which electronically stored information is to be produced.

The party upon whom the request is served shall serve a written response within 30 days after the service of the request, except that a defendant may serve a response within 45 days after service of the summons and complaint upon that defendant. The court may allow a shorter or longer time. The response shall state, with respect to each item or category, that inspection and related activities will be permitted as requested, unless the request is objected to, in which event the reasons for objection shall be stated. If objection is made to part of an item or category, the part shall be specified. In addition to other bases for objection, the response may state an objection to production of electronically stored information from sources that the party identifies as not reasonably accessible because of undue burden or cost. The response may also state an objection to a requested form for producing electronically stored information. If the responding party objects to a requested form, or if no form is specified in the request, the party must state the form or forms it intends to use. The party submitting the request may move for an order under Rule 37(a) with respect to any objection to or other failure to respond to the request or any part thereof, or any failure to permit inspection as requested.

Unless otherwise stipulated by the parties or ordered by the court, the following procedures apply to producing documents or electronically stored information:

(1) A party must produce documents as they are kept in the usual course of business or must organize and label them to correspond to the categories in the request;

(2) If a request does not specify a form for producing the electronically stored information, a party must produce it in a reasonably usable form or forms; and

(3) A party need not produce the same electronically stored information in more than one form.

(b1) Form of response. – There shall be sufficient space following each request in which the respondent may state the response. The respondent shall: (1) state the response in the space provided, using additional pages if necessary; or (2) restate the request to be followed by the response. An objection to a request shall be made by stating the objection and the reason therefor either in the space following the request or following the restated request.

(c) Persons not parties. – This rule does not preclude an independent action against a person not a party for production of documents and things and permission to enter upon land. (1967, c. 954, s. 1; 1969, c. 895, s. 8; 1973, c. 923, s. 1; 1975, c. 762, s. 2; 1987, c. 613, s. 2; 2011-199, s. 4.)

Rule 35. Physical and mental examination of persons
(a) Order for examination. – When the mental or physical condition (including the blood group) of a party, or of an agent or a person in the custody or under the legal control of a party, is in controversy, a judge of the court in which the action is pending as defined by Rule 30(h) may order the party to submit to a physical or mental examination by a physician or to produce for examination his agent or the person in his custody or legal control. The order may be made only on motion for good cause shown and upon notice to the person to be examined and to all parties and shall specify the time, place, manner, conditions, and scope of the examination and the person or persons by whom it is to be made.

(b) Report of examining physician. –

(1) If requested by the party against whom an order is made under Rule 35(a) or the person examined, the party causing the examination to be made shall deliver to him a copy of a detailed written report of the examining physician setting out his findings, including results of all tests made, diagnoses and conclusions, together with like reports of all earlier examinations of the same condition. After such request and delivery the party causing the examination

shall be entitled upon request to receive from the party against whom the order is made a like report of any examination, previously or thereafter made, of the same condition, unless, in the case of a report of examination of a person not a party, the party shows that he is unable to obtain it. The court on motion may make an order against a party requiring delivery of a report on such terms as are just, and if a physician fails or refuses to make a report the court may exclude his testimony if offered at the trial.

(2)   By requesting and obtaining a report of the examination so ordered or by taking the deposition of the examiner, the party examined waives any privilege he may have in that action or any other involving the same controversy, regarding the testimony of every other person who has examined or may thereafter examine him in respect of the same mental or physical condition.

(3)   This subsection applies to examinations made by agreement of the parties, unless the agreement expressly provides otherwise. This subsection does not preclude discovery of a report of an examining physician or the taking of a deposition of the physician in accordance with the provisions of any other rule. (1967, c. 954, s. 1; 1975, c. 762, s. 2.)

Rule 36. Requests for admission; effect of admission

(a)   Request for admission. – A party may serve upon any other party a written request for the admission, for purposes of the pending action only, of the truth of any matters within the scope of Rule 26(b) set forth in the request that relate to statements or opinions of fact or of the application of law to fact, including the genuineness of any documents described in the request. Copies of documents shall be served with the request unless they have been or are otherwise furnished or made available for inspection and copying. The request may, without leave of court, be served upon the plaintiff after commencement of the action and upon any other party with or after service of the summons and complaint upon that party. If the request is served with service of the summons and complaint, the summons shall so state.

Each matter of which an admission is requested shall be separately set forth. The matter is admitted unless, within 30 days after service of the request, or within such shorter or longer time as the court may allow, the party to whom the request is directed serves upon the party requesting the admission a written answer or objection addressed to the matter, signed by the party or by his attorney, but, unless the court shortens the time, a defendant shall not be required to serve answers or objections before the expiration of 60 days after service of the summons and complaint upon him. If objection is made, the reasons therefor shall be stated. The answer shall specifically deny the matter or set forth in detail the reasons why the answering party cannot truthfully admit or deny the matter. A denial shall fairly meet the substance of the requested admission, and when good faith requires that a party qualify his answer or deny only a part of the matter of which an admission is requested, he shall specify so much of it as is true and qualify or deny the remainder. An answering party may not give lack of information or knowledge as a reason for failure to admit or deny unless he states that he has made reasonable inquiry and that the information known or readily obtainable by him is insufficient to enable him to admit or deny. A party who considers that a matter of which an admission has been requested presents a genuine issue for trial may not, on that ground alone, object to the request; he may, subject to the provisions of Rule 37(c), deny the matter or set forth reasons why he cannot admit or deny it.

There shall be sufficient space following each request in which the respondent may state the response. The respondent shall:

(1) State the response in the space provided, using additional pages if necessary; or

(2) Restate the request to be followed by the response. An objection to a request shall be made by stating the objection and the reason therefor either in the space following the request or following the restated request.

The party who has requested the admissions may move to determine the sufficiency of the answers or objections. Unless the court determines that an objection is justified, it shall order that an answer be served. If the court determines that an answer does not comply with the requirements of this rule, it may order either that the matter is admitted or that an amended answer be served. The court may, in lieu of these orders, determine that final disposition of the request be made at a pretrial conference or at a designated time prior to trial. The provisions of Rule 37(a)(4) apply to the award of expenses incurred in relation to the motion.

(b) Effect of admission. – Any matter admitted under this rule is conclusively established unless the court on motion permits withdrawal or amendment of the admission. Subject to the provisions of Rule 16 governing amendment of a pretrial order, the court may permit withdrawal or amendment when the presentation of the merits of the action will be subserved thereby and the party who obtained the admission fails to satisfy the court that withdrawal or amendment will prejudice him in maintaining his action or defense on the merits. Any admission made by a party under this rule is for the purpose of pending action only and is not an admission by him for any other purpose nor may it be used against him in any other proceeding. (1967, c. 954, s. 1; 1975, c. 762, s. 2; 1981, c. 384, ss. 1, 2; 1987, c. 613, s. 3.)

Rule 37. Failure to make discovery; sanctions

(a) Motion for order compelling discovery. – A party, upon reasonable notice to other parties and all persons affected thereby, may apply for an order compelling discovery as follows:

(1) Appropriate Court. – An application for an order to a party or a deponent who is not a party may be made to a judge of the court in which the action is pending, or, on matters relating to a deposition where the deposition is being taken in this State, to a judge of the court in the county where the deposition is being taken, as defined by Rule 30(h).

(2) Motion. – If a deponent fails to answer a question propounded or submitted under Rules 30 or 31, or a corporation or other entity fails to make a designation under Rule 30(b)(6) or 31(a), or a party fails to answer an interrogatory submitted under Rule 33, or if a party, in response to a request for inspection submitted under Rule 34, fails to respond that inspection will be permitted as requested or fails to permit inspection as requested, the discovering party may move for an order compelling an answer, or a designation, or an order compelling inspection in accordance with the request. The motion must include a certification that the movant has in good faith conferred or attempted to confer with the person or party failing to make the discovery in an effort to secure the information or material without court action. When taking a deposition on oral examination, the proponent of the question shall complete the examination on all other matters before the examination is adjourned, in order to apply for an order. If the motion is based upon an objection to production of electronically stored information from sources the objecting party identified as not reasonably accessible because of undue burden or cost, the objecting party has the burden of showing that the basis for the objection exists.

If the court denies the motion in whole or in part, it may make such protective order as it would have been empowered to make on a motion made pursuant to Rule 26(c).

(3) Evasive or Incomplete Answer. – For purposes of this subdivision an evasive or incomplete answer is to be treated as a failure to answer.

(4) Award of Expenses of Motion. – If the motion is granted, the court shall, after opportunity for hearing, require the party or deponent whose conduct necessitated the motion or the party advising such conduct or both of them to pay to the moving party the reasonable expenses incurred in obtaining the order, including attorney's fees, unless the court finds that the opposition to the motion was substantially justified or that other circumstances make an award of expenses unjust.

If the motion is denied, the court shall, after opportunity for hearing, require the moving party to pay to the party or deponent who opposed the motion the reasonable expenses incurred in opposing the motion, including attorney's fees, unless the court finds that the making of the motion was substantially justified or that other circumstances make an award of expenses unjust.

If the motion is granted in part and denied in part, the court may apportion the reasonable expenses incurred in relation to the motion among the parties and persons in a just manner.

(b) Failure to comply with order. –

(1) Sanctions by Court in County Where Deposition Is Taken. – If a deponent fails to be sworn or to answer a question after being directed to do so by a judge of the court in the county in which the deposition is being taken, the failure may be considered a contempt of that court.

(2) Sanctions by Court in Which Action Is Pending. – If a party or an officer, director, or managing agent of a party or a person designated under Rule 30(b)(6) or 31(a) to testify on behalf of a party fails to obey an order to provide or permit discovery, including an order made under section (a) of this rule or Rule 35, or if a party fails to obey an order entered under Rule 26(f) a judge of the court in which the action is pending may make such orders in regard to the failure as are just, and among others the following:

a. An order that the matters regarding which the order was made or any other designated facts shall be taken to be established for the purposes of the action in accordance with the claim of the party obtaining the order;

b. An order refusing to allow the disobedient party to support or oppose designated claims or defenses, or prohibiting the party from introducing designated matters in evidence;

c. An order striking out pleadings or parts thereof, or staying further proceedings until the order is obeyed, or dismissing the action or proceeding or any part thereof, or rendering a judgment by default against the disobedient party;

d. In lieu of any of the foregoing orders or in addition thereto, an order treating as a contempt of court the failure to obey any orders except an order to submit to a physical or mental examination;

e. Where a party has failed to comply with an order under Rule 35(a) requiring the party to produce another for examination, such orders as are listed in subdivisions a, b, and c of this subsection, unless the party failing to comply shows that the party is unable to produce such person for examination.

In lieu of any of the foregoing orders or in addition thereto, the court shall require the party failing to obey the order to pay the reasonable expenses, including attorney's fees, caused by the failure, unless the court finds that the failure was substantially justified or that other circumstances make an award of expenses unjust.

(b1) Failure to provide electronically stored information. – Absent exceptional circumstances, a court may not impose sanctions under these rules on a party for failing to provide electronically stored information lost as a result of routine, good-faith operation of an electronic information system.

(c) Expenses on failure to admit. – If a party fails to admit the genuineness of any document or the truth of any matter as requested under Rule 36, and if the party requesting the admissions thereafter proves the genuineness of the document or the truth of the matter, the requesting party may apply to the court for an order requiring the other party to pay to him or her the reasonable expenses incurred in making that proof, including reasonable attorney's fees. The court shall make the order unless it finds that (i) the request was held objectionable pursuant to Rule 36(a), or (ii) the admission sought was of no substantial importance, or (iii) the party failing to admit had reasonable ground to believe that he or she might prevail on the matter, or (iv) there was other good reason for the failure to admit.

(d) Failure of party to attend at own deposition or serve answers to interrogatories or respond to request for inspection. – If a party or an officer, director, or managing agent of a party or a person designated under Rule 30(b)(6) or 31(a) to testify on behalf of a party fails (i) to appear before the person who is to take the deposition, after being served with a proper notice, or (ii) to serve answers or objections to interrogatories submitted under Rule 33, after proper service of the interrogatories, or (iii) to serve a written response to a request for inspection submitted under Rule 34, after proper service of the request, the court in which the action is pending on motion may make such orders in regard to the failure as are just, and among others it may take any action authorized under subdivisions a, b, and c of subsection (b)(2) of this rule. In lieu of any order or in addition thereto, the court shall require the party failing to act to pay the reasonable expenses, including attorney's fees, caused by the failure, unless the court finds that the failure was substantially justified or that other circumstances make an award of expenses unjust.

The failure to act described in this section may not be excused on the ground that the discovery sought is objectionable unless the party failing to act has applied for a protective order as provided by Rule 26(c).

(e), (f) Reserved for future codification purposes.

(g) Failure to participate in the framing of a discovery plan. – If a party or the party's attorney fails to participate in good faith in the framing of a discovery plan by agreement as is required by Rule 26(f), the court may, after opportunity for hearing, require such party or the party's attorney to pay to any other party the reasonable expenses, including attorney's fees, caused by the failure. (1967, c. 954, s. 1; 1973, c. 827, s. 1; 1975, c. 762, s. 2; 1985, c. 603, ss. 5-7; 2001-379, s. 5; 2011-199, s. 5.)

Article 6

Trials

Rule 38. Jury trial of right

(a) Right preserved. – The right of trial by jury as declared by the Constitution or statutes of North Carolina shall be preserved to the parties inviolate.

(b) Demand. – Any party may demand a trial by jury of any issue triable of right by a jury by serving upon the other parties a demand therefor in writing at any time after commencement of the action and not later than 10 days after the service of the last pleading directed to such issue. Such demand may be made in the pleading of the party or endorsed on the pleading.

(c) Demand – Specification of issues. – In his demand a party may specify the issues which he wishes so tried; otherwise, he shall be deemed to have demanded trial by jury for all the issues so triable. If a party has demanded trial by jury for only some of the issues, any other party within 10 days after service of the last pleading directed to such issues or within 10 days after service of the demand, whichever is later, or such lesser time as the court may order, may serve a demand for trial by jury of any other or all of the issues in the action.

(d) Waiver. – Except in actions wherein jury trial cannot be waived, the failure of a party to serve a demand as required by this rule and file it as required by Rule 5(d) constitutes a waiver by him of trial by jury. A demand for trial by jury as herein provided may not be withdrawn without the consent of the parties who have pleaded or otherwise appear in the action.

(e) Right granted. – The right of trial by jury as to the issue of just compensation shall be granted to the parties involved in any condemnation proceeding brought by bodies politic, corporations or persons which possess the power of eminent domain. (1967, c. 954, s. 1; 1973, c. 149.)

Rule 39. Trial by jury or by the court

(a) By jury. – When trial by jury has been demanded and has not been withdrawn as provided in Rule 38, the action shall be designated upon the docket as a jury action. The trial of all issues so demanded shall be by jury, unless

(1) The parties who have pleaded or otherwise appeared in the action or their attorneys of record, by written stipulation filed with the court or by an oral stipulation made in open court and entered in the minutes, consent to trial by the court sitting without a jury, or

(2) The court upon motion or of its own initiative finds that a right of trial by jury of some or all of those issues does not exist under the Constitution or statutes.

(b) By the court. – Issues not demanded for trial by jury as provided in Rule 38 shall be tried by the court; but, notwithstanding the failure of a party to demand a trial by jury in an action in which such a demand might have been made of right, the court in its discretion upon motion or of its own initiative may order a trial by jury of any or all issues.

(c) Advisory jury and trial by consent. – In all actions not triable of right by a jury the court upon motion or if its own initiative may try any issue or question of fact with an advisory jury or the court, with the consent of the parties, may order a trial with a jury whose verdict has the same effect as if trial by jury had been a matter of right. In either event the jury shall be selected in the manner provided by Rule 47(a). (1967, c. 954, s. 1.)

Rule 40. Assignment of cases for trial; continuances
(a) The senior resident superior court judge of any superior court district or set of districts as defined in G.S. 7A-41.1 may provide by rule for the calendaring of actions for trial in the superior court division of the various counties within his district or set of districts. Calendaring of actions for trial in the district court shall be in accordance with G.S. 7A-146. Precedence shall be given to actions entitled thereto by any statute of this State.

(b) No continuance shall be granted except upon application to the court. A continuance may be granted only for good cause shown and upon such terms and conditions as justice may require. Good cause for granting a continuance shall include those instances when a party to the proceeding, a witness, or counsel of record has an obligation of service to the State of North Carolina, including service as a member of the General Assembly or the Rules Review Commission. (1967, c. 954, s. 1; 1969, c. 895, s. 9; 1985, c. 603, s. 8; 1987 (Reg. Sess., 1988), c. 1037, s. 43; 1997-34, s. 10.)

Rule 41. Dismissal of actions

(a) Voluntary dismissal; effect thereof. –

(1) By Plaintiff; by Stipulation. – Subject to the provisions of Rule 23(c) and of any statute of this State, an action or any claim therein may be dismissed by the plaintiff without order of court (i) by filing a notice of dismissal at any time before the plaintiff rests his case, or; (ii) by filing a stipulation of dismissal signed by all parties who have appeared in the action. Unless otherwise stated in the notice of dismissal or stipulation, the dismissal is without prejudice, except that a notice of dismissal operates as an adjudication upon the merits when filed by a plaintiff who has once dismissed in any court of this or any other state or of the United States, an action based on or including the same claim. If an action commenced within the time prescribed therefor, or any claim therein, is dismissed without prejudice under this subsection, a new action based on the same claim may be commenced within one year after such dismissal unless a stipulation filed under (ii) of this subsection shall specify a shorter time.

(2) By Order of Judge. – Except as provided in subsection (1) of this section, an action or any claim therein shall not be dismissed at the plaintiff's instance save upon order of the judge and upon such terms and conditions as justice requires. Unless otherwise specified in the order, a dismissal under this subsection is without prejudice. If an action commenced within the time prescribed therefor, or any claim therein, is dismissed without prejudice under this subsection, a new action based on the same claim may be commenced within one year after such dismissal unless the judge shall specify in his order a shorter time.

(b) Involuntary dismissal; effect thereof. – For failure of the plaintiff to prosecute or to comply with these rules or any order of court, a defendant may move for dismissal of an action or of any claim therein against him. After the plaintiff, in an action tried by the court without a jury, has completed the presentation of his evidence, the defendant, without waiving his right to offer evidence in the event the motion is not granted, may move for a dismissal on the ground that upon the facts and the law the plaintiff has shown no right to relief. The court as trier of the facts may then determine them and render judgment against the plaintiff or may decline to render any judgment until the close of all the evidence. If the court renders judgment on the merits against the plaintiff, the court shall make findings as provided in Rule 52(a). Unless the court in its order for dismissal otherwise specifies, a dismissal under this section and any dismissal not provided for in this rule, other than a dismissal for lack of jurisdiction, for improper venue, or for failure to join a necessary party, operates as an adjudication upon the merits. If the court specifies that the dismissal of an action commenced within the time prescribed therefor, or any claim therein, is without prejudice, it may also specify in its order that a new action based on the same claim may be commenced within one year or less after such dismissal.

(c) Dismissal of counterclaim; crossclaim, or third-party claim. – The provisions of this rule apply to the dismissal of any counterclaim, crossclaim, or third-party claim.

(d) Costs. – A plaintiff who dismisses an action or claim under section (a) of this rule shall be taxed with the costs of the action unless the action was brought in forma pauperis. If a plaintiff who has once dismissed an action in any court commences an action based upon or including the same claim against the same defendant before the payment of the costs of the action previously dismissed, unless such previous action was brought in forma pauperis, the court, upon motion of the defendant, shall make an order for the payment of such costs by the plaintiff within 30 days and shall stay the proceedings in the action until the plaintiff has complied with the order. If the plaintiff does not comply with the order, the court shall dismiss the action. (1967, c. 954, s. 1; 1969, c. 895, s. 10; 1977, c. 290.)

Rule 42. Consolidation; separate trials

(a) Consolidation. – Except as provided in subdivision (b)(2) of this section, when actions involving a common question of law or fact are pending in one division of the court, the judge may order a joint hearing or trial of any or all the matters in issue in the actions; he may order all the actions consolidated; and he may make such orders concerning proceedings therein as may tend to avoid unnecessary costs or delay. When actions involving a common question of law or fact are pending in both the superior and the district court of the same county, a judge of the superior court in which the action is pending may order all the actions consolidated, and he may make such orders concerning proceedings therein as may tend to avoid unnecessary costs or delay.

(b) Separate trials

(1) The court may in furtherance of convenience or to avoid prejudice and shall for considerations of venue upon timely motion order a separate trial of any claim, cross-claim, counterclaim, or third-party claim, or of any separate issue or of any number of claims, cross-claims, counterclaims, third-party claims, or issues.

(2) Upon motion of any party in an action that includes a claim commenced under Article 1G of Chapter 90 of the General Statutes involving a managed

care entity as defined in G.S. 90-21.50, the court shall order separate discovery and a separate trial of any claim, cross-claim, counterclaim, or third-party claim against a physician or other medical provider.

(3) Upon motion of any party in an action in tort wherein the plaintiff seeks damages exceeding one hundred fifty thousand dollars ($150,000), the court shall order separate trials for the issue of liability and the issue of damages, unless the court for good cause shown orders a single trial. Evidence relating solely to compensatory damages shall not be admissible until the trier of fact has determined that the defendant is liable. The same trier of fact that tries the issues relating to liability shall try the issues relating to damages. (1967, c. 954, s. 1; 2001-446, s. 4.8; 2011-400, s. 2.)

Rule 43. Evidence

(a) Form. – In all trials the testimony of witnesses shall be taken orally in open court, unless otherwise provided by these rules.

(b) Examination of hostile witnesses and adverse parties. – A party may interrogate any unwilling or hostile witness by leading questions and may contradict and impeach him in all respects as if he had been called by the adverse party. A party may call an adverse party or an agent or employee of an adverse party, or an officer, director, or employee of a public or private corporation or of a partnership or association which is an adverse party, or an officer, agent or employee of a state, county or municipal government or agency thereof which is an adverse party, and interrogate him by leading questions and contradict and impeach him in all respects as if he had been called by the adverse party.

(c) Record of excluded evidence. – In an action tried before a jury, if an objection to a question propounded to a witness is sustained by the court, the court on request of the examining attorney shall order a record made of the answer the witness would have given. The court may add such other or further statement as clearly shows the character of the evidence, the form in which it was offered, the objection made and the ruling thereon. In actions tried without a jury the same procedure may be followed, except that the court upon request shall take and report the evidence in full, unless it clearly appears that the evidence is not admissible on any grounds or that the witness is privileged.

(d) Affirmation in lieu of oath. – Whenever under these rules an oath is required to be taken, a solemn affirmation may be accepted in lieu thereof.

(e) Evidence on motions. – When a motion is based on facts not appearing of record the court may hear the matter on affidavits presented by the respective parties, but the court may direct that the matter be heard wholly or partly on oral testimony or depositions. (1967, c. 954, s. 1.)

Rule 44. Proof of official record

(a) Authentication of copy. – An official record or an entry therein, when admissible for any purpose, may be evidence by an official publication thereof or by a copy attested by the officer having the legal custody of the record, or by his deputy, and accompanied with a certificate that such officer has the custody. If the office in which the record is kept is without the State of North Carolina but within the United States or within a territory or insular possession subject to the dominion of the United States, the certificate may be made by a judge of a court of record of the political subdivision in which the record is kept, authenticated by the seal of the court, or may be made by any public officer having a seal of office and having official duties in the political subdivision in which the record is kept, authenticated by the seal of his office. If the office in which the record is kept is in a foreign state or country, the certificate may be made by a secretary of embassy or legation, consul general, consul, vice-consul, or consular agent or by any officer in the foreign service of the United States stationed in the foreign state or country in which the record is kept, and authenticated by the seal of his office.

(b) Proof of lack of record. – A written statement signed by an officer having the custody of an official record or by his deputy that after diligent search no record or entry of a specified tenor is found to exist in the records of his office, accompanied by a certificate as above provided, is admissible as evidence that the records of his office contain no such record or entry.

(c) Other proof. – This rule does not prevent the proof of official records specified in Title 28, U.S.C. §§ 1738 and 1739 in the manner therein provided; nor of entry or lack of entry in official records by any method authorized by any other applicable statute or by the rules of evidence at common law. (1967, c. 954, s. 1.)

Rule 44.1. Determination of foreign law

A party who intends to raise an issue concerning the law of a foreign country shall give notice by pleadings or by other reasonable written notice. The court, in determining foreign law, may consider any relevant material or source, including testimony, whether or not submitted by a party or admissible under Chapter 8 of the General Statutes and State law. The court's determination shall be treated as a ruling on a question of law. (1995, c. 389, s. 5.)

Rule 45. Subpoena

(a)   Form; Issuance. –

(1)   Every subpoena shall state all of the following:
a.   The title of the action, the name of the court in which the action is pending, the number of the civil action, and the name of the party at whose instance the witness is summoned.

b.   A command to each person to whom it is directed to attend and give testimony or to produce and permit inspection and copying of designated records, books, papers, documents, electronically stored information, or tangible things in the possession, custody, or control of that person therein specified.

c.   The protections of persons subject to subpoenas under subsection (c) of this rule.

d.   The requirements for responses to subpoenas under subsection (d) of this rule.

(2)   A command to produce records, books, papers, electronically stored information, or tangible things may be joined with a command to appear at trial or hearing or at a deposition, or any subpoena may be issued separately. A subpoena may specify the form or forms in which electronically stored information is to be produced.

(3)   A subpoena shall issue from the court in which the action is pending.

(4)   The clerk of court in which the action is pending shall issue a subpoena, signed but otherwise blank, to a party requesting it, who shall complete it before

service. Any judge of the superior court, judge of the district court, magistrate, or attorney, as officer of the court, may also issue and sign a subpoena.

(b) Service

(1) Manner. – Any subpoena may be served by the sheriff, by the sheriff's deputy, by a coroner, or by any person who is not a party and is not less than 18 years of age. Service of a subpoena upon a person named therein shall be made by delivering a copy thereof to that person or by registered or certified mail, return receipt requested. Service of a subpoena for the attendance of a witness only may also be made by telephone communication with the person named therein only by a sheriff, the sheriff's designee who is not less than 18 years of age and is not a party, or a coroner.

(2) Service of copy. – A copy of the subpoena served under subdivision (b)(1) of this subsection shall also be served upon each party in the manner prescribed by Rule 5(b).

(3) Subdivision (b)(2) of this subsection does not apply to subpoenas issued under G.S. 15A-801 or G.S. 15A-802.
(c) Protection of Persons Subject to Subpoena

(1) Avoid undue burden or expense. – A party or an attorney responsible for the issuance and service of a subpoena shall take reasonable steps to avoid imposing an undue burden or expense on a person subject to the subpoena. The court shall enforce this subdivision and impose upon the party or attorney in violation of this requirement an appropriate sanction that may include compensating the person unduly burdened for lost earnings and for reasonable attorney's fees.

(2) For production of public records or hospital medical records. – Where the subpoena commands any custodian of public records or any custodian of hospital medical records, as defined in G.S. 8-44.1, to appear for the sole purpose of producing certain records in the custodian's custody, the custodian subpoenaed may, in lieu of personal appearance, tender to the court in which the action is pending by registered or certified mail or by personal delivery, on or before the time specified in the subpoena, certified copies of the records requested together with a copy of the subpoena and an affidavit by the custodian testifying that the copies are true and correct copies and that the records were made and kept in the regular course of business, or if no such records are in the custodian's custody, an affidavit to that effect. When the

copies of records are personally delivered under this subdivision, a receipt shall be obtained from the person receiving the records. Any original or certified copy of records or an affidavit delivered according to the provisions of this subdivision, unless otherwise objectionable, shall be admissible in any action or proceeding without further certification or authentication. Copies of hospital medical records tendered under this subdivision shall not be open to inspection or copied by any person, except to the parties to the case or proceedings and their attorneys in depositions, until ordered published by the judge at the time of the hearing or trial. Nothing contained herein shall be construed to waive the physician-patient privilege or to require any privileged communication under law to be disclosed.

(3) Written objection to subpoenas. – Subject to subsection (d) of this rule, a person commanded to appear at a deposition or to produce and permit the inspection and copying of records, books, papers, documents, electronically stored information, or tangible things may, within 10 days after service of the subpoena or before the time specified for compliance if the time is less than 10 days after service, serve upon the party or the attorney designated in the subpoena written objection to the subpoena, setting forth the specific grounds for the objection. The written objection shall comply with the requirements of Rule 11. Each of the following grounds may be sufficient for objecting to a subpoena:

a. The subpoena fails to allow reasonable time for compliance.

b. The subpoena requires disclosure of privileged or other protected matter and no exception or waiver applies to the privilege or protection.

c. The subpoena subjects a person to an undue burden or expense.

d. The subpoena is otherwise unreasonable or oppressive.

e. The subpoena is procedurally defective.

(4) Order of court required to override objection. – If objection is made under subdivision (3) of this subsection, the party serving the subpoena shall not be entitled to compel the subpoenaed person's appearance at a deposition or to inspect and copy materials to which an objection has been made except pursuant to an order of the court. If objection is made, the party serving the subpoena may, upon notice to the subpoenaed person, move at any time for an order to compel the subpoenaed person's appearance at the deposition or the production of the materials designated in the subpoena. The motion shall be

filed in the court in the county in which the deposition or production of materials is to occur.

(5) Motion to quash or modify subpoena. – A person commanded to appear at a trial, hearing, deposition, or to produce and permit the inspection and copying of records, books, papers, documents, electronically stored information, or other tangible things, within 10 days after service of the subpoena or before the time specified for compliance if the time is less than 10 days after service, may file a motion to quash or modify the subpoena. The court shall quash or modify the subpoena if the subpoenaed person demonstrates the existence of any of the reasons set forth in subdivision (3) of this subsection. The motion shall be filed in the court in the county in which the trial, hearing, deposition, or production of materials is to occur.

(6) Order to compel; expenses to comply with subpoena. – When a court enters an order compelling a deposition or the production of records, books, papers, documents, electronically stored information, or other tangible things, the order shall protect any person who is not a party or an agent of a party from significant expense resulting from complying with the subpoena. The court may order that the person to whom the subpoena is addressed will be reasonably compensated for the cost of producing the records, books, papers, documents, electronically stored information, or tangible things specified in the subpoena.

(7) Trade secrets; confidential information. – When a subpoena requires disclosure of a trade secret or other confidential research, development, or commercial information, a court may, to protect a person subject to or affected by the subpoena, quash or modify the subpoena, or when the party on whose behalf the subpoena is issued shows a substantial need for the testimony or material that cannot otherwise be met without undue hardship, the court may order a person to make an appearance or produce the materials only on specified conditions stated in the order.

(8) Order to quash; expenses. – When a court enters an order quashing or modifying the subpoena, the court may order the party on whose behalf the subpoena is issued to pay all or part of the subpoenaed person's reasonable expenses including attorney's fees.

(d) Duties in Responding to Subpoenas

(1) Form of response. – A person responding to a subpoena to produce records, books, documents, electronically stored information, or tangible things

shall produce them as they are kept in the usual course of business or shall organize and label them to correspond with the categories in the request.

(2) Form of producing electronically stored information not specified. – If a subpoena does not specify a form for producing electronically stored information, the person responding must produce it in a form or forms in which it ordinarily is maintained or in a reasonably useable form or forms.

(3) Electronically stored information in only one form. – The person responding need not produce the same electronically stored information in more than one form.

(4) Inaccessible electronically stored information. – The person responding need not provide discovery of electronically stored information from sources that the person identifies as not reasonably accessible because of undue burden or cost. On motion to compel discovery or for a protective order, the person responding must show that the information is not reasonably accessible because of undue burden or cost. If that showing is made, the court may nonetheless order discovery from such sources if the requesting party shows good cause, after considering the limitations of Rule 26(b)(1a). The court may specify conditions for discovery, including requiring the party that seeks discovery from a nonparty to bear the costs of locating, preserving, collecting, and producing the electronically stored information involved.

(5) Specificity of objection. – When information subject to a subpoena is withheld on the objection that it is subject to protection as trial preparation materials, or that it is otherwise privileged, the objection shall be made with specificity and shall be supported by a description of the nature of the communications, records, books, papers, documents, electronically stored information, or other tangible things not produced, sufficient for the requesting party to contest the objection.

(d1) Opportunity for Inspection of Subpoenaed Material. – A party or attorney responsible for the issuance and service of a subpoena shall, within five business days after the receipt of material produced in compliance with the subpoena, serve all other parties with notice of receipt of the material produced in compliance with the subpoena and, upon request, shall provide all other parties a reasonable opportunity to copy and inspect such material at the expense of the inspecting party.

(e) Contempt; Expenses to Force Compliance With Subpoena. –

(1) Failure by any person without adequate excuse to obey a subpoena served upon the person may be deemed a contempt of court. Failure by any party without adequate cause to obey a subpoena served upon the party shall also subject the party to the sanctions provided in Rule 37(d).

(2) The court may award costs and attorney's fees to the party who issued a subpoena if the court determines that a person objected to the subpoena or filed a motion to quash or modify the subpoena, and the objection or motion was unreasonable or was made for improper purposes such as unnecessary delay.

(f) Discovery From Persons Residing Outside the State. –

(1) Any party may obtain discovery from a person residing in another state of the United States or a territory or an insular possession subject to its jurisdiction in any one or more of the following forms: (i) oral depositions, (ii) depositions upon written questions, or (iii) requests for production of documents and tangible things. In doing so, the party shall use and follow any applicable process and procedures required and available under the laws of the state, territory, or insular possession where the discovery is to be obtained. If required by the process or procedure of the state, territory, or insular possession where the discovery is to be obtained, a commission may issue from the court in which the action is pending in accordance with the procedures set forth in subdivision (2) of this subsection.

(2) Obtaining a commission

a. The party desiring a commission to obtain discovery outside the State shall prepare and file a motion indicating the party's intent to obtain a commission and requesting that the commission be issued.

b. The motion shall indicate that the moving party has conferred, or describe fully the moving party's good faith attempts to confer, with counsel for all other parties regarding the request and shall indicate whether the motion is unopposed. The motion shall also attach a copy of any proposed subpoena, notice of deposition, or other papers to be served on the person from whom the moving party is seeking to obtain discovery.

c. The motion shall indicate that counsel for the moving party has read the applicable rules and procedures of the foreign state and that the moving party will comply with those rules and procedures in obtaining the requested discovery.

d. If the motion reflects that it is unopposed or indicates that the moving party has made reasonable, good faith efforts to confer with all other parties and that no other party has indicated that it opposes the motion, the motion shall immediately be placed on the calendar for a hearing within 20 days before the court in which the action is pending where the commission shall be issued. However, if the court determines, in its discretion, that the moving party has failed to make reasonable, good faith efforts to confer with all other parties prior to filing the motion, the court shall refuse to issue the commission, and the motion shall be denied.

e. If the motion does not reflect that it is unopposed or that the moving party has made reasonable, good faith efforts to confer with all other parties and that no other party has indicated that it opposes the motion, any party wishing to oppose the motion shall file written objections to issuance of the commission within 10 days of being served with the motion, and the motion shall immediately be placed on the calendar for a hearing to be held within 20 days before the court in which the action is pending. The hearing may be held by telephone in the court's discretion. The court may refuse to issue the commission only upon a showing of substantial good cause to deny the motion.

f. If the court, in its discretion, determines that any party opposing the motion did so without good cause, the court shall require the party opposing the motion to pay the moving party the reasonable costs and expenses incurred in obtaining the order, including attorneys' fees, unless circumstances exist which make an award of expenses unjust.

(3) In addition to any terms required by the foreign jurisdiction to initiate the process of obtaining the requested discovery, the commission shall:

a. State the time and place at which the requested discovery is to occur;

b. State the name and address of the person from whom the discovery is sought, if known, and, if unknown, a general description sufficient to identify the person or the particular class or group to which he or she belongs; and

c. Attach a copy of any case management order, discovery order, local rule, or other rule or order establishing any discovery deadlines in the North Carolina action. (1967, c. 954, s. 1; 1969, c. 886, s. 1; 1971, c. 159; 1975, c.

762, s. 3; 1983, c. 665, s. 1; c. 722; 1989, c. 262, s. 1; 2003-276, s. 1; 2007-514, s. 1; 2011-199, s. 6; 2011-247, s. 3.)

Rule 46. Objections and exceptions

(a)   Rulings on admissibility of evidence

(1)   When there is objection to the admission of evidence on the ground that the witness is for a specified reason incompetent or not qualified or disqualified, it shall be deemed that a like objection has been made to any subsequent admission of evidence from the witness in question. Similarly, when there is objection to the admission of evidence involving a specified line of questioning, it shall be deemed that a like objection has been taken to any subsequent admission of evidence involving the same line of questioning.

(2)   If there is proper objection to the admission of evidence and the objection is overruled, the ruling of the court shall be deemed excepted to by the party making the objection. If an objection to the admission of evidence is sustained or if the court for any reason excludes evidence offered by a party, the ruling of the court shall be deemed excepted to by the party offering the evidence.

(3)   No objections are necessary with respect to questions propounded to a witness by the court or a juror but it shall be deemed that each such question has been properly objected to and that the objection has been overruled and that an exception has been taken to the ruling of the court by all parties to the action.

(b)   Pretrial rulings, interlocutory orders, trial rulings, and other orders not directed to the admissibility of evidence. – With respect to pretrial rulings, interlocutory orders, trial rulings, and other orders of the court not directed to the admissibility of evidence, formal objections and exceptions are unnecessary. In order to preserve an exception to any such ruling or order or to the court's failure to make any such ruling or order, it shall be sufficient if a party, at the time the ruling or order is made or sought, makes known to the court the party's objection to the action of the court or makes known the action that the party desires the court to take and the party's grounds for its position. If a party has no opportunity to object or except to a ruling or order at the time it is made, the absence of an objection or exception does not thereafter prejudice that party.

(c) Repealed by Session Laws 2001-379, s. 6. (1967, c. 954, s. 1; 2001-379, s. 6.)

Rule 47. Jurors

Inquiry as to the fitness and competency of any person to serve as a juror and the challenging of such person shall be as provided in Chapter 9 of the General Statutes. (1967, c. 954, s. 1.)

Rule 48. Juries of less than twelve – majority verdict

Except in actions in which a jury is required by statute, the parties may stipulate that the jury will consist of any number less than 12 or that a verdict or a finding of a stated majority of the jurors shall be taken as the verdict or finding of the jury. (1967, c. 954, s. 1.)

Rule 49. Verdicts
(a) General and special verdicts. – The judge may require a jury to return either a general or a special verdict and in all cases may instruct the jury, if it renders a general verdict, to find upon particular questions of fact, to be stated in writing, and may direct a written finding thereon. A general verdict is that by which the jury pronounces generally upon all or any of the issues, either in favor of the plaintiff or defendant. A special verdict is that by which the jury finds the facts only.
(b) Framing of issues. – Issues shall be framed in concise and direct terms, and prolixity and confusion must be avoided by not having too many issues. The issues, material to be tried, must be made up by the attorneys appearing in the action, or by the judge presiding, and reducing to writing, before or during the trial.

(c) Waiver of jury trial on issue. – If, in submitting the issues to the jury, the judge omits any issue of fact raised by the pleadings or by the evidence, each party waives his right to a trial by jury of the issue so omitted unless before the jury retires he demands its submission to the jury. As to an issue omitted without such demand the judge may make a finding; or, if he fails to do so, he shall be deemed to have made a finding in accord with the judgment entered.

(d) Special finding inconsistent with general verdict. – Where a special finding of facts is inconsistent with the general verdict, the former controls, and the judge shall give judgment accordingly. (1967, c. 954, s. 1.)

Rule 50. Motion for a directed verdict and for judgment notwithstanding the verdict

(a) When made; effect. – A party who moves for a directed verdict at the close of the evidence offered by an opponent may offer evidence in the event that the motion is not granted, without having reserved the right so to do and to the same extent as if the motion had not been made. A motion for a directed verdict which is not granted is not a waiver of trial by jury even though all parties to the action have moved for directed verdicts. A motion for a directed verdict shall state the specific grounds therefor. The order granting a motion for a directed verdict shall be effective without any assent of the jury.

(b) Motion for judgment notwithstanding the verdict. –

(1) Whenever a motion for a directed verdict made at the close of all the evidence is denied or for any reason is not granted, the submission of the action to the jury shall be deemed to be subject to a later determination of the legal questions raised by the motion. Not later than 10 days after entry of judgment, a party who has moved for a directed verdict may move to have the verdict and any judgment entered thereon set aside and to have judgment entered in accordance with his motion for a directed verdict; or if a verdict was not returned such party, within 10 days after the jury has been discharged, may move for judgment in accordance with his motion for a directed verdict. In either case the motion shall be granted if it appears that the motion for directed verdict could properly have been granted. A motion for a new trial may be joined with this motion, or a new trial may be prayed for in the alternative. If a verdict was returned the judge may allow the judgment to stand or may set aside the judgment and either order a new trial or direct the entry of judgment as if the requested verdict had been directed. If no verdict was returned the judge may direct the entry of judgment as if the requested verdict had been directed or may order a new trial. Not later than ten (10) days after entry of judgment or the discharge of the jury if a verdict was not returned, the judge on his own motion may, with or without further notice and hearing, grant, deny, or redeny a motion for directed verdict made at the close of all the evidence that was denied or for any reason was not granted.

(2) An appellate court, on finding that a trial judge should have granted a motion for directed verdict made at the close of all the evidence, may not direct entry of judgment in accordance with the motion unless the party who made the motion for a directed verdict also moved for judgment in accordance with Rule 50(b)(1) or the trial judge on his own motion granted, denied or redenied the motion for a directed verdict in accordance with Rule 50(b)(1).

(c) Motion for judgment notwithstanding the verdict – Conditional rulings on grant of motion. –

(1) If the motion for judgment notwithstanding the verdict, provided for in section (b) of this rule, is granted, the court shall also rule on the motion for new trial, if any, by determining whether it should be granted if the judgment is thereafter vacated or reversed, and shall specify the grounds for granting or denying the motion for the new trial. If the motion for new trial is thus conditionally granted, the order thereon does not affect the finality of the judgment. In case the motion for new trial has been conditionally granted and the judgment is reversed on appeal, the new trial shall proceed unless the appellate division has otherwise ordered. In case the motion for new trial has been conditionally denied, the appellee on appeal may assert error in that denial; and if the judgment is reversed on appeal, subsequent proceedings shall be in accordance with the order of the appellate division.

(2) The party whose verdict has been set aside on motion for judgment notwithstanding the verdict may serve a motion for a new trial pursuant to Rule 59 not later than 10 days after entry of the judgment notwithstanding the verdict.

(d) Motion for judgment notwithstanding the verdict – Denial of motion. – If the motion for judgment notwithstanding the verdict is denied, the party who prevailed on that motion may, as appellee, assert grounds entitling him to a new trial in the event the appellate division concludes that the trial court erred in denying the motion for judgment notwithstanding the verdict. If the appellate division reverses the judgment, nothing in this rule precludes it from determining that the appellee is entitled to a new trial, or from directing the trial court to determine whether a new trial shall be granted. (1967, c. 954, s. 1; 1969, c. 895, s. 11.)

Rule 51. Instructions to jury

(a) Judge to explain law but give no opinion on facts. - In charging the jury in any action governed by these rules, a judge shall not give an opinion as to whether or not a fact is fully or sufficiently proved and shall not be required to state, summarize or recapitulate the evidence, or to explain the application of the law to the evidence. If the judge undertakes to state the contentions of the parties, he shall give equal stress to the contentions of each party.

(b) Requests for special instructions. - Requests for special instructions must be in writing, entitled in the cause, and signed by the counsel or party submitting them. Such requests for special instructions must be submitted to the judge before the judge's charge to the jury is begun. The judge may, in his discretion, consider such requests regardless of the time they are made. Written requests for special instructions shall, after their submission to the judge, be filed with the clerk as a part of the record.

(c) Judge not to comment on verdict. - The judge shall make no comment on any verdict in open court in the presence or hearing of any member of the jury panel; and if any judge shall make any comment as herein prohibited or shall praise or criticize any jury on account of its verdict, whether such praise, criticism or comment be made inadvertently or intentionally, such praise, criticism or comment by the judge shall for any party to any other action remaining to be tried constitute valid grounds as a matter of right for a continuance of any action to a time when all members of the jury panel are no longer serving. The provisions of this section shall not be applicable upon the hearing of motions for a new trial or for judgment notwithstanding the verdict. (1967, c. 954, s. 1; 1985, c. 537, s. 2.)

Rule 52. Findings by the court.

(a) Findings. –

(1) In all actions tried upon the facts without a jury or with an advisory jury, the court shall find the facts specially and state separately its conclusions of law thereon and direct the entry of the appropriate judgment.

(2) Findings of fact and conclusions of law are necessary on decisions of any motion or order ex mero motu only when requested by a party and as provided by Rule 41(b). Similarly, findings of fact and conclusions of law are necessary on the granting or denying of a preliminary injunction or any other provisional remedy only when required by statute expressly relating to such remedy or requested by a party.

(3) If an opinion or memorandum of decision is filed, it will be sufficient if the findings of fact and conclusions of law appear therein.

(b) Amendment. – Upon motion of a party made not later than 10 days after entry of judgment the court may amend its findings or make additional findings and may amend the judgment accordingly. The motion may be made with a motion for a new trial pursuant to Rule 59.

(c) Review on appeal. – When findings of fact are made in actions tried by the court without a jury, the question of Rule 52. Findings by the court.

(a) Findings. -

(1) In all actions tried upon the facts without a jury or with an advisory jury, the court shall find the facts specially and state separately its conclusions of law thereon and direct the entry of the appropriate judgment.

(2) Findings of fact and conclusions of law are necessary on decisions of any motion or order ex mero motu only when requested by a party and as provided by Rule 41(b). Similarly, findings of fact and conclusions of law are necessary on the granting or denying of a preliminary injunction or any other provisional remedy only when required by statute expressly relating to such remedy or requested by a party.

(3) If an opinion or memorandum of decision is filed, it will be sufficient if the findings of fact and conclusions of law appear therein.
(b) Amendment. - Upon motion of a party made not later than 10 days after entry of judgment the court may amend its findings or make additional findings and may amend the judgment accordingly. The motion may be made with a motion for a new trial pursuant to Rule 59.

(c) Review on appeal. - When findings of fact are made in actions tried by the court without a jury, the question of the sufficiency of the evidence to support the findings may be raised on appeal whether or not the party raising the question has made in the trial court an objection to such findings or has made a motion to amend them or a motion for judgment, or a request for specific findings. (1967, c. 954, s. 1; 1969, c. 895, s. 12.)

Rule 53. Referees

(a) Kinds of reference. -

(1) By Consent. - Any or all of the issues in an action may be referred upon the written consent of the parties except in actions to annul a marriage, actions for divorce, actions for divorce from bed and board, actions for alimony without the divorce or actions in which a ground of annulment or divorce is in issue.

(2) Compulsory. - Where the parties do not consent to a reference, the court may, upon the application of any party or on its own motion, order a reference in the following cases:

a. Where the trial of an issue requires the examination of a long or complicated account; in which case the referee may be directed to hear and decide the whole issue, or to report upon any specific question of fact involved therein.

b. Where the taking of an account is necessary for the information of the court before judgment, or for carrying a judgment or order into effect.

c. Where the case involves a complicated question of boundary, or requires a personal view of the premises.

d. Where a question of fact arises outside the pleadings, upon motion or otherwise, at any stage of the action.

(b) Jury trial. -
(1) Where the reference is by consent, the parties waive the right to have any of the issues within the scope of the reference passed on by a jury.

(2) A compulsory reference does not deprive any party of his right to a trial by jury, which right he may preserve by

a. Objecting to the order of compulsory reference at the time it is made, and

b. By filing specific exceptions to particular findings of fact made by the referee within 30 days after the referee files his report with the clerk of the court in which the action is pending, and

c. By formulating appropriate issues based upon the exceptions taken and demanding a jury trial upon such issues. Such issues shall be tendered at the same time the exceptions to the referee's report are filed. If there is a trial by jury upon any issue referred, the trial shall be only upon the evidence taken before the referee.

(c) Appointment. - The parties may agree in writing upon one or more persons not exceeding three, and a reference shall be ordered to such person or persons in appropriate cases. If the parties do not agree, the court shall appoint one or more referees, not exceeding three, but no person shall be appointed referee to whom all parties in the action object.

(d) Compensation. - The compensation to be allowed a referee shall be fixed by the court and charged in the bill of costs. After appointment of a referee, the court may from time to time order advancements by one or more of the parties of sums to be applied to the referee's compensation. Such advancements may be apportioned between the parties in such manner as the court sees fit. Advancements so made shall be taken into account in the final fixing of costs and such adjustments made as the court then deems proper.

(e) Powers. - The order of reference to the referee may specify or limit his powers and may direct him to report only upon particular issues or to do or perform particular acts or to receive and report evidence only and may fix the time and place for beginning and closing the hearings and for the filing of the referee's report. Subject to the specifications and limitations stated in the order, every referee has power to administer oaths in any proceeding before him, and has generally the power vested in a referee by law. The referee shall have the same power to grant adjournments and to allow amendments to pleadings and to the summons as the judge and upon the same terms and with like effect. The referee shall have the same power as the judge to preserve order and punish all violations thereof, to compel the attendance of witnesses before him by attachment, and to punish them as for contempt for nonattendance or for refusal to be sworn or to testify. The parties may procure the attendance of witnesses before the referee by the issuance and service of subpoenas as provided in Rule 45.

(f) Proceedings. -

(1) Meetings. - When a reference is made, the clerk shall forthwith furnish the referee with a copy of the order of reference. Upon receipt thereof unless the order of reference otherwise provides, the referee shall forthwith set a time and place for the first meeting of the parties or their attorneys to be held within 20 days after the date of the order of reference and shall notify the parties or their attorneys. It is the duty of the referee to proceed with all reasonable

diligence. Any party, on notice to all other parties and the referee, may apply to the court for an order requiring the referee to expedite the proceedings and to make his report. If a party fails to appear at the time and place appointed, the referee may proceed ex parte, or, in his discretion, may adjourn the proceedings to a future day, giving notice to the absent party of the adjournment.

(2)   Statement of Accounts. - When matters of accounting are in issue before the referee, he may prescribe the form in which the accounts shall be submitted and in any proper case may require or receive in evidence a statement by a certified public accountant or other qualified accountant who is called as a witness. Upon objection of a party to any of the items thus submitted or upon a showing that the form of statement is insufficient, the referee may require a different form of statement to be furnished, or the accounts of specific items thereof to be proved by oral examination of the accounting parties or upon written interrogatories or in such other manner as he directs.

(3)   Testimony Reduced to Writing. - The testimony of all witnesses must be reduced to writing by the referee, or by someone acting under his direction and shall be filed in the cause and constitute a part of the record.

(g)   Report. -
(1)   Contents and Filing. - The referee shall prepare a report upon the matters submitted to him by the order of reference and shall include therein his decision on all matters so submitted. If required to make findings of fact and conclusions of law, he shall set them forth separately in the report. He shall file the report with the clerk of the court in which the action is pending and unless otherwise directed by the order of reference, shall file with it a transcript of the proceedings and of the evidence and the original exhibits. Before filing his report a referee may submit a draft thereof to counsel for all parties for the purpose of receiving their suggestions. The clerk shall forthwith mail to all parties notice of the filing.

(2)   Exceptions and Review. - All or any part of the report may be excepted to by any party within 30 days from the filing of the report. Thereafter, and upon 10 days' notice to the other parties, any party may apply to the judge for action on the report. The judge after hearing may adopt, modify or reject the report in whole or in part, render judgment, or may remand the proceedings to the referee with instructions. No judgment may be rendered on any reference except by the judge. (1967, c. 954, s. 1; 1969, c. 895, s. 13.)

Article 7

Judgment.

Rule 54. Judgments.

(a) Definition. - A judgment is either interlocutory or the final determination of the rights of the parties.

(b) Judgment upon multiple claims or involving multiple parties. - When more than one claim for relief is presented in an action, whether as a claim, counterclaim, crossclaim, or third-party claim, or when multiple parties are involved, the court may enter a final judgment as to one or more but fewer than all of the claims or parties only if there is no just reason for delay and it is so determined in the judgment. Such judgment shall then be subject to review by appeal or as otherwise provided by these rules or other statutes. In the absence of entry of such a final judgment, any order or other form of decision, however designated, which adjudicates fewer than all the claims or the rights and liabilities of fewer than all the parties shall not terminate the action as to any of the claims or parties and shall not then be subject to review either by appeal or otherwise except as expressly provided by these rules or other statutes. Similarly, in the absence of entry of such a final judgment, any order or other form of decision is subject to revision at any time before the entry of judgment adjudicating all the claims and the rights and liabilities of all the parties.

(c) Demand for judgment. - A judgment by default shall not be different in kind from or exceed in amount that prayed for in the demand for judgment. Except as to a party against whom a judgment is entered by default, every final judgment shall grant the relief to which the party in whose favor it is rendered is entitled, even if the party has not demanded such relief in his pleadings. (1967, c. 954, s. 1.)

Rule 55. Default.

(a) Entry. - When a party against whom a judgment for affirmative relief is sought has failed to plead or is otherwise subject to default judgment as provided by these rules or by statute and that fact is made to appear by affidavit, motion of attorney for the plaintiff, or otherwise, the clerk shall enter his default.

(b) Judgment. - Judgment by default may be entered as follows:

(1) By the Clerk. - When the plaintiff's claim against a defendant is for a sum certain or for a sum which can by computation be made certain, the clerk upon request of the plaintiff and upon affidavit of the amount due shall enter judgment for that amount and costs against the defendant, if the defendant has been defaulted for failure to appear and if the defendant is not an infant or incompetent person. A verified pleading may be used in lieu of an affidavit when the pleading contains information sufficient to determine or compute the sum certain.

In all cases wherein, pursuant to this rule, the clerk enters judgment by default upon a claim for debt which is secured by any pledge, mortgage, deed of trust or other contractual security in respect of which foreclosure may be had, or upon a claim to enforce a lien for unpaid taxes or assessments under G.S. 105-414, the clerk may likewise make all further orders required to consummate foreclosure in accordance with the procedure provided in Article 29A of Chapter 1 of the General Statutes, entitled "Judicial Sales."

(2) By the Judge. -

a. In all other cases the party entitled to a judgment by default shall apply to the judge therefor; but no judgment by default shall be entered against an infant or incompetent person unless represented in the action by a guardian ad litem or other such representative who has appeared therein. If the party against whom judgment by default is sought has appeared in the action, that party (or, if appearing by representative, the representative) shall be served with written notice of the application for judgment at least three days prior to the hearing on such application. If, in order to enable the judge to enter judgment or to carry it into effect, it is necessary to take an account or to determine the amount of damages or to establish the truth of any averment by evidence or to take an investigation of any other matter, the judge may conduct such hearings or order such references as the judge deems necessary and proper and shall accord a right of trial by jury to the parties when and as required by the Constitution or by any statute of North Carolina. If the plaintiff seeks to establish paternity under Article 3 of Chapter 49 of the General Statutes and the defendant fails to appear, the judge shall enter judgment by default.

b. A motion for judgment by default may be decided by the court without a hearing if:

1. The motion specifically provides that the court will decide the motion for judgment by default without a hearing if the party against whom judgment is sought fails to serve a written response, stating the grounds for opposing the motion, within 30 days of service of the motion; and

2. The party against whom judgment is sought fails to serve the response in accordance with this sub-subdivision.

(c) Service by publication. - When service of the summons has been made by published notice, no judgment shall be entered on default until the plaintiff shall have filed a bond, approved by the court, conditioned to abide such order as the court may make touching the restitution of any property collected or obtained by virtue of the judgment in case a defense is thereafter permitted and sustained; provided, that in actions involving the title to real estate or to foreclose mortgages thereon or in actions in which the State of North Carolina or a county or municipality thereof is the plaintiff such bond shall not be required.

(d) Setting aside default. - For good cause shown the court may set aside an entry of default, and, if a judgment by default has been entered, the judge may set it aside in accordance with Rule 60(b).

(e) Plaintiffs, counterclaimants, cross claimants. - The provisions of this rule apply whether the party entitled to the judgment by default is a plaintiff, a third-party plaintiff, or a party who has pleaded a crossclaim or counterclaim. In all cases a judgment by default is subject to the limitations of Rule 54(c).
(f) Judgment against the State of North Carolina. - No judgment by default shall be entered against the State of North Carolina or an officer in his official capacity or agency thereof unless the claimant establishes his claim or right to relief by evidence. (1967, c. 954, s. 1; 1971, cc. 542, 1101; 1977, c. 675; 1991, c. 278, s. 1; 1993 (Reg. Sess., 1994), c. 733, s. 3; 1999-187, s. 1.)

Rule 56. Summary judgment.

(a) For claimant. - A party seeking to recover upon a claim, counterclaim, or crossclaim or to obtain a declaratory judgment may, at any time after the expiration of 30 days from the commencement of the action or after service of a motion for summary judgment by the adverse party, move with or without supporting affidavits for a summary judgment in his favor upon all or any part thereof.

(b) For defending party. - A party against whom a claim, counterclaim, or crossclaim is asserted or a declaratory judgment is sought, may, at any time, move with or without supporting affidavits for a summary judgment in his favor as to all or any part thereof.

(c) Motion and proceedings thereon. - The motion shall be served at least 10 days before the time fixed for the hearing. The adverse party may serve opposing affidavits at least two days before the hearing. If the opposing affidavit is not served on the other parties at least two days before the hearing on the motion, the court may continue the matter for a reasonable period to allow the responding party to prepare a response, proceed with the matter without considering the untimely served affidavit, or take such other action as the ends of justice require. For the purpose of this two-day requirement only, service shall mean personal delivery, facsimile transmission, or other means such that the party actually receives the affidavit within the required time.

The judgment sought shall be rendered forthwith if the pleadings, depositions, answers to interrogatories, and admissions on file, together with the affidavits, if any, show that there is no genuine issue as to any material fact and that any party is entitled to a judgment as a matter of law. A summary judgment, interlocutory in character, may be rendered on the issue of liability alone although there is genuine issue as to the amount of damages. Summary judgment, when appropriate, may be rendered against the moving party.

(d) Case not fully adjudicated on motion. - If on motion under this rule judgment is not rendered upon the whole case or for all the relief asked and a trial is necessary, the court at the hearing of the motion, by examining the pleadings and the evidence before it and by interrogating counsel, shall if practicable ascertain what material facts exist without substantial controversy and what material facts are actually and in good faith controverted. It shall thereupon make an order specifying the facts that appear without substantial controversy, including the extent to which the amount of damages or other relief is not in controversy, and directing such further proceedings in the action as are just. Upon the trial of the action the facts so specified shall be deemed established.

(e) Form of affidavits; further testimony; defense required. - Supporting and opposing affidavits shall be made on personal knowledge, shall set forth such facts as would be admissible in evidence, and shall show affirmatively that the affiant is competent to testify to the matters stated therein. Sworn or certified copies of all papers or parts thereof referred to in an affidavit shall be attached thereto or served therewith. The court may permit affidavits to be supplemented or opposed by depositions, answers to interrogatories, or further affidavits. When a motion for summary judgment is made and supported as provided in this rule, an adverse party may not rest upon the mere allegations or denials of his pleading, but his response, by affidavits or as otherwise provided in this rule, must set forth specific facts showing that there is a genuine issue for trial. If he does not so respond, summary judgment, if appropriate, shall be entered against him.

(f)   When affidavits are unavailable. - Should it appear from the affidavits of a party opposing the motion that he cannot for reasons stated present by affidavit facts essential to justify his opposition, the court may refuse the application for judgment or may order a continuance to permit affidavits to be obtained or depositions to be taken or discovery to be had or may make such other order as is just.

(g)   Affidavits made in bad faith. - Should it appear to the satisfaction of the court at any time that any of the affidavits presented pursuant to this rule are presented in bad faith or solely for the purpose of delay, the court shall forthwith order the party employing them to pay to the other party the amount of the reasonable expenses which the filing of the affidavits caused him to incur, including reasonable attorney's fees. (1967, c. 954, s. 1; 2000-127, s. 6.)

Rule 57. Declaratory judgments.

The procedure for obtaining a declaratory judgment pursuant to Article 26, Chapter 1, General Statutes of North Carolina, shall be in accordance with these rules, and the right to trial by jury may be demanded under the circumstances and in the manner provided in Rules 38 and 39. The existence of another adequate remedy does not preclude a judgment for declaratory relief in cases where it is appropriate. The court may order a prompt hearing of an action for a declaratory judgment and may advance it on the calendar. (1967, c. 954, s. 1.)

Rule 58. Entry of judgment

Subject to the provisions of Rule 54(b), a judgment is entered when it is reduced to writing, signed by the judge, and filed with the clerk of court. The party designated by the judge or, if the judge does not otherwise designate, the party who prepares the judgment, shall serve a copy of the judgment upon all other parties within three days after the judgment is entered. Service and proof of service shall be in accordance with Rule 5. If service is by mail, three days shall be added to the time periods prescribed by Rule 50(b), Rule 52(b), and Rule 59. All time periods within which a party may further act pursuant to Rule 50(b), Rule 52(b), or Rule 59 shall be tolled for the duration of any period of noncompliance with this service requirement, provided however that no time period under Rule 50(b), Rule 52(b), or Rule 59 shall be tolled longer than 90 days from the date the judgment is entered. Subject to the provisions of Rule 7(b)(4), consent for the signing and entry of a judgment out of term, session, county, and district shall be deemed to have been given unless an express objection to such action was made on the record prior to the end of the term or session at which the matter was heard.

Notwithstanding any other law to the contrary, any judgment entered by a magistrate in a small claims action pursuant to Article 19 of Chapter 7A shall be entered in accordance with this Rule except judgments announced and signed in open court at the conclusion of a trial are considered to be served on the parties, and copies of any judgment not announced and signed in open court at the conclusion of a trial shall be served by the magistrate on all parties in accordance with this Rule, within three days after the judgment is entered. If service is by mail, three days shall be added to the time periods prescribed by G.S. 7A-228. All time periods within which a party may further act pursuant to G.S. 7A-228 shall be tolled for the duration of any period of noncompliance of this service requirement, provided that no time period shall be tolled longer than 90 days from the date judgment is entered. (1967, c. 954, s. 1; 1993 (Reg. Sess., 1994), c. 594, s. 1; 2005-163, s. 2.)

Rule 59. New trials; amendment of judgments

(a)   Grounds. - A new trial may be granted to all or any of the parties and on all or part of the issues for any of the following causes or grounds:

(1)   Any irregularity by which any party was prevented from having a fair trial;

(2)   Misconduct of the jury or prevailing party;

(3)   Accident or surprise which ordinary prudence could not have guarded against;

(4)   Newly discovered evidence material for the party making the motion which he could not, with reasonable diligence, have discovered and produced at the trial;

(5)   Manifest disregard by the jury of the instructions of the court;

(6)   Excessive or inadequate damages appearing to have been given under the influence of passion or prejudice;

(7)   Insufficiency of the evidence to justify the verdict or that the verdict is contrary to law;

(8)   Error in law occurring at the trial and objected to by the party making the motion, or

(9)   Any other reason heretofore recognized as grounds for new trial.

On a motion for a new trial in an action tried without a jury, the court may open the judgment if one has been entered, take additional testimony, amend findings of fact and conclusions of law or make new findings and conclusions, and direct the entry of a new judgment.

(b)   Time for motion. - A motion for a new trial shall be served not later than 10 days after entry of the judgment.

(c)   Time for serving affidavits. - When a motion for new trial is based upon affidavits they shall be served with the motion. The opposing party has 10 days after such service within which to serve opposing affidavits, which period may be extended for an additional period not exceeding 30 days either by the court for good cause shown or by the parties by written stipulation. The court may permit reply affidavits.

(d)   On initiative of court. - Not later than 10 days after entry of judgment the court of its own initiative, on notice to the parties and hearing, may order a new trial for any reason for which it might have granted a new trial on motion of a party, and in the order shall specify the grounds therefor.

(e) Motion to alter or amend a judgment. - A motion to alter or amend the judgment under section (a) of this rule shall be served not later than 10 days after entry of the judgment. (1967, c. 954, s. 1.)

Rule 60. Relief from judgment or order

(a) Clerical mistakes. - Clerical mistakes in judgments, orders or other parts of the record and errors therein arising from oversight or omission may be corrected by the judge at any time on his own initiative or on the motion of any party and after such notice, if any, as the judge orders. During the pendency of an appeal, such mistakes may be so corrected before the appeal is docketed in the appellate division, and thereafter while the appeal is pending may be so corrected with leave of the appellate division.

(b) Mistakes; inadvertence; excusable neglect; newly discovered evidence; fraud, etc. - On motion and upon such terms as are just, the court may relieve a party or his legal representative from a final judgment, order, or proceeding for the following reasons:

(1) Mistake, inadvertence, surprise, or excusable neglect;

(2) Newly discovered evidence which by due diligence could not have been discovered in time to move for a new trial under Rule 59(b);

(3) Fraud (whether heretofore denominated intrinsic or extrinsic), misrepresentation, or other misconduct of an adverse party;

(4) The judgment is void;

(5) The judgment has been satisfied, released, or discharged, or a prior judgment upon which it is based has been reversed or otherwise vacated, or it is no longer equitable that the judgment should have prospective application; or

(6) Any other reason justifying relief from the operation of the judgment.

The motion shall be made within a reasonable time, and for reasons (1), (2) and (3) not more than one year after the judgment, order, or proceeding was entered or taken. A motion under this section does not affect the finality of a judgment or suspend its operation. This rule does not limit the power of a court to entertain an independent action to relieve a party from a judgment, order, or proceeding, or to set aside a judgment for fraud upon the court. The procedure for obtaining any relief from a judgment, order, or proceeding shall be by motion as prescribed in these rules or by an independent action.

(c)   Judgments rendered by the clerk. - The clerk may, in respect of judgments rendered by himself, exercise the same powers authorized in sections (a) and (b). The judge has like powers in respect of such judgments. Where such powers are exercised by the clerk, appeals may be had to the judge in the manner provided by law. (1967, c. 954, s. 1.)

Rule 61. Harmless error

No error in either the admission or exclusion of evidence and no error or defect in any ruling or order or in anything done or omitted by any of the parties is ground for granting a new trial or for setting aside a verdict or for vacating, modifying, or otherwise disturbing a judgment or order, unless refusal to take such action amounts to the denial of a substantial right. (1967, c. 954, s. 1.)

Rule 62. Stay of proceedings to enforce a judgment

(a)   Automatic stay; exceptions - Injunctions and receiverships. - Except as otherwise stated herein, no execution shall issue upon a judgment nor shall proceedings be taken for its enforcement until the expiration of the time provided in the controlling statute or rule of appellate procedure for giving notice of appeal from the judgment. Unless otherwise ordered by the court, an interlocutory or final judgment in an action for an injunction or in a receivership action shall not be stayed during the period after its entry and until an appeal is taken or during the pendency of an appeal. The provisions of section (c) govern the suspending, modifying, restoring, or granting of an injunction during the pendency of an appeal.

(b)   Stay on motion for new trial or for judgment. - In its discretion and on such conditions for the security of the adverse party as are proper, the court may stay the execution of or any proceedings to enforce a judgment pending the disposition of a motion for a new trial or to alter or amend a judgment made pursuant to Rule 59, or of a motion for relief from a judgment or order made pursuant to Rule 60, or of a motion for judgment made pursuant to Rule 50, or of a motion for amendment to the findings or for additional findings made pursuant to Rule 52(b). If the time provided in the controlling statute or rule of appellate procedure for giving notice of appeal from the judgment had not expired before a stay under this subsection was entered, that time shall begin to run immediately upon the expiration of any stay under this section, and no execution shall issue nor shall proceedings be taken for enforcement of the judgment until the expiration of that time.

(c) Injunction pending appeal. - When an appeal is taken from an interlocutory or final judgment granting, dissolving, or denying an injunction, the court in its discretion may suspend, modify, restore, or grant an injunction during the pendency of the appeal upon such terms as to bond or otherwise as it considers proper for the security of the rights of the adverse party.

(d) Stay upon appeal. - When an appeal is taken, the appellant may obtain a stay of execution, subject to the exceptions contained in section (a), by proceeding in accordance with and subject to the conditions of G.S. 1-289, G.S. 1-290, G.S. 1-291, G.S. 1-292, G.S. 1-293, G.S. 1-294, and G.S. 1-295.

When stay is had by giving supersedeas bond, the bond may be given at or after the time of filing the notice of appeal or of procuring the order allowing the appeal as the case may be, and stay is then effective when the supersedeas bond is approved by the court.

(e) Stay in favor of North Carolina, city, county, local board of education, or agency thereof. - When an appeal is taken by the State of North Carolina, or a city or a county thereof, a local board of education, or an officer in his official capacity or agency thereof or by direction of any department or agency of the State of North Carolina or a city or county thereof or a local board of education and the operation or enforcement of the judgment is stayed, no bond, obligation, or other security shall be required from the appellant.

(f) Power of appellate court not limited. - The provisions of this rule do not limit any power of an appellate court or of a judge or justice thereof to stay proceedings during the pendency of an appeal or to suspend, modify, restore, or grant an injunction during the pendency of an appeal or to make any order appropriate to preserve the status quo or the effectiveness of the judgment subsequently to be entered.

(g) Stay of judgment as to multiple claims or multiple parties. - When a court has ordered a final judgment under the conditions stated in Rule 54(b), the court may stay enforcement of that judgment until the entering of a subsequent judgment or judgments and may prescribe such conditions as are necessary to secure the benefit thereof to the party in whose favor the judgment is entered. (1967, c. 954, s. 1; 1973, c. 91; 1979, c. 820, s. 10; 1987, c. 462, s. 1; 1989, c. 377, ss. 3, 4.)

Rule 63. Disability of a judge

If by reason of death, sickness or other disability, resignation, retirement, expiration of term, removal from office, or other reason, a judge before whom an action has been tried or a hearing has been held is unable to perform the duties to be performed by the court under these rules after a verdict is returned or a trial or hearing is otherwise concluded, then those duties, including entry of judgment, may be performed:

(1)   In actions in the superior court by the judge senior in point of continuous service on the superior court regularly holding the courts of the district. If this judge is under a disability, then the resident judge of the district senior in point of service on the superior court may perform those duties. If a resident judge, while holding court in the judge's own district suffers disability and there is no other resident judge of the district, such duties may be performed by a judge of the superior court designated by the Chief Justice of the Supreme Court.

(2)   In actions in the district court, by the chief judge of the district, or if the chief judge is disabled, by any judge of the district court designated by the Director of the Administrative Office of the Courts.

If the substituted judge is satisfied that he or she cannot perform those duties because the judge did not preside at the trial or hearing or for any other reason, the judge may, in the judge's discretion, grant a new trial or hearing. (1967, c. 954, s. 1; 2001-379, s. 7.)

Article 8

Miscellaneous

Rule 64. Seizure of person or property

At the commencement of and during the course of an action, all remedies providing for seizure of person or property for the purpose of securing satisfaction of the judgment ultimately to be entered in the action are available under the circumstances and in the manner provided by the law of this State. (1967, c. 954, s. 1.)

Rule 65. Injunctions

(a)   Preliminary injunction; notice. - No preliminary injunction shall be issued without notice to the adverse party.

(b)   Temporary restraining order; notice; hearing; duration. - A temporary restraining order may be granted without written or oral notice to the adverse party or that party's attorney only if (i) it clearly appears from specific facts shown by affidavit or by verified complaint that immediate and irreparable injury, loss, or damage will result to the applicant before the adverse party or that party's attorney can be heard in opposition, and (ii) the applicant's attorney certifies to the court in writing the efforts, if any, that have been made to give the notice and the reasons supporting the claim that notice should not be required. Every temporary restraining order granted without notice shall be endorsed with the date and hour of issuance; shall be filed forthwith in the clerk's office and entered of record; shall define the injury and state why it is irreparable and why the order was granted without notice; and shall expire by its terms within such time after entry, not to exceed 10 days, as the judge fixes, unless within the time so fixed the order, for good cause shown, is extended for a like period or unless the party against whom the order is directed consents that it may be extended for a longer period. The reasons for the extension shall be entered of record. In case a temporary restraining order is granted without notice and a motion for a preliminary injunction is made, it shall be set down for hearing at the earliest possible time and takes precedence over all matters except older matters of the same character; and when the motion comes on for hearing, the party who obtained the temporary restraining order shall proceed with a motion for a preliminary injunction, and, if he does not do so, the judge shall dissolve the temporary restraining order. On two days' notice to the party who obtained the temporary restraining order without notice or on such shorter notice to that party as the judge may prescribe, the adverse party may appear and move its dissolution or modification and in that event the judge shall proceed to hear and determine such motion as expeditiously as the ends of justice require. Damages may be awarded in an order for dissolution as provided in section (e).

(c)   Security. - No restraining order or preliminary injunction shall issue except upon the giving of security by the applicant, in such sum as the judge deems proper, for the payment of such costs and damages as may be incurred or suffered by any party who is found to have been wrongfully enjoined or restrained. No such security shall be required of the State of North Carolina or of any county or municipality thereof, or any officer or agency thereof acting in an official capacity, but damages may be awarded against such party in accord with this rule. In suits between spouses relating to support, alimony, custody of children, separation, divorce from bed and board, and absolute divorce no such security shall be required of the plaintiff spouse as a condition precedent to the issuing of a temporary restraining order or preliminary injunction enjoining the defendant spouse from interfering with, threatening, or in any way molesting the plaintiff spouse during pendency of the suit, until further order of the court, but damages may be awarded against such party in accord with this rule.

A surety upon a bond or undertaking under this rule submits himself to the jurisdiction of the court and irrevocably appoints the clerk of the court as his agent upon whom any papers affecting his liability on the bond or undertaking may be served. His liability may be enforced on motion without the necessity of an independent action. The motion and such notice of the motion as the court prescribes may be served on the clerk of the court, who shall forthwith mail copies to the persons giving the security and the sureties thereon if their addresses are known.

(d)   Form and scope of injunction or restraining order. - Every order granting an injunction and every restraining order shall set forth the reasons for its issuance; shall be specific in terms; shall describe in reasonable detail, and not by reference to the complaint or other document, the act or acts enjoined or restrained; and is binding only upon the parties to the action, their officers, agents, servants, employees, and attorneys, and upon those persons in active concert or participation with them who receive actual notice in any manner of the order by personal service or otherwise.

(e)   Damages on dissolution. - An order or judgment dissolving an injunction or restraining order may include an award of damages against the party procuring the injunction and the sureties on his undertaking without a showing of malice or want of probable cause in procuring the injunction. The damages may be determined by the judge, or he may direct that they be determined by a referee or jury. (1967, c. 954, s. 1; 2001-379, s. 8.)

Rule 66 through Rule 67. Omitted.

Rule 68. Offer of judgment and disclaimer

(a) Offer of judgment. - At any time more than 10 days before the trial begins, a party defending against a claim may serve upon the adverse party an offer to allow judgment to be taken against him for the money or property or to the effect specified in his offer, with costs then accrued. If within 10 days after the service of the offer the adverse party serves written notice that the offer is accepted, either party may then file the offer and notice of acceptance together with proof of service thereof and thereupon the clerk shall enter judgment. An offer not accepted within 10 days after its service shall be deemed withdrawn and evidence of the offer is not admissible except in a proceeding to determine costs. If the judgment finally obtained by the offeree is not more favorable than the offer, the offeree must pay the costs incurred after the making of the offer. The fact that an offer is made but not accepted does not preclude a subsequent offer.

(b) Conditional offer of judgment for damages. - A party defending against a claim arising in contract or quasi contract may, with his responsive pleading, serve upon the claimant an offer in writing that if he fails in his defense, the damages shall be assessed at a specified sum; and if the claimant signifies his acceptance thereof in writing within 20 days of the service of such offer, and on the trial prevails, his damages shall be assessed accordingly. If the claimant does not accept the offer, he must prove his damages as if the offer had not been made. If the damages assessed in the claimant's favor do not exceed the sum stated in the offer, the party defending shall recover the costs in respect to the question of damages. (1967, c. 954, s. 1.)

Rule 68.1. Confession of judgment

(a) For present or future liability. - A judgment by confession may be entered without action at any time in accordance with the procedure prescribed by this rule. Such judgment may be for money due or for money that may become due. Such judgment may also be entered for alimony or for support of minor children.

(b) Procedure. - A prospective defendant desiring to confess judgment shall file with the clerk of the superior court as provided in section (c) a statement in writing signed and verified or sworn to by such defendant authorizing the entry of judgment for the amount stated. The statement shall contain the name of the prospective plaintiff, his county of residence, the name of the defendant, his county of residence, and shall concisely show why the defendant is or may become liable to the plaintiff.

If either the plaintiff or defendant is not a natural person, for the purposes of this rule its county of residence shall be considered to be the county in which it has its principal place of business, whether in this State or not.

(c)   Where entered. - Judgment by confession may be entered only in the county where the defendant resides or has real property or in the county where the plaintiff resides but the entry of judgment in any county shall be conclusive evidence that this section has been complied with.

(d)   Form of entry. - When a statement in conformity with this rule is filed with the clerk of the superior court, the clerk shall enter judgment thereon for the amount confessed, and docket the judgment as in other cases, with costs, together with disbursements. The statement, with the judgment, shall become the judgment roll.

(e)   Force and effect. - Judgments entered in conformity with this rule shall have the same effect as other judgments except that no judgment by confession shall be held to be res judicata as to any fact in any civil action except in an action on the judgment confessed. When such judgment is for alimony or support of minor children, the failure of the defendant to make any payments as required by such judgment shall subject him to such penalties as may be adjudged by the court as in any other case of contempt of its orders. Executions may be issued and enforced in the same manner as upon other judgments. When the full amount of the judgment is not all due, or is payable in installments, and the installments are not all due, execution may issue upon such judgment for the collection of such sums as have become due and shall be in usual form. Notwithstanding the issue and satisfaction of such execution, the judgment remains as security for the sums thereafter to become due; and whenever any further sum becomes due, execution may in like manner be issued. (1967, c. 954, s. 1; 1987, c. 288.)

Rule 69. Omitted.

Rule 70. Judgment for specific acts; vesting title

If a judgment directs a party to execute a conveyance of land or to deliver deeds or other documents or to perform any other specific act and the party fails to comply within the time specified, the judge may direct the act to be done at the cost of the disobedient party by some other person appointed by the judge and the act when so done has like effect as if done by the party. On application of the party entitled to performance, the clerk shall issue a writ of attachment or sequestration against the property of the disobedient party to compel obedience to the judgment. The judge may also in proper cases adjudge the party in contempt. If real or personal property is within the State, the judge in lieu of directing a conveyance thereof may enter a judgment divesting the title of any party and vesting it in others and such judgment has the effect of a conveyance executed in due form of law. When any order or judgment is for the delivery of possession, the party in whose favor it is entered is entitled to execution upon application to the clerk upon payment of the necessary fees. (1967, c. 954, s. 1.)

Rule 71 through Rule 83. Omitted.

Rule 84. Forms

The following forms are sufficient under these rules and are intended to indicate the simplicity and brevity of statement which the rules contemplate:

(1) Complaint on a Promissory Note.

1. On or about _____, _____, defendant executed and delivered to plaintiff a promissory note [in the following words and figures: (here set out the note verbatim)]; [a copy of which is hereto annexed as Exhibit A]; [whereby defendant promised to pay to plaintiff or order on _____, _____, the sum of _____ dollars with interest thereon at the rate of _____ percent per annum].

2. Defendant owes to plaintiff the amount of said note and interest.

Wherefore, plaintiff demands judgment against defendant for the sum of _____ dollars, interest and costs.

(2) Complaint on Account.

Defendant owes plaintiff _____ dollars according to the account hereto annexed as Exhibit A.

Wherefore, plaintiff demands judgment against defendant for the sum of _____ dollars, interest and costs.

(3) Complaint for Negligence.

1. On _____, _____, at [name of place where accident occurred], defendant negligently drove a motor vehicle against plaintiff who was then crossing said street.

2. Defendant was negligent in that:

(a)   Defendant drove at an excessive speed.

(b)   Defendant drove through a red light.

(c)   Defendant failed to yield the right-of-way to plaintiff in a marked crosswalk.

3. As a result plaintiff was thrown down and had his leg broken and was otherwise injured, was prevented from transacting his business, suffered great pain of body and mind, and incurred expenses for medical attention and hospitalization [in the sum of one thousand dollars] (or) [in an amount not yet determined].

Wherefore, plaintiff demands judgment against defendant in the sum of _____ dollars and costs.

(4) Complaint for Negligence.

(Where Plaintiff Is Unable to Determine Definitely Whether

One or the Other of Two Persons Is Responsible or

Whether Both Are Responsible and Where His

Evidence May Justify a Finding of Willfulness or of Recklessness or of Negligence.

1. On _____, _____, at _____, defendant X or defendant Y, or both defendants X and Y, willfully or recklessly or negligently drove or caused to be driven a motor vehicle against plaintiff who was then crossing said street.

2. Defendant X or defendant Y, or both defendants X and Y were negligent in that:

(a) Either defendant or both defendants drove at an excessive speed.

(b) Either defendant or both defendants drove through a red light.

(c) Either defendant or both defendants failed to yield the right-of-way to plaintiff in a marked crosswalk.

3. As a result plaintiff was thrown down and had his leg broken and was otherwise injured, was prevented from transacting his business, suffered great pain of body and mind, and incurred expenses for medical attention and hospitalization [in the sum of one thousand dollars] (or) [in an amount not yet determined].

Wherefore, plaintiff demands judgment against X or against Y or against both in the sum of _____ dollars and costs.

(5) Complaint for Specific Performance.

1. On or about _____, _____, plaintiff and defendant entered into an agreement in writing, a copy of which is hereto annexed as Exhibit A.

2. In accord with the provisions of said agreement plaintiff tendered to defendant the purchase price and requested a conveyance of the land, but defendant refused to accept the tender and refused to make the conveyance.

3. Plaintiff now offers to pay the purchase price.

Wherefore, plaintiff demands (1) that defendant be required specifically to perform said agreement, (2) damages in the sum of _____ dollars, and (3) that if specific performance is not granted plaintiff have judgment against defendant in the sum of _____ dollars.

(6) Complaint in the Alternative.

I.

Defendant owes plaintiff _____ dollars according to the account hereto annexed as Exhibit A.

II. ALTERNATIVE COUNT

Plaintiff claims in the alternative that defendant owes plaintiff _____ dollars for goods sold and delivered by plaintiff to defendant between _____, _____, and _____, _____.

(7) Complaint for Fraud.

1. On _____, _____, at _____, defendant with intent to defraud plaintiff represented to plaintiff that _____.

2. Said representations were known by defendant to be and were false. In truth, [what the facts actually were].

3. Plaintiff believed and relied upon the false representations, and thus was induced to _____.

4. As a result of the foregoing, plaintiff has been damaged [nature and amount of damage].

Wherefore, plaintiff demands judgment against defendant for _____ dollars, interest and costs.

(8) Complaint for Money Paid by Mistake.

Defendant owes plaintiff _____ dollars for money paid by plaintiff to defendant by mistake under the following circumstances:

1. On _____, _____, at _____, pursuant to a contract _____, plaintiff paid defendant _____ dollars.

(9) Motion for Judgment on the Pleadings.

Plaintiff moves that judgment be entered for plaintiff on the pleadings, on the ground that the undisputed facts appearing therein entitle plaintiff to such judgment as a matter of law.

(10) Motion for More Definite Statement.

Defendant moves for an order directing plaintiff to file a more definite statement of the following matters: [set out]

The ground of this motion is that plaintiff's complaint is so [vague] [ambiguous] in respect to these matters that defendant cannot reasonably be required to frame an answer hereto, in that the complaint _____.

(11) Answer to Complaint.

First Defense

The complaint fails to state a claim against defendant upon which relief can be granted.

Second Defense

If defendant is indebted to plaintiff as alleged in the complaint, he is indebted to plaintiff jointly with X. X is alive; is a resident of the State of North Carolina, and is subject to the jurisdiction of this court as to serve of process; and has not been made a party.

Third Defense

1. Defendant admits the allegations contained in paragraphs _____ and _____ of the complaint.

2. Defendant alleges that he is without knowledge or information sufficient to form a belief as to the truth of the allegations contained in paragraph _____ of the complaint.

3. Defendant denies each and every other allegation contained in the complaint.

Fourth Defense

The right of action set forth in the complaint did not accrue within _____ year next before the commencement of this action.

Counterclaim

[Here set forth any claim as a counterclaim in the manner in which a claim is pleaded in a complaint.]Crossclaim Against Defendant Y

[Here set forth the claim constituting a crossclaim against defendant Y in the manner in which a claim is pleaded in a complaint.]

Dated: _____.

_____

Attorney for Defendant

(12) Motion to Bring in Third-Party Defendant.

Defendant moves for leave to make X a party to this action and that there be served upon him summons and third-party complaint as set forth in Exhibit A attached.

(13) Third-Party Complaint.

_____,

Plaintiff,

v.

_____,

Defendant and Third-Party Complaint

Third-Party Plaintiff,

v.

_____

Third-Party Defendant.

Civil Action No. _____

1. Plaintiff _____ has filed against defendant _____ a complaint, a copy of which is attached as "Exhibit C."

2. [Here state the grounds upon which the defendant and third-party plaintiff is entitled to recover from the third-party defendant all or part of what plaintiff may recover from the defendant and third-party plaintiff.]

Wherefore, plaintiff demands judgment against third-party defendant _____ for all sums that may be adjudged against defendant _____ in favor of plaintiff.

(14) Complaint for Negligence Under Federal Employer's Liability Act.

1. During all the times herein mentioned defendant owned and operated in interstate commerce a railroad which passed through a tunnel located at _____ and known as Tunnel No. _____.

2. On or about June 1, _____, defendant was repairing and enlarging the tunnel in order to protect interstate trains and passengers and freight from injury and in order to make the tunnel more conveniently usable for interstate commerce.

3. In the course of thus repairing and enlarging the tunnel on said day defendant employed plaintiff as one of its workmen, and negligently put plaintiff to work in a portion of the tunnel which defendant had left unprotected and unsupported.

4. By reason of defendant's negligence in thus putting plaintiff to work in that portion of the tunnel, plaintiff was, while so working pursuant to defendant's orders, struck and crushed by a rock which fell from the unsupported portion of the tunnel, and was (here describe plaintiff's injuries).

5. Prior to these injuries, plaintiff was a strong, able-bodied man, capable of earning and actually earning _____ dollars per day. By these injuries he has been made incapable of any gainful activity, has suffered great physical and mental pain, and has incurred expense in the amount of _____ dollars for medicine, medical attendance, and hospitalization.

Wherefore, plaintiff demands judgment against defendant in the sum of _____ dollars and costs.

(15) Complaint for Interpleader and Declaratory Relief.

1. On or about June 1, _____, plaintiff issued to G. H. a policy of life insurance whereby plaintiff promised to pay to K. L. as beneficiary the sum of _____ dollars upon the death of G. H. The policy required the payment by G. H. of a stipulated premium on June 1, _____, and annually thereafter as a condition precedent to its continuance in force.

2. No part of the premium due June 1, _____, was ever paid and the policy ceased to have any force of effect on July 1, _____.

3. Thereafter, on September 1, _____, G. H. and K. L. died as the result of a collision between a locomotive and the automobile in which G. H. and K. L. were riding.

4. Defendant C. D. is the duly appointed and acting executor of the will of G. H.; defendant E. F. is the duly appointed and acting executor of the will of K. L.; defendant X. Y. claims to have been duly designed as beneficiary of said policy in place of K. L.

5. Each of defendants, C. D., E. F., and X. Y. is claiming that the above-mentioned policy was in full force and effect at the time of the death of G. H.; each of them is claiming to be the only person entitled to receive payment of the amount of the policy and has made demand for payment thereof.

6. By reason of these conflicting claims of the defendants, plaintiff is in great doubt as to which defendant is entitled to be paid the amount of the policy, if it was in force at the death of G. H.

Wherefore plaintiff demands that the court adjudge:

(1) That none of the defendants is entitled to recover from plaintiff the amount of said policy or any part thereof.

(2) That each of the defendants be restrained from instituting any action against plaintiff for the recovery of the amount of said policy or any part thereof.

(3)   That, if the court shall determine that said policy was in force at the death of G. H., the defendants be required to interplead and settle between themselves their rights to the money due under said policy, and that plaintiff be discharged from all liability in the premises except to the person whom the court shall adjudge entitled to the amount of said policy.

(4)   That plaintiff recover its costs.

(16) Averment of Capacity Under Rule 9(a).

(North Carolina Corporation)

Plaintiff is a corporation incorporated under the law of North Carolina having its principal office in [address].

(Foreign Corporation)

Plaintiff is a corporation incorporated under the law of the State of Delaware having [not having] a registered office in the State of North Carolina.

(Unincorporated Association)
Plaintiff is an unincorporated association organized under the law of the State of New York having its principal office in [address] and (if applicable) having a principal office in the State of North Carolina at [address], and as such has the capacity to sue in its own name in North Carolina. (1967, c. 954, s. 1; 1999-456, s. 59.)the sufficiency of the evidence to support the findings may be raised on appeal whether or not the party raising the question has made in the trial court an objection to such findings or has made a motion to amend them or a motion for judgment, or a request for specific findings. (1967, c. 954, s. 1; 1969, c. 895, s. 12.)

Chapter 1B

Contribution.

Article 1.

Uniform Contribution among Tort-Feasors Act.

§ 1B-1. Right to contribution.

(a) Except as otherwise provided in this Article, where two or more persons become jointly or severally liable in tort for the same injury to person or property or for the same wrongful death, there is a right of contribution among them even though judgment has not been recovered against all or any of them.

(b) The right of contribution exists only in favor of a tort-feasor who has paid more than his pro rata share of the common liability, and his total recovery is limited to the amount paid by him in excess of his pro rata share. No tort-feasor is compelled to make contribution beyond his own pro rata share of the entire liability.

(c) There is no right of contribution in favor of any tort-feasor who has intentionally caused or contributed to the injury or wrongful death.

(d) A tort-feasor who enters into a settlement with a claimant is not entitled to recover contribution from another tort-feasor whose liability for the injury or wrongful death has not been extinguished nor in respect to any amount paid in a settlement which is in excess of what was reasonable.

(e) A liability insurer, who by payment has discharged in full or in part the liability of a tort-feasor and has thereby discharged in full its obligation as insurer, succeeds to the tort-feasor's right of contribution to the extent of the amount it has paid in excess of the tort-feasor's pro rata share of the common liability. This provision does not limit or impair any right of subrogation arising from any other relationship.

(f) This Article does not impair any right of indemnity under existing law. Where one tort-feasor is entitled to indemnity from another, the right of the indemnity obligee is for indemnity and not contribution, and the indemnity obligor is not entitled to contribution from the obligee for any portion of his indemnity obligation.

(g) This Article shall not apply to breaches of trust or of other fiduciary obligation.

(h) The provisions of this Article shall apply to tort claims against the State. However, in such cases, the same rules governing liability and the limits of liability shall apply to the State and its agencies as in cases heard before the Industrial Commission. The State's share in such cases shall not exceed the pro rata share based upon the maximum amount of liability under the Tort Claims Act.

(i)   The provisions of this Article shall apply to the injury or death of an employee of any common carrier by rail which is subject to the provisions of Chapter 2 of Title 45 of the United States Code (45 U.S.C. § 51 et seq.) or G.S. 62-242 where such injury or death is caused by the joint or concurring negligence of such common carrier by rail and any other person or persons. In any such instance, the following will apply:

(1)   Where liability is imposed or sought to be imposed only on such common carrier by rail, the railroad is entitled to contribution from any other such person or persons;

(2)   Where liability is imposed or sought to be imposed only on a person or persons other than a common carrier by rail, such other person or persons are entitled to contribution from the railroad;

(3)   Where liability is imposed or sought to be imposed on both a common carrier by rail and any other person or persons, damages shall be determined as provided in Chapter 2 of Title 45 of the United States Code (45 U.S.C. § 51 et seq.) or G.S. 62-242 whichever controls the claim. (1967, c. 847, s. 1; 1975, c. 587, s. 2; 1979, c. 620.)

§ 1B-2. Pro rata shares.

In determining the pro rata shares of tort-feasors in the entire liability

(1)   Their relative degree of fault shall not be considered;

(2)   If equity requires, the collective liability of some as a group shall constitute a single share; and

(3)   Principles of equity applicable to contribution generally shall apply. (1967, c. 847, s. 1.)

§ 1B-3. Enforcement.

(a)   Whether or not judgment has been entered in an action against two or more tort-feasors for the same injury or wrongful death, contribution may be enforced by separate action.

(b) Where a judgment has been entered in an action against two or more tort-feasors for the same injury or wrongful death, contribution may be enforced in that action by judgment in favor of one against other judgment defendants by motion upon notice to all parties to the action.

(c) If there is a judgment for the injury or wrongful death against the tort-feasor seeking contribution, any separate action by him to enforce contribution must be commenced within one year after the judgment has become final by lapse of time for appeal or after final judgment is entered in the trial court in conformity with the decisions of the appellate court.

(d) If there is no judgment for the injury or wrongful death against the tort-feasor seeking contribution, his right of contribution is barred unless he has either

(1) Discharged by payment the common liability within the statute of limitations period applicable to claimant's right of action against him and has commenced his action for contribution within one year after payment,

(2) Agreed while action is pending against him to discharge the common liability and has within one year after the agreement paid the liability and commenced his action for contribution, or

(3) While action is pending against him, joined the other tort-feasors as third-party defendants for the purpose of contribution.

(e) The recovery of judgment against one tort-feasor for the injury or wrongful death does not of itself discharge the other tort-feasors from liability to the claimant. The satisfaction of the judgment discharges the other tort-feasors from liability to the claimant for the same injury or wrongful death, but does not impair any right of contribution. Provided, however, that a consent judgment in a civil action brought on behalf of a minor, or other person under disability, for the sole purpose of obtaining court approval of a settlement between the injured minor or other person under disability and one of two or more tort-feasors, shall not be deemed to be a judgment as that term is used herein, but shall be treated as a release or covenant not to sue as those terms are used in G.S. 1B-4 unless the judgment shall specifically provide otherwise.

(f) The judgment of the court in determining the liability of the several defendants to the claimant for the same injury or wrongful death shall be binding as among such defendants in determining their right to contribution. (1967, c. 847, s. 1; 1973, c. 465, s. 1; 1975, c. 866, s. 5.)

§ 1B-4. Release or covenant not to sue.

When a release or a covenant not to sue or not to enforce judgment is given in good faith to one of two or more persons liable in tort for the same injury or the same wrongful death:

(1) It does not discharge any of the other tort-feasors from liability for the injury or wrongful death unless its terms so provide; but it reduces the claim against the others to the extent of any amount stipulated by the release or the covenant, or in the amount of the consideration paid for it, whichever is the greater; and,

(2) It discharges the tort-feasor to whom it is given from all liability for contribution to any other tort-feasor. (1967, c. 847, s. 1.)

§ 1B-5. Uniformity of interpretation.

This Article shall be so interpreted and construed as to effectuate its general purpose to make uniform the law of those states that enact it. (1967, c. 847, s. 1.)

§ 1B-6. Short title.

This Article may be cited as the Uniform Contribution among Tort-Feasors Act. (1967, c. 847, s. 1.)

Article 2

Judgment against Joint Obligors or Joint Tort-Feasors.

§ 1B-7. Payment of judgment by one of several.

(a) In all cases in the courts of this State wherein judgment has been, or may hereafter be, rendered against two or more persons or corporations, who are jointly and severally liable for its payment either as joint obligors or joint tort-feasors, and the same has not been paid by all the judgment debtors by each paying his pro rata share thereof, if one or more of the judgment debtors shall pay the judgment creditor, either before or after execution has been issued, the full amount due on said judgment, and shall have entered on the judgment docket in the manner hereinafter set out a notation of the preservation of the right of contribution, such notation shall have the effect of preserving the lien of the judgment and of keeping the same in full force as against any judgment debtor who does not pay his pro rata share thereof to the extent of his liability thereunder in law and equity. Such judgment may be enforced by execution or otherwise in behalf of the judgment debtor or debtors who have so preserved the judgment.

(b) The entry on the judgment docket shall be made in the same manner as other cancellations of judgment, and shall recite that the same has been satisfied, released and discharged, together with all costs and interest, as to the paying judgment debtor, naming him, but that the lien of the judgment is preserved as to the other judgment debtors for the purpose of contribution. No entry of cancellation as to such other judgment debtors shall be made upon the judgment docket or judgment index by virtue of such payment.

(c) If the judgment debtors disagree as to their pro rata shares of the liability, on the grounds that any judgment debtor is insolvent or is a nonresident of the State and cannot be forced under the execution of the court to contribute to the payment of the judgment, or upon other grounds in law and equity, their shares may be determined upon motion in the cause and notice to all parties to the action. Issues of fact arising therein shall be tried by jury as in other civil actions. (1967, c. 847, s. 1.)

Article 3

Cross Claims and Joinder of Third Parties for Contribution.

§ 1B-8. Repealed by Session Laws 1969, c. 895, s. 19.

Chapter 1C

Enforcement of Judgments.

Articles 1 to 15

Reserved for Future Codification Purposes.

§§ 1C-1 through 1C-1599. Reserved for future codification purposes.

Article 16

Exempt Property.

§ 1C-1601. What property exempt; waiver; exceptions.

(a) Exempt property. - Each individual, resident of this State, who is a debtor is entitled to retain free of the enforcement of the claims of creditors:

(1) The debtor's aggregate interest, not to exceed thirty-five thousand dollars ($35,000) in value, in real property or personal property that the debtor or a dependent of the debtor uses as a residence, in a cooperative that owns property that the debtor or a dependent of the debtor uses as a residence, or in a burial plot for the debtor or a dependent of the debtor; however, an unmarried debtor who is 65 years of age or older is entitled to retain an aggregate interest in the property not to exceed sixty thousand dollars ($60,000) in value so long as the property was previously owned by the debtor as a tenant by the entireties or as a joint tenant with rights of survivorship and the former co-owner of the property is deceased.

(2) The debtor's aggregate interest in any property, not to exceed five thousand dollars ($5,000) in value of any unused exemption amount to which the debtor is entitled under subdivision (1) of this subsection.

(3) The debtor's interest, not to exceed three thousand five hundred dollars ($3,500) in value, in one motor vehicle.

(4) The debtor's aggregate interest, not to exceed five thousand dollars ($5,000) in value for the debtor plus one thousand dollars ($1,000) for each dependent of the debtor, not to exceed four thousand dollars ($4,000) total for dependents, in household furnishings, household goods, wearing apparel, appliances, books, animals, crops, or musical instruments, that are held primarily for the personal, family, or household use of the debtor or a dependent of the debtor.

(5) The debtor's aggregate interest, not to exceed two thousand dollars ($2,000) in value, in any implements, professional books, or tools of the trade of the debtor or the trade of a dependent of the debtor.

(6) Life insurance as provided in Article X, Section 5 of the Constitution of North Carolina.

(7) Professionally prescribed health aids for the debtor or a dependent of the debtor.

(8) Compensation for personal injury, including compensation from private disability policies or annuities, or compensation for the death of a person upon whom the debtor was dependent for support, but such compensation is not exempt from claims for funeral, legal, medical, dental, hospital, and health care charges related to the accident or injury giving rise to the compensation.

(9) Individual retirement plans as defined in the Internal Revenue Code and any plan treated in the same manner as an individual retirement plan under the Internal Revenue Code, including individual retirement accounts and Roth retirement accounts as described in section 408(a) and section 408A of the Internal Revenue Code, individual retirement annuities as described in section 408(b) of the Internal Revenue Code, and accounts established as part of a trust described in section 408(c) of the Internal Revenue Code.

(10) Funds in a college savings plan qualified under section 529 of the Internal Revenue Code, not to exceed a cumulative limit of twenty-five thousand dollars ($25,000), but excluding any funds placed in a college savings plan account within the preceding 12 months (except to the extent any of the contributions were made in the ordinary course of the debtor's financial affairs and were consistent with the debtor's past pattern of contributions) and only to the extent that the funds are for a child of the debtor and will actually be used for the child's college or university expenses.

(11) Retirement benefits under the retirement plans of other states and governmental units of other states, to the extent that these benefits are exempt under the laws of the state or governmental unit under which the benefit plan is established.

(12) Alimony, support, separate maintenance, and child support payments or funds that have been received or to which the debtor is entitled, to the extent the

payments or funds are reasonably necessary for the support of the debtor or any dependent of the debtor.

(b) Definitions. - As used in this section, the following definitions apply:

(1) "Internal Revenue Code" means Code as defined in G.S. 105-228.90.

(2) "Value" means fair market value of an individual's interest in property, less valid liens superior to the judgment lien sought to be enforced.

(c) Waiver. - The exemptions provided in this Article cannot be waived except by:

(1) Transfer of property allocated as exempt (and in that event only as to the specific property transferred);

(2) Written waiver, after judgment, approved by the clerk or district court judge. The clerk or district court judge must find that the waiver is made freely, voluntarily, and with full knowledge of the debtor's rights to exemptions and that he is not required to waive them; or

(3) Failure to assert the exemption after notice to do so pursuant to G.S. 1C-1603. The clerk or district court judge may relieve such a waiver made by reason of mistake, surprise or excusable neglect, to the extent that the rights of innocent third parties are not affected.

(d) Recent purchases. - The exemptions provided in subdivisions (2), (3), (4), and (5) of subsection (a) of this section are inapplicable with respect to tangible personal property purchased by the debtor less than 90 days preceding the initiation of judgment collection proceedings or the filing of a petition for bankruptcy, unless the purchase of the property is directly traceable to the liquidation or conversion of property that may be exempt and no additional property was transferred into or used to acquire the replacement property.

(e) Exceptions. - The exemptions provided in this Article are inapplicable to claims:

(1) Of the United States or its agencies as provided by federal law;

(2) Of the State or its subdivisions for taxes, appearance bonds or fiduciary bonds;

(3) Of lien by a laborer for work done and performed for the person claiming the exemption, but only as to the specific property affected;

(4) Of lien by a mechanic for work done on the premises, but only as to the specific property affected;

(5) For payment of obligations contracted for the purchase of the specific real property affected;

(6) Repealed by Session Laws 1981 (Regular Session, 1982), c. 1224, s. 6, effective September 1, 1982;

(7) For contractual security interests in the specific property affected; provided, that the exemptions shall apply to the debtor's household goods notwithstanding any contract for a nonpossessory, nonpurchase money security interest in any such goods;

(8) For statutory liens, on the specific property affected, other than judicial liens;

(9) For child support, alimony or distributive award order pursuant to Chapter 50 of the General Statutes;

(10) For criminal restitution orders docketed as civil judgments pursuant to G.S. 15A-1340.38.

(f) Federal Bankruptcy Code. - The exemptions provided in The Bankruptcy Code, 11 U.S.C. § 522(d), are not applicable to residents of this State. The exemptions provided by this Article and by other statutory or common law of this State shall apply for purposes of The Bankruptcy Code, 11 U.S.C. § 522(b).

(g) Effect of exemptions. - Notwithstanding any other provision of law, a creditor shall not obtain possession of a debtor's household goods and furnishings in which the creditor holds a nonpossessory, nonpurchase money security interest until the creditor has fully complied with the procedures required by G.S. 1C-1603. (1981, c. 490, s. 1; 1981 (Reg. Sess., 1982), c. 1224, ss. 1-7, 20; 1991, c. 506, s. 1; 1995, c. 250, s. 1; 1998-212, s. 19.4(j); 1999-337, s. 2; 2005-401, s. 1; 2009-417, s. 1.)

§ 1C-1602. Alternative exemptions.

The debtor may elect to take the personal property and homestead exemptions provided in Article X of the Constitution of North Carolina instead of the exemptions provided by G.S. 1C-1601. If the debtor elects to take his constitutional exemptions, the exemptions provided in G.S. 1C-1601 shall not apply and in that event the exemptions provided in this Article shall not be construed so as to affect the personal property and homestead exemptions granted by Article X of the Constitution of North Carolina. If the debtor elects to take his constitutional exemptions, the clerk or district court judge must designate the property to be exempt under the procedure set out in G.S. 1C-1603. The debtor is entitled to have one thousand dollars ($1,000) in value in real property owned and occupied by him and five hundred dollars ($500.00) in value in his personal property exempted from sale under execution. If the value of the property in which the debtor claims his constitutional exemption is in excess of his exemptions, the clerk, in an execution, may order the sale of the property with the proceeds of the sale being distributed first to the debtor to satisfy his exemption and the excess to be distributed as ordered. (1981, c. 490, s. 1; 1981 (Reg. Sess., 1982), c. 1224, s. 8.)

§ 1C-1603. Procedure for setting aside exempt property.

(a) Motion or Petition; Notice. -

(1) A judgment debtor may have his exempt property designated by motion after judgment has been entered against him.

(2) Repealed by Session Laws 1981 (Regular Session, 1982), c. 1224, s. 10.

(3) The clerk or district court judge may determine that particular property is not exempt even though there has been no proceeding to designate the exemption.

(4) After judgment, except as provided in G.S. 1C-1603(a)(3) or when exemptions have already been designated, the clerk may not issue an execution or writ of possession unless notice from the court has been served upon the judgment debtor advising the debtor of the debtor's rights. The judgment creditor shall cause the notice, which shall be accompanied by the form for the statement by the debtor under subsection (c) of this section, to be served on the debtor as provided in G.S. 1A-1, Rule 4(j)(1). If the judgment debtor cannot be served as provided above, the judgment creditor may serve the judgment debtor

by mailing a copy of the notice to the judgment debtor at the debtor's last known address. Proof of service by certified or registered mail or personal service is as provided in G.S. 1A-1, Rule 4. The judgment creditor may prove service by mailing to last known address by filing a certificate that the notice was served indicating the circumstances warranting the use of such service and the date and address of service. The notice shall be substantially in the following form:

NORTH CAROLINA
_____ COUNTY

IN THE GENERAL COURT
OF JUSTICE DISTRICT
COURT DIVISION
CvD

_____) NOTICE OF
Judgment Creditor) PETITION (OR
) MOTION) TO SET
    vs.) OFF DEBTOR'S
_____) EXEMPT
PROPERTY

GREETINGS:

You have been named as a "judgment debtor" in a proceeding initiated by a "judgment creditor". A "judgment debtor" is a person who a court has declared owes money to another, the "judgment creditor". The purpose of this proceeding is to make arrangements to collect that debt from you personally or from property you own.

It is important that you respond to this notice no later than 20 days after you receive it because you may lose valuable rights if you do nothing. You may wish to consider hiring an attorney to help you with this proceeding to make certain that you receive all the protections to which you are entitled under the North Carolina Constitution and laws.

NOTICE TO JUDGMENT DEBTOR:

THERE ARE CERTAIN EXEMPTIONS UNDER STATE AND FEDERAL LAW THAT YOU ARE ENTITLED TO CLAIM IN ADDITION TO THE EXEMPTIONS LISTED ON THE "SCHEDULE OF DEBTOR'S PROPERTY AND REQUEST TO SET ASIDE EXEMPT PROPERTY" THAT IS ENCLOSED WITH THIS NOTICE.

These exemptions may include social security benefits, unemployment benefits, workers' compensation benefits, and earnings for your personal services rendered within the last 60 days. There is available to you a prompt procedure for challenging an attachment or levy on your property.

(b)   Contents of Motion or Petition. - The motion or petition must:

(1)   Name the judgment debtor;
(2)   Name the judgment creditors of the debtor insofar as they are known to the movant;

(3)   If it is a motion to modify a previously allocated exemption, describe the change of condition (if the movant received notice of the exemption hearing) and the modification desired.

(c)   Statement by the Debtor. - When proceedings are instituted, the debtor shall file with the court a schedule of:

(1)   The debtor's assets, including their location;

(2)   The debtor's debts and the names and addresses of the debtor's creditors;

(3)   The property that the debtor desires designated as exempt.

The form for the statement shall be substantially as follows:

NORTH CAROLINA   IN THE GENERAL COURT

_____ COUNTY   OF JUSTICE DISTRICT
                                          COURT DIVISION
                                          CvD

Judgment Creditor   )   SCHEDULE OF DEBTOR'S
)   PROPERTY
)   AND REQUEST TO
)   SET ASIDE EXEMPT

Judgment Debtor   )   PROPERTY
NOTICE TO JUDGMENT DEBTOR:

THERE ARE CERTAIN EXEMPTIONS UNDER STATE AND FEDERAL LAW THAT YOU ARE ENTITLED TO CLAIM IN ADDITION TO THE EXEMPTIONS LISTED BELOW.

These exemptions may include social security benefits, unemployment benefits, workers' compensation benefits, and earnings for your personal services rendered within the last 60 days. There is available to you a prompt procedure for challenging an attachment or levy on your property.

I, _____, being duly sworn do depose and say:
(fill in your name)

1. That I am a citizen and resident of _____
County, North Carolina;

2. That I was born on _____;
(date of birth)

3. That I am (married to _____)
(spouse's name)
_____;
(not married)

4. That the following persons live in my household and are in substantial need of my support:

NAME   RELATIONSHIP TO DEBTOR   AGE

235

_____   _____   _____   _____
_____   _____   _____   _____
_____   _____   _____   _____

(Use additional space, as necessary)

5. That (I own) (I am purchasing) (I rent) (choose one; mark out the other choices) a (house) (trailer) (apartment) (choose one; mark out the other choices)

located at

_____
which is my residence.   (address, city, zip code)

6. That I (do) (do not) own any other real property. If other real property is owned, list that property on the following lines; if no other real property is owned, mark "not applicable" on the first line.

_____
_____
_____
_____

7. That the following persons are, so far as I am able to tell, all of the persons or companies to whom I owe money:

_____
_____
_____
_____

8. That I wish to claim my interest in the following real or personal property, or in a cooperative that owns property, that I use as a residence or my dependent uses as a residence. I also wish to claim my interest in the following burial plots for myself or my dependents. I understand that my total interest claimed in the residence and burial plots may not exceed $35,000, except that if I am unmarried and am 65 years of age or older, I am entitled to claim a total exemption in the residence and burial plots not to exceed $60,000 so long as the property was previously owned by me as a tenant by the entireties or as a

joint tenant with rights of survivorship, and the former co-owner of the property is deceased.

I understand that I am not entitled to this exemption if I take the homestead exemption provided by the Constitution of North Carolina in other property. I understand that if I wish to claim more than one parcel exempt I must attach additional pages setting forth the following information for each parcel claimed exempt.

Property Location:

County _____ Township _____
Street Address
_____

Legal Description:

Number by which county tax assessor identifies property

_____

Description (Attach a copy of your deed or other instrument of conveyance that describes the property and indicate here: _____ or describe the property in as much detail as possible.

Attach additional sheets if necessary.)

_____
_____
_____

Record Owner(s)
_____
_____
_____

Estimated Value:
_____

Lienholders:

(1) Name _____ Current Balance _____

Address
_____

(2) Name _____ Current Balance _____
Address
_____

(3) Name _____ Current Balance _____
Address
_____

(4) If others, attach additional pages.
If you are unmarried and 65 years of age or older, specify which, if any, property listed above was previously owned by you as a tenant by the entireties or as a joint tenant with rights of survivorship and as to which the former co-owner of the property is deceased:

9. That I wish to claim the following life insurance policies whose sole beneficiaries are (my wife) (my children) (my wife and children) as exempt:

Name of Insurer	Policy Number	Face Value	Beneficiary(ies)
_____	_____	_____	_____
_____	_____	_____	_____
_____	_____	_____	_____

10. That I wish to claim the following items of health care aid necessary for (myself) (my dependents) to work or sustain health:

Item	Purpose	Person using item
_____	_____	_____
_____	_____	_____
_____	_____	_____

11. That I wish to claim the following implements, professional books, or tools (not to exceed $2,000), of my trade or the trade of my dependent. I understand that such property purchased within 90 days of this proceeding may not be exempt:

Item   Estimated Value

_____   _____
_____   _____
_____   _____

12. That I wish to claim the following personal property consisting of household furnishings, household goods, wearing apparel, appliances, books, animals, crops or musical instruments as exempt from the claims of my creditors. I affirm, that these items of personal property are held primarily for my personal, family or household use or for such use by my dependents.

I understand that I am entitled to personal property worth the sum of $5,000. I understand that I am also entitled to $1,000 for each person dependent on me for support, but not to exceed $4,000 for dependents. I further understand that I am entitled to this amount after deduction from the value of the property the amount of any valid lien or purchase money security interest and that property purchased within 90 days of this proceeding may not be exempt.

Item (or class) of Property	Amount of Lien or Security Interest	Location	Estimated Value of Debtor's Interest
_____	_____	_____	_____
_____	_____	_____	_____
_____	_____	_____	_____

13. That I wish to claim my interest in the following motor vehicle as exempt from the claims of my creditors. I understand that I am entitled to my interest in a motor vehicle worth the sum of $3,500 after deduction of the amount of any valid liens or purchase money security interest. I understand that a motor vehicle purchased within 90 days of this proceeding may not be exempt.

Make and Model of Motor Vehicle Interest	Year	Name(s) of Title Owner of Record	Name(s) of Lien Holder(s) of Record	Estimated Value of Debtor's
_____	____	_____	_____	_____

14. That I wish to claim as exempt the following compensation that I received or to which I am entitled for the personal injury of myself or a person upon whom I was dependent for support, including compensation from a private disability

policy or an annuity, or compensation that I received for the death of a person upon whom I was dependent for support. I understand that this compensation is not exempt from claims for funeral, legal, medical, dental, hospital or health care charges related to the accident or injury that resulted in the payment of the compensation to me. I understand that if I wish to claim more than one amount of compensation exempt, I must attach additional pages setting forth the following information for each amount of compensation claimed exempt.

(a) amount of compensation

(b) method of payment: lump sum or installments
(If installments, state amount, frequency and duration of payments)

(c) name and relationship to debtor of person(s) injured or killed giving rise to compensation

(d) location/source of compensation if received in lump or installments, including name and account number of any disability policy or annuity

(e) unpaid debts arising out of the injury or death giving rise to compensation

Name and Address	Services Rendered	Amount of Debt
_____	_____	_____
_____	_____	_____

15. That I wish to claim the following property as exempt because I claimed residential real or personal property as exempt that is worth less than $35,000 or I made no claim for a residential exemption under section (8) above. I understand that I am entitled to an exemption of up to $5,000 in any property only if I made no claim under section (8) above or a claim that was less than $35,000 under section (8) above. I understand that I am entitled to claim any unused amount that I was permitted to make under section (8) above up to a maximum of $5,000 in any property. (Examples: (a) if you claim $34,000 under section (8), $1,000 allowed here; (b) if you claim $30,000 under section (8), $5,000 allowed here; (c) if you claim $35,000 under section (8), no claim allowed here.) I further understand that the amount of my claim under this section is after the deduction from the value of this property of the amount of any valid lien or purchase money security interests and that tangible personal property purchased within 90 days of this proceeding may not be exempt.

PERSONAL PROPERTY:

Property Location	Amount of Liens or Purchase Money Security Interests	Value of Debtor's Interest
_____	_____	

PROPERTY (I understand that if I wish to claim more than one parcel exempt, I must attach additional pages setting forth the following information for each parcel claimed exempt):

Property Location

County _____ Township _____
Street Address_____
Legal Description:

Number by which county tax assessor identifies property
_____
_____

Description (Attach a copy of your deed or other instrument of conveyance that describes the property and indicate here: _____ or describe the property in as much detail as possible.

Attach additional sheets if necessary.)

_____
_____
_____
_____
_____
_____

Record Owner(s):

_____
_____
_____
_____

Estimated Value:

Lienholders:

(1) Name _____ Current Balance_____
Address_____
(2) Name _____ Current Balance _____
Address_____
(3) Name _____ Current Balance _____
Address_____

(4) If others, attach additional pages.

16. That I wish to claim as exempt the following retirement plans that I have that are individual retirement plans as described in the Internal Revenue Code or that are treated in the same manner as an individual retirement plan under the Internal Revenue Code, including individual retirement accounts and Roth retirement accounts as described in section 408(a) and section 408A of the Internal Revenue Code, individual retirement annuities as described in section 408(b) of the Internal Revenue Code, and accounts established as part of a trust described in section 408(c) of the Internal Revenue Code.

Type of Retirement Account	Name of Account	Account Number
_____	_____	_____
_____	_____	_____
_____	_____	_____

17. That I wish to claim as exempt the following funds I hold in a college savings plan, not to exceed $25,000. I understand that to qualify for this exemption, the college savings plan must qualify as a college savings plan under section 529 of the Internal Revenue Code, and the college savings plan must be for my child and must actually be used for my child's college or university expenses. I understand I may not exempt any funds I placed in this account within the preceding 12 months, except to the extent that any contributions were made in

the ordinary course of my financial affairs and were consistent with my past pattern of contributions.

College Savings Plan Beneficiaries	Account Number	Value	Name(s) of Child(ren)
_____	_____	_____	_____
_____	_____	_____	_____
_____	_____	_____	_____

18. That I wish to claim as exempt the following retirement benefits to which I am entitled to under the retirement plans of other states and governmental units of other states. I understand that these benefits are exempt only to the extent these benefits are exempt under the laws of the state or governmental unit under which the benefit plan was established.

State/Government Unit	Name of Retirement Plan	Identifying Number
_____	_____	_____
_____	_____	_____
_____	_____	_____

19. That I wish to claim as exempt any alimony, support, separate maintenance, or child support payments or funds that I have received or that I am entitled to receive. I understand that these payments are exempt only to the extent that they are reasonably necessary for my support or for the support of a person dependent on me for support.

Type of Support of Funds	Person Paying Support	Amount & Location
_____	_____	_____
_____	_____	_____
_____	_____	_____

20. That the following is a complete listing of all of my assets that I have not claimed as exempt under any of the preceding paragraphs:

Item	Location	Estimated value
_____	_____	_____

_____   _____   _____
_____   _____   _____

This the ____ day of ____, ____.

_____
Judgment Debtor

Sworn to and Subscribed before me this ____ day of ____, ____.

Notary Public _____   My Commission Expires: ____

(d) Notice to Persons Affected. - If the judgment debtor moves to designate his exemptions, a copy of the motion and schedule must be served on the judgment creditor as provided in G.S. 1A-1, Rule 5.

(e) Procedure for Setting Aside Exempt Property. -

(1) When served with the notice provided in G.S. 1C-1603(a)(4), the judgment debtor may either file a motion to designate his exemptions with a schedule of assets or may request, in writing, a hearing before the clerk to claim exemptions.

(2) If the judgment debtor does not file a motion to designate exemptions with a schedule of assets within 20 days after notice of his rights was served in accordance with G.S. 1C-1603(a)(4) or if he does not request a hearing before the clerk within 20 days after service of the notice of rights and appear at the requested hearing, the judgment debtor has waived the exemptions provided in this Article and in Sections 1 and 2 of Article X of the North Carolina Constitution. Upon request of the judgment creditor, the clerk shall issue a writ of execution or writ of possession.

(3) If the judgment debtor moves to designate his exemptions by filing a motion and schedule of assets, the judgment creditor is served as provided in G.S. 1C-1603(d).

(4) If the judgment debtor requests a hearing before the clerk to claim exemptions, the clerk sets a hearing date and gives notice of the hearing to the

judgment debtor and judgment creditor. At the hearing, the judgment debtor may claim his exemptions.

(5) The judgment creditor has 10 days from the date served with a motion and schedule of assets or from the date of a hearing to claim exemptions to file an objection to the judgment debtor's schedule of exemptions.

(6) If the judgment creditor files no objection to the schedule filed by the judgment debtor or claimed at the requested hearing, the clerk shall enter an order designating the property allowed by law and scheduled by the judgment debtor as exempt property. Upon request of the judgment creditor, the clerk shall issue an execution or writ of possession except for exempt property.

(7) If the judgment creditor objects to the schedule filed or claimed by the judgment debtor, the clerk must place the motion for hearing by the district court judge, without a jury, at the next civil session.

(8) The district court judge must determine the value of the property. The district court judge or the clerk, upon order of the judge, may appoint a qualified person to examine the property and report its value to the judge. Compensation of that person must be advanced by the person requesting the valuation and is a court cost having priority over the claims.

(9) The district court judge must enter an order designating exempt property. Supplemental reports and orders may be filed and entered as necessary to implement the order.

(10) Where the order designating exemptions indicates excess value in exempt property, the clerk, in an execution, may order the sale of property having excess value and appropriate distribution of the proceeds.

(11) The clerk or district court judge may permit a particular item of property having value in excess of the allowable exemption to be retained by the judgment debtor upon his making available to judgment creditors money or property not otherwise available to them in an amount equivalent to the excess value. Priorities of judgment creditors are the same in the substituted property as they were in the original property.

(12) Appeal from a designation of exempt property by the clerk is to the district court judge. A party has 10 days from the date of entry of an order to appeal. Appeal from a designation of exempt property by a district court judge is to the Court of Appeals. Decisions of the Court of Appeals with regard to

questions of valuation of property are final as provided in G.S. 7A-28. Other questions may be appealed as provided in G.S. 7A-30 and 7A-31.

(f) Notation of Order on Judgment Docket. - A notation of the order setting aside exempt property must be entered by the clerk of court on the judgment docket opposite the judgment that was the subject of the enforcement proceeding. If real property located in a county other than the county in which the judgment was rendered is designated as exempt and the judgment has already been docketed in that county, the clerk must send a notice of the designation of exempt property to the county where the property is located. The clerk of the county where the land is located shall enter a notation of the designation of exempt property on the judgment docket. If a judgment is docketed in a county where real property is located after that real property has been designated as exempt, the transcript of judgment must indicate that the exemptions have been designated. The clerk in the county receiving the transcript must enter the notation of designation of exempt property as well as docket the judgment.

(g) Modification. - The debtor's exemption may be modified by motion in the original exemption proceeding by anyone who did not receive notice of the exemption hearing. Also, the debtor's exemption may be modified upon a change of circumstances, by motion in the original exemption proceeding, made by the debtor or anyone interested. A substantial change in value may constitute changed circumstances. Modification may include the substitution of different property for the exempt property.

(h) Repealed by Session Laws 1981 (Regular Session, 1982), c. 1224, s. 14. (1981, c. 490, s. 1; 1981 (Reg. Sess., 1982), c. 1224, ss. 9-14, 18, 19; 1991, c. 607, s. 1; 1999-456, s. 59; 2005-401, ss. 2, 3; 2011-326, s. 1.)

§ 1C-1604. Effect of exemption.

(a) Property allocated to the debtor as exempt is free of the enforcement of the claims of creditors for indebtedness incurred before or after the exempt property is set aside, other than claims exempted by G.S. 1C-1601(e), for so long as the debtor owns it. When the property is conveyed to another, the exemption ceases as to liens attaching prior to the conveyance. Creation of a security interest in the property does not constitute a conveyance within the meaning of this section, but a transfer in satisfaction of, or for the enforcement of, a security interest is a conveyance. When exempt property is conveyed, the debtor may have other exemptions allotted.

(a1)   The statute of limitations on judgments is suspended for the period of exemption as to the property which is exempt. However, the statute of limitations is not suspended as to the exempt property unless the judgment creditor shall have, prior to the expiration of the statute of limitations, recorded a copy of the order designating exempt property in the office of the register of deeds in the county where the exempt real property is located.

(b)   Exempt property which passes by devise, intestate succession or gift to a dependent spouse, child or person to whom the debtor stands in loco parentis, continues to be exempt while held by that person. The exemption is terminated if the spouse remarries, or, with regard to a dependent, when the court determinates that dependency no longer exists. (1981, c. 490, s. 1; 1991, c. 607, s. 2; 2011-284, s. 6.)

§§ 1C-1605 through 1C-1700. Reserved for future codification purposes.

Article 17

Uniform Enforcement of Foreign Judgments Act.
§ 1C-1701. Short title.

This Article shall be known and may be cited as the Uniform Enforcement of Foreign Judgments Act. (1989, c. 747.)

§ 1C-1702. Definitions.

As used in this Article, unless the context requires otherwise:

(1)   "Foreign Judgment" means any judgment, decree, or order of a court of the United States or a court of any other state which is entitled to full faith and credit in this State, except a "child support order," as defined in G.S. 52C-1-101 (The Uniform Interstate Family Support Act), a "custody decree," as defined in G.S. 50A-102 (The Uniform Child-Custody Jurisdiction and Enforcement Act), or a domestic violence protective order as provided in G.S. 50B-4(d).

(2)   "Judgment Debtor" means the party against whom a foreign judgment has been rendered.

(3) "Judgment Creditor" means the party in whose favor a foreign judgment has been rendered. (1989, c. 747, s. 1; 1999-23, s. 3; 1999-223, s. 4.)

§ 1C-1703. Filing and status of foreign judgments.

(a) A copy of any foreign judgment authenticated in accordance with an act of Congress or the statutes of this State may be filed in the office of the clerk of superior court of any county of this State in which the judgment debtor resides, or owns real or personal property. Along with the foreign judgment, the judgment creditor or his attorney shall make and file with the clerk an affidavit which states that the foreign judgment is final and that it is unsatisfied in whole or in part, and which sets forth the amount remaining unpaid on the judgment.
(b) Upon the filing of the foreign judgment and the affidavit, the foreign judgment shall be docketed and indexed in the same manner as a judgment of this State; however, no execution shall issue upon the foreign judgment nor shall any other proceeding be taken for its enforcement until the expiration of 30 days from the date upon which notice of filing is served in accordance with G.S. 1C-1704.

(c) A judgment so filed has the same effect and is subject to the same defenses as a judgment of this State and shall be enforced or satisfied in like manner; provided however, if the judgment debtor files a motion for relief or notice of defense pursuant to G.S. 1C-1705, enforcement of the foreign judgment is automatically stayed, without security, until the court finally disposes of the matter. (1989, c. 747.)

§ 1C-1704. Notice of filing; service.

(a) Promptly upon the filing of a foreign judgment and affidavit, the judgment creditor shall serve the notice of filing provided for in subsection (b) on the judgment debtor and shall attach thereto a filed-stamped copy of the foreign judgment and affidavit. Service and proof of service of the notice may be made in any manner provided for in Rule 4(j) of the Rules of Civil Procedure.

(b) The notice shall set forth the name and address of the judgment creditor, of his attorney if any, and of the clerk's office in which the foreign judgment is filed in this State, and shall state that the judgment attached thereto has been filed in that office, that the judgment debtor has 30 days from the date of receipt of the notice to seek relief from the enforcement of the judgment, and that if the judgment is not satisfied and no such relief is sought within that 30 days, the judgment will be enforced in this State in the same manner as any judgment of this State. (1989, c. 747.)

§ 1C-1705. Defenses; procedure; stay.

(a) The judgment debtor may file a motion for relief from, or notice of defense to, the foreign judgment on the grounds that the foreign judgment has been appealed from, or enforcement has been stayed by, the court which rendered it, or on any other ground for which relief from a judgment of this State would be allowed. Notwithstanding subsection (b) of this section, the court shall stay enforcement of the foreign judgment for an appropriate period if the judgment debtor shows that:

(1) The foreign judgment has been stayed by the court that rendered it; or

(2) An appeal from the foreign judgment is pending or the time for taking an appeal has not expired and the judgment debtor executes a written undertaking in the same manner and amount as would be required in the case of a judgment entered by a court of this State under G.S. 1-289.

(b) If the judgment debtor has filed a motion for relief or notice of defenses then the judgment creditor may move for enforcement of the foreign judgment as a judgment of this State, unless the court stays enforcement of the judgment under subsection (a) of this section. The judgment creditor's motion shall be heard before a judge of the trial division which would be the proper division for the trial of an action in which the amount in controversy is the same as the amount remaining unpaid on the foreign judgment. The Rules of Civil Procedure (G.S. 1A-1) shall apply. The judgment creditor shall have the burden of proving that the foreign judgment is entitled to full faith and credit. (1989, c. 747, s. 1; 2003-19, s. 2.)

§ 1C-1706. Fees.

The enforcement of a foreign judgment under this Article shall be subject to the costs and fees set forth in Article 28 of Chapter 7A of the General Statutes. The amount remaining unpaid on the foreign judgment as set forth in the affidavit filed under G.S. 1C-1703(b) shall determine the amount of the costs to be collected at the time of the filing of the foreign judgment and assessed pursuant to G.S. 7A-305. (1989, c. 747.)

§ 1C-1707. Optional procedure.

This Article may not be construed to impair a judgment creditor's right to bring a civil action in this State to enforce such creditor's judgment. (1989, c. 747.)

§ 1C-1708. Judgments against public policy.

The provisions of this Article shall not apply to foreign judgments based on claims which are contrary to the public policies of North Carolina. (1989, c. 747.)

§§ 1C-1709 through 1C-1749. Reserved for future codification purposes.

Article 17A

Enforcement of Foreign Judgments for Noncompensatory Damages.

§ 1C-1750: Repealed by Session Laws 2003-19, s. 1, effective April 23, 2003.

§§ 1C-1751 through 1C-1759. Reserved for future codification purposes.

§ 1C-1760: Repealed by Session Laws 2003-19, s. 1, effective April 23, 2003.

§§ 1C-1761 through 1C-1799. Reserved for future codification purposes.

Article 18

North Carolina Foreign Money Judgments Recognition Act.

§ 1C-1800: Repealed by Session Laws 2009-325, s. 1, effective October 1, 2009, and applicable to all actions commenced on or after that date in which the issue of recognition of a foreign-country judgment is raised.

§ 1C-1801: Repealed by Session Laws 2009-325, s. 1, effective October 1, 2009, and applicable to all actions commenced on or after that date in which the issue of recognition of a foreign-country judgment is raised.

§ 1C-1802: Repealed by Session Laws 2009-325, s. 1, effective October 1, 2009, and applicable to all actions commenced on or after that date in which the issue of recognition of a foreign-country judgment is raised.

§ 1C-1803: Repealed by Session Laws 2009-325, s. 1, effective October 1, 2009, and applicable to all actions commenced on or after that date in which the issue of recognition of a foreign-country judgment is raised.

§ 1C-1804: Repealed by Session Laws 2009-325, s. 1, effective October 1, 2009, and applicable to all actions commenced on or after that date in which the issue of recognition of a foreign-country judgment is raised.

§ 1C-1805: Repealed by Session Laws 2009-325, s. 1, effective October 1, 2009, and applicable to all actions commenced on or after that date in which the issue of recognition of a foreign-country judgment is raised.

§ 1C-1806: Repealed by Session Laws 2009-325, s. 1, effective October 1, 2009, and applicable to all actions commenced on or after that date in which the issue of recognition of a foreign-country judgment is raised.

§ 1C-1807: Repealed by Session Laws 2009-325, s. 1, effective October 1, 2009, and applicable to all actions commenced on or after that date in which the issue of recognition of a foreign-country judgment is raised.

§ 1C-1808: Repealed by Session Laws 2009-325, s. 1, effective October 1, 2009, and applicable to all actions commenced on or after that date in which the issue of recognition of a foreign-country judgment is raised.

§§ 1C-1809 through 1C-1819. Reserved for future codification purposes.

Article 19
The North Carolina Foreign-Money Claims Act.

§ 1C-1820. Definitions.

As used in this Article:

(1) "Action" means a judicial proceeding or arbitration in which a payment in money may be awarded or enforced with respect to a foreign-money claim.

(2) "Bank-offered spot rate" means the spot rate of exchange at which a bank will sell foreign money at a spot rate.

(3) "Conversion date" means the banking day next preceding the date on which money, in accordance with this Article, is:

a. Paid to a claimant in an action or distribution proceeding;

b. Paid to the official designated by law to enforce a judgment or award on behalf of a claimant; or

c. Used to recoup, set off, or counterclaim in different moneys in an action or distribution proceeding.

(4) "Distribution proceeding" means a judicial or nonjudicial proceeding for the distribution of a fund in which one or more foreign-money claims is asserted and includes an accounting, an assignment for the benefit of creditors, a foreclosure, the liquidation or rehabilitation of a corporation or other entity, and the distribution of an estate, trust, or other fund.

(5) "Foreign money" means money other than money of the United States.

(6) "Foreign-money claim" means a claim upon an obligation to pay, or a claim for recovery of a loss, expressed in or measured by a foreign money.

(7) "Money" means a medium of exchange for the payment of obligations or a store of value authorized or adopted by a government or by intergovernmental agreement.

(8) "Money of the claim" means the money determined as proper for payment of the claim pursuant to G.S. 1C-1823.

(9) "Person" means an individual, a corporation, government or governmental subdivision or agency, business trust, estate, trust, joint venture, partnership, association, two or more persons having a joint or common interest, or any other legal or commercial entity.

(10) "Rate of exchange" means the rate at which money of one country may be converted into money of another country in a free financial market convenient to or reasonably usable by a person obligated to pay or to state a rate of conversion. "Rate of exchange" means, if separate rates of exchange apply to different kinds of transactions, the rate applicable to the particular transaction giving rise to the foreign-money claim.

(11) "Spot rate" means the rate of exchange at which foreign money is sold by a bank or other dealer in foreign exchange for immediate or next day

availability or for settlement by immediate payment in cash or its equivalent, by charge to an account, or by an agreed delayed settlement not exceeding two days.

(12)   "State" means a state of the United States, the District of Columbia, the Commonwealth of Puerto Rico, or a territory or insular possession subject to the jurisdiction of the United States. (1995, c. 213, s. 1.)

§ 1C-1821. Scope of Article.

(a)   This Article applies only to a foreign-money claim in an action or distribution proceeding.

(b)   This Article applies to foreign-money issues even if other law under the conflict of laws rules of this State applies to other issues in the action or distribution proceeding. (1995, c. 213, s. 1.)

§ 1C-1822. Variation by agreement.

(a)   The effect of this Article may be varied by agreement of the parties made before or after commencement of an action or distribution proceeding or the entry of judgment.

(b)   Parties to a transaction may agree upon the money to be used in a transaction giving rise to a foreign-money claim and may agree to use different moneys for different aspects of the transaction. Stating the price in a foreign money for one aspect of a transaction does not alone require the use of that money for other aspects of the transaction. (1995, c. 213, s. 1.)

§ 1C-1823. Determining proper money of the claim.

(a)   The money in which the parties to a transaction have agreed that payment is to be made is the proper money of the claim for payment.

(b)   If the parties to a transaction have not otherwise agreed, the proper money of the claim, as in each case may be appropriate, is the money:

(1) Regularly used between the parties as a matter of usage or course of dealing;

(2) Used at the time of a transaction in international trade, by trade usage or common practice, for valuing or settling transactions in the particular commodity or service involved; or

(3) In which the loss was ultimately felt or will be incurred by the party claimant. (1995, c. 213, s. 1.)

§ 1C-1824. Determining amount of the money of certain contract claims.

(a) If an amount contracted to be paid in a foreign money is measured by a specified amount of a different money, the amount to be paid shall be determined on the conversion date.

(b) If an amount contracted to be paid in a foreign money is to be measured by a different money at the rate of exchange prevailing on a date before default, that rate of exchange applies only to payments made within a reasonable time after default, not exceeding 30 days. Thereafter, conversion is made at the bank-offered spot rate on the conversion date.

(c) A monetary claim is neither usurious nor unconscionable for the reason that the agreement on which it is based provides that the amount of the debtor's obligation to be paid in the debtor's money, when received by the creditor, must equal a specified amount of the foreign money of the country of the creditor. If, because of unexcused delay in payment of a judgment or award, the amount received by the creditor does not equal the amount of the foreign money specified in the agreement, the court or arbitrator shall amend the judgment or award accordingly. (1995, c. 213, s. 1.)

§ 1C-1825. Asserting and defending foreign-money claims.

(a) A person may assert a claim in a specified foreign money. If a foreign-money claim is not asserted, the claimant shall make the claim in United States dollars.

(b) An opposing party may allege and prove that a claim, in whole or in part, is in a different money than that asserted by the claimant.

(c) A person may assert a defense, setoff, recoupment, or counterclaim in any money without regard to the money of other claims.

(d) The determination of the proper money of the claim pursuant to G.S. 1C-1823 is a question of law. (1995, c. 213, s. 1.)

§ 1C-1826. Judgments and awards on foreign-money claims, times of money conversion; form of judgments.

(a) Except as provided in subsection (c) of this section, a judgment or award on a foreign-money claim must be stated in an amount of the money of the claim.

(b) A judgment or award on a foreign-money claim is payable in that foreign money or, at the option of the debtor, in the amount of United States dollars that will purchase that foreign money on the conversion date at a bank-offered spot rate.

(c) A judgment or award on a foreign-money claim shall assess costs in United States dollars.

(d) Each payment in United States dollars shall be accepted and credited on a judgment or award on a foreign-money claim in the amount of the foreign money that could be purchased by the dollars at a bank-offered spot rate of exchange at or near the close of business on the conversion date for that payment.

(e) A judgment or award made in an action or distribution proceeding on:
(1) A defense, setoff, recoupment, or counterclaim, and
(2) The adverse party's claim

shall be netted by converting the money of the smaller into the money of the larger, and by subtracting the smaller from the larger and shall specify the rates of exchange used.

(f) A judgment substantially in the following form satisfies the provisions of this section:

"It is ORDERED, ADJUDGED, AND DECREED that defendant (insert name) pay to Plaintiff (insert name) the sum of (insert amount in the foreign money) plus interest on that sum at the rate of (insert rate pursuant to G.S. 1C-1828) percent a year or, at the option of the judgment debtor, the number of United States dollars that will purchase the (insert name of foreign money) with interest due, at a bank-offered spot rate at or near the close of business on the banking day next before the day of payment, together with assessed costs of (insert amount) United States dollars."

(g) If a contract claim is of the type covered by G.S. 1C-1824(a) or G.S. 1C-1824(b), the judgment or award shall be entered for the amount of money stated to measure the obligation to be paid in the money specified for payment or, at the option of the debtor, the number of United States dollars that will purchase the computed amount of the money of payment on the conversion date at a bank-offered spot rate.

(h) A judgment shall be filed, docketed, and indexed in foreign money in the same manner as other judgments and has the same effect as a lien. A judgment may be discharged by payment.

(i) A party seeking enforcement of a judgment entered as provided in this section shall file with each request or application an affidavit or certificate executed in good faith by its counsel or a bank officer, stating the rate of exchange used and how it was obtained and setting forth the calculation and the amount of United States dollars that would satisfy the judgment on the date of the affidavit or certificate by applying that rate of exchange. Affected court officials shall incur no liability, after a filing of the affidavit or certificate, for acting as if the judgment were in the amount of United States dollars stated in the affidavit or certificate. The computation contained in the affidavit or certificate shall remain in effect for 90 days following the filing of the affidavit or certificate and may be recomputed before the expiration of 90 days by filing additional affidavits or certificates. Recomputation shall not affect any payment obtained before the filing of the recomputation.

(j) When a payment is made to a clerk's office pursuant to G.S. 1-239, the clerk may determine the spot rate of exchange on the conversion date on the basis of information received in good faith from any bank officer or other reliable source and shall incur no liability to any person for crediting a payment toward a judgment, or for marking a judgment satisfied in full, on the basis of the rate so determined. (1995, c. 213, s. 1.)

§ 1C-1827. Conversions of foreign money in distribution proceedings.

The rate of exchange prevailing at or near the close of business on the day the distribution proceeding is initiated shall govern all exchanges of foreign money in a distribution proceeding. A foreign-money claimant in a distribution proceeding shall assert its claim in the named foreign money and show the amount of United States dollars resulting from a conversion as of the date the proceeding was initiated. (1995, c. 213, s. 1.)

§ 1C-1828. Prejudgment and judgment interest.

(a) Except as provided in subsection (b) of this section, recovery of prejudgment or pre-award interest and the rate of interest to be applied in the action or distribution proceeding shall be determined by the substantive law governing the right to recovery under the conflict of laws rules of this State.

(b) The court or arbitrator shall increase or decrease the amount of prejudgment or pre-award interest otherwise payable in a judgment or award in foreign money to the extent required by the law of this State governing a failure to make or accept an offer of settlement or offer of judgment, or conduct by a party or its attorney causing undue delay or expense.

(c) A judgment or award on a foreign-money claim bears interest at the rate applicable to judgments of this State. (1995, c. 213, s. 1.)

§ 1C-1829. Enforcement of foreign judgments.

Subject to the provisions of Article 17 and 18 of this Chapter:

(a) If an action is brought to enforce a judgment of another jurisdiction expressed in a foreign money and the judgment is recognized in this State as enforceable, the enforcing judgment shall be entered as provided in G.S. 1C-1826, whether or not the foreign judgment confers an option to pay in an equivalent amount of United States dollars.

(b) A foreign judgment may be filed or docketed in accordance with any rule or statute of this State providing a procedure for its recognition and enforcement.

(c) A satisfaction or partial payment made upon the foreign judgment, on proof thereof, shall be credited against the amount of foreign money specified in the judgment, notwithstanding the entry of judgment in this State.

(d) A judgment entered on a foreign-money claim only in United States dollars in another state shall be enforced in this State in United States dollars only. (1995, c. 213, s. 1.)

§ 1C-1830. Determining United States dollar value of assets to be seized or restrained.

(a) Computations under this section shall not affect computation of the United States dollar equivalent of the money of the judgment for the purpose of payment.

(b) For the limited purpose of facilitating the enforcement of provisional remedies in an action, the value in United States dollars of assets to be seized or restrained pursuant to a writ of attachment, garnishment, execution, or other legal process, the amount of United States dollars at issue for assessing costs, or the amount of United States dollars involved for a surety bond or other court-required undertaking, shall be ascertained as provided in subsections (c) and (d) of this section.

(c) A party seeking process, costs, bond, or other undertaking under subsection (b) of this section shall compute in United States dollars the amount of the foreign-money claim from a bank-offered spot rate prevailing at or near the close of business on the banking day next preceding the filing of a request or application for the issuance of process or for the determination of costs, or an application for a bond or other court-required undertaking.

(d) A party seeking the process, costs, bond, or other undertaking under subsection (b) of this section shall file with each request or application an affidavit or certificate executed in good faith by its counsel or a bank officer, stating the market quotation used and how it was obtained, and setting forth the calculation. Affected court officials shall incur no liability, after a filing of the affidavit or certificate, for acting as if the judgment were in the amount of United States dollars stated in the affidavit or certificate. (1995, c. 213, s. 1.)

§ 1C-1831. Effect of currency revalorization.

(a) If, after an obligation is expressed or a loss is incurred in a foreign money, the country issuing or adopting that money substitutes a new money in place of that money, the obligation or the loss shall be treated as if expressed or incurred in the new money at the rate of conversion the issuing country established for the payment of like obligations or losses denominated in the former money.

(b) If substitution under subsection (a) of this section occurs after a judgment or award is entered on a foreign-money claim, the court or arbitrator shall amend the judgment or award by a like conversion of the former money. (1995, c. 213, s. 1.)

§ 1C-1832. Supplementary general principles of law.

Unless displaced by particular provisions of this Article, the principles of law and equity, including the law merchant, and the law relative to capacity to contract, principal and agent, estoppel, fraud, misrepresentation, duress, coercion, mistake, bankruptcy, or other validating or invalidating causes shall supplement its provisions. (1995, c. 213, s. 1.)

§ 1C-1833. Uniformity of application and construction.

This Article shall be applied and construed to effectuate its general purpose to make uniform the law with respect to the subject of this Article among states enacting it. (1995, c. 213, s. 1.)

§ 1C-1834. Short title.

This Article may be cited as the North Carolina Foreign-Money Claims Act. (1995, c. 213, s. 1.)

§ 1C-1835. Reserved for future codification purposes.

§ 1C-1836. Reserved for future codification purposes.

§ 1C-1837. Reserved for future codification purposes.

§ 1C-1838. Reserved for future codification purposes.

§ 1C-1839. Reserved for future codification purposes.

§ 1C-1840. Reserved for future codification purposes.

§ 1C-1841. Reserved for future codification purposes.

§ 1C-1842. Reserved for future codification purposes.

§ 1C-1843. Reserved for future codification purposes.

§ 1C-1844. Reserved for future codification purposes.

§ 1C-1845. Reserved for future codification purposes.

§ 1C-1846. Reserved for future codification purposes.

§ 1C-1847. Reserved for future codification purposes.

§ 1C-1848. Reserved for future codification purposes.

§ 1C-1849. Reserved for future codification purposes.

Article 20

North Carolina Uniform Foreign-Country Money Judgments Recognition Act.

§ 1C-1850. Short title.

This Article may be cited as the North Carolina Uniform Foreign-Country Money Judgments Recognition Act. (2009-325, s. 2.)

§ 1C-1851. Definitions.
The following definitions apply in this Article:

(1) Foreign country. - A government other than:

a. The United States;

b. A state, district, commonwealth, territory, or insular possession of the United States; or

c. Any other government with regard to which the decision in this State as to whether to recognize a judgment of that government's courts is initially subject to determination under the Full Faith and Credit Clause of the United States Constitution.

(2) Foreign-country judgment. - A judgment of a court of a foreign country. (2009-325, s. 2.)

§ 1C-1852. Applicability; saving clause.

(a) Except as otherwise provided in subsection (b) of this section, this Article applies to a foreign-country judgment to the extent that the judgment:

(1) Grants or denies recovery of a sum of money; and

(2) Under the law of the foreign country where rendered, is final, conclusive, and enforceable.

(b) This Article does not apply to a foreign-country judgment, even if the judgment grants or denies recovery of a sum of money, to the extent that the judgment is:

(1) A judgment for taxes;

(2) A fine or other penalty; or

(3) A judgment for alimony, support, or maintenance in matrimonial or family matters.

(c) A party seeking recognition of a foreign-country judgment has the burden of establishing that this Article applies to the foreign-country judgment.

(d) This Article does not prevent the recognition under principles of comity or otherwise of a foreign-country judgment to which this Article does not apply. (2009-325, s. 2.)

§ 1C-1853. Standards for recognition and nonrecognition of foreign-country judgment.

(a) Except as otherwise provided in this section, a court of this State shall recognize a foreign-country judgment to which this Article applies.
(b) A court of this State shall not recognize a foreign-country judgment if:

(1) The judgment was rendered under a judicial system that, taken as a whole, does not provide impartial tribunals or procedures compatible with the requirements of due process of law;

(2) The foreign court did not have personal jurisdiction over the defendant; or

(3) The foreign court did not have jurisdiction over the subject matter.

(c) If a court of this State finds that any of the following exist with respect to a foreign-country judgment for which recognition is sought, recognition of the judgment shall be denied unless the court determines, as a matter of law, that recognition would nevertheless be reasonable under the circumstances:

(1) The defendant in the proceeding in the foreign court did not receive notice of the proceeding in sufficient time to enable the defendant to defend.

(2) The judgment was obtained by fraud that deprived the losing party of an adequate opportunity to present its case.

(3) The judgment, or the cause of action or claim for relief on which the judgment is based, is repugnant to the public policy of this State or of the United States.

(4) Reserved for future codification.

(5) The proceeding in the foreign court was contrary to an agreement between the parties under which the dispute in question was to be determined otherwise than by proceedings in that foreign court.

(6) In the case of jurisdiction based only on personal service, the foreign court was a seriously inconvenient forum for the trial of the action.

(7) The judgment was rendered in circumstances that raise substantial doubt about the integrity of the rendering court with respect to the judgment.

(8) The specific proceeding in the foreign court leading to the judgment was fundamentally unfair.

(d) If a foreign-country judgment for which recognition is sought is otherwise entitled to recognition under this Article but conflicts with a prior final and conclusive judgment, a court of this State shall recognize the judgment for which recognition is sought unless the court determines that nonrecognition would nevertheless be reasonable under the circumstances.

(e) If a foreign-country judgment for which recognition is sought is otherwise entitled to recognition under this Article but conflicts with a subsequent final and conclusive judgment, a court of this State shall deny recognition of the judgment for which recognition is sought unless the court determines that recognition would nevertheless be reasonable under the circumstances.

(f) A party resisting recognition of a foreign-country judgment has the burden of establishing that a ground for nonrecognition stated in subsection (b) of this section exists.

(g) A party resisting recognition of a foreign-country judgment has the burden of establishing that a ground for nonrecognition stated in subsection (c) of this section exists. The party seeking recognition of the judgment has the burden of establishing that, as a matter of law, recognition would nevertheless be reasonable under the circumstances.

(h) A party resisting recognition of a foreign-country judgment under subsection (d) or (e) of this section has the burden of establishing that another final and conclusive judgment exists and that the other judgment conflicts with the judgment for which recognition is sought. Under subsection (d) of this section, the party resisting recognition also has the burden of establishing that nonrecognition of the judgment for which recognition is sought would be reasonable under the circumstances. Under subsection (e) of this section, the party seeking recognition of the foreign-country judgment has the burden of establishing that recognition would be reasonable under the circumstances.

(i) When a court of this State rules on recognition of a foreign-country judgment, the court shall state the facts specially and state separately its conclusions of law. (2009-325, s. 2.)

§ 1C-1854. Personal jurisdiction.

(a) A foreign-country judgment shall not be refused recognition for lack of personal jurisdiction if any of the following exist:

(1) The defendant was served with process personally in the foreign country.

(2) The defendant voluntarily appeared in the proceeding, other than for the purpose of protecting property seized or threatened with seizure in the proceeding or of contesting the jurisdiction of the court over the defendant.

(3) The defendant, before the commencement of the proceeding, had agreed to submit to the jurisdiction of the foreign court with respect to the subject matter involved.

(4) The defendant was domiciled in the foreign country when the proceeding was instituted or was a corporation or other form of business organization that had its principal place of business in, or was organized under the laws of, the foreign country.

(5) The defendant had a business office in the foreign country and the proceeding in the foreign court involved a cause of action or claim for relief arising out of business done by the defendant through that office in the foreign country.

(6) The defendant operated a motor vehicle or airplane in the foreign country and the proceeding involved a cause of action or claim for relief arising out of that operation.

(7) There was any other basis for personal jurisdiction that would be consistent with the Due Process Clause of the Fourteenth Amendment to the United States Constitution.

(b) The list of bases for personal jurisdiction in subsection (a) of this section is not exclusive. The courts of this State may recognize reasonable bases of personal jurisdiction other than those listed in subsection (a) of this section as sufficient to support a foreign-country judgment. (2009-325, s. 2.)

§ 1C-1855. Procedure for recognition and nonrecognition of foreign-country judgment.

(a) If recognition of a foreign-country judgment is sought as an original matter, the issue of recognition shall be raised by filing an action seeking recognition of the foreign-country judgment.

(b) If recognition or nonrecognition of a foreign-country judgment is sought in some other action, the issue of recognition may be raised by complaint, counterclaim, cross-claim, or affirmative defense. (2009-325, s. 2.)

§ 1C-1856. Effect of recognition of foreign-country judgment.

(a) If the court in a proceeding under G.S. 1C-1855 finds that the foreign-country judgment is entitled to recognition under this Article then, to the extent that the foreign-country judgment grants or denies recovery of a sum of money, the foreign-country judgment is:

(1) Conclusive between the parties to the same extent as the judgment of a sister state entitled to full faith and credit in this State would be conclusive; and

(2) Enforceable in the same manner and to the same extent as a judgment rendered in this State.

(b) Article 17 of this Chapter does not apply to the enforcement of foreign-country judgments recognized under this Article. (2009-325, s. 2.)

§ 1C-1857. Stay of proceedings pending appeal of foreign-country judgment.

If a party establishes that an appeal from a foreign-country judgment is pending or will be taken, the court may stay any proceedings with regard to the foreign-country judgment until the appeal is concluded, the time for appeal expires without an appeal being taken, or the appellant has had sufficient time to prosecute the appeal and has failed to do so. (2009-325, s. 2.)

§ 1C-1858. Statute of limitations.

An action to recognize a foreign-country judgment must be commenced within the earlier of the time during which the foreign-country judgment is effective in the foreign country or 10 years from the date that the foreign-country judgment became effective in the foreign country. (2009-325, s. 2.)

§ 1C-1859. Uniformity of interpretation.

In applying and construing this Article, consideration may be given to promoting uniformity of interpretation with respect to its subject matter among states that enact it. (2009-325, s. 2.)

Chapter 1D

Punitive Damages.

§ 1D-1. Purpose of punitive damages.

Punitive damages may be awarded, in an appropriate case and subject to the provisions of this Chapter, to punish a defendant for egregiously wrongful acts and to deter the defendant and others from committing similar wrongful acts. (1995, c. 514, s. 1.)
§ 1D-5. Definitions.

As used in this Chapter:

(1) "Claimant" means a party, including a plaintiff, counterclaimant, cross-claimant, or third-party plaintiff, seeking recovery of punitive damages. In a claim for relief in which a party seeks recovery of punitive damages related to injury to another person, damage to the property of another person, death of another person, or other harm to another person, "claimant" includes any party seeking recovery of punitive damages.

(2) "Compensatory damages" includes nominal damages.

(3) "Defendant" means a party, including a counterdefendant, cross-defendant, or third-party defendant, from whom a claimant seeks relief with respect to punitive damages.

(4) "Fraud" does not include constructive fraud unless an element of intent is present.
(5) "Malice" means a sense of personal ill will toward the claimant that activated or incited the defendant to perform the act or undertake the conduct that resulted in harm to the claimant.

(6) "Punitive damages" means extracompensatory damages awarded for the purposes set forth in G.S. 1D-1.

(7) "Willful or wanton conduct" means the conscious and intentional disregard of and indifference to the rights and safety of others, which the defendant knows or should know is reasonably likely to result in injury, damage, or other harm. "Willful or wanton conduct" means more than gross negligence. (1995, c. 514, s. 1.)

§ 1D-10. Scope of the Chapter.

This Chapter applies to every claim for punitive damages, regardless of whether the claim for relief is based on a statutory or a common-law right of action or based in equity. In an action subject to this Chapter, in whole or in part, the provisions of this Chapter prevail over any other law to the contrary. (1995, c. 514, s. 1.)

§ 1D-15. Standards for recovery of punitive damages.

(a) Punitive damages may be awarded only if the claimant proves that the defendant is liable for compensatory damages and that one of the following aggravating factors was present and was related to the injury for which compensatory damages were awarded:

(1) Fraud.

(2) Malice.

(3) Willful or wanton conduct.

(b) The claimant must prove the existence of an aggravating factor by clear and convincing evidence.

(c) Punitive damages shall not be awarded against a person solely on the basis of vicarious liability for the acts or omissions of another. Punitive damages may be awarded against a person only if that person participated in the conduct constituting the aggravating factor giving rise to the punitive damages, or if, in the case of a corporation, the officers, directors, or managers of the corporation participated in or condoned the conduct constituting the aggravating factor giving rise to punitive damages.

(d) Punitive damages shall not be awarded against a person solely for breach of contract. (1995, c. 514, s. 1.)

§ 1D-20. Election of extracompensatory remedies.

A claimant must elect, prior to judgment, between punitive damages and any other remedy pursuant to another statute that provides for multiple damages. (1995, c. 514, s. 1.)

§ 1D-25. Limitation of amount of recovery.

(a) In all actions seeking an award of punitive damages, the trier of fact shall determine the amount of punitive damages separately from the amount of compensation for all other damages.

(b) Punitive damages awarded against a defendant shall not exceed three times the amount of compensatory damages or two hundred fifty thousand dollars ($250,000), whichever is greater. If a trier of fact returns a verdict for punitive damages in excess of the maximum amount specified under this subsection, the trial court shall reduce the award and enter judgment for punitive damages in the maximum amount.

(c) The provisions of subsection (b) of this section shall not be made known to the trier of fact through any means, including voir dire, the introduction into evidence, argument, or instructions to the jury. (1995, c. 514, s. 1.)

§ 1D-26. Driving while impaired; exemption from cap.

G.S. 1D-25(b) shall not apply to a claim for punitive damages for injury or harm arising from a defendant's operation of a motor vehicle if the actions of the defendant in operating the motor vehicle would give rise to an offense of driving while impaired under G.S. 20-138.1, 20-138.2, or 20-138.5. (1995, c. 514, s. 1.)

§ 1D-30. Bifurcated trial.

Upon the motion of a defendant, the issues of liability for compensatory damages and the amount of compensatory damages, if any, shall be tried separately from the issues of liability for punitive damages and the amount of punitive damages, if any. Evidence relating solely to punitive damages shall not be admissible until the trier of fact has determined that the defendant is liable for compensatory damages and has determined the amount of compensatory damages. The same trier of fact that tried the issues relating to compensatory damages shall try the issues relating to punitive damages. (1995, c. 514, s. 1.)

§ 1D-35. Punitive damages awards.

In determining the amount of punitive damages, if any, to be awarded, the trier of fact:

(1) Shall consider the purposes of punitive damages set forth in G.S. 1D-1; and

(2) May consider only that evidence that relates to the following:

a. The reprehensibility of the defendant's motives and conduct.

b. The likelihood, at the relevant time, of serious harm.

c. The degree of the defendant's awareness of the probable consequences of its conduct.

d. The duration of the defendant's conduct.

e. The actual damages suffered by the claimant.

f. Any concealment by the defendant of the facts or consequences of its conduct.

g. The existence and frequency of any similar past conduct by the defendant.

h. Whether the defendant profited from the conduct.

i. The defendant's ability to pay punitive damages, as evidenced by its revenues or net worth. (1995, c. 514, s. 1.)

§ 1D-40. Jury instructions.

In a jury trial, the court shall instruct the jury with regard to subdivisions (1) and (2) of G.S. 1D-35. (1995, c. 514, s. 1.)

§ 1D-45. Frivolous or malicious actions; attorneys' fees.
The court shall award reasonable attorneys' fees, resulting from the defense against the punitive damages claim, against a claimant who files a claim for punitive damages that the claimant knows or should have known to be frivolous or malicious. The court shall award reasonable attorney fees against a defendant who asserts a defense in a punitive damages claim that the defendant knows or should have known to be frivolous or malicious. (1995, c. 514, s. 1.)

§ 1D-50. Judicial review of award.

When reviewing the evidence regarding a finding by the trier of fact concerning liability for punitive damages in accordance with G.S. 1D-15(a), or regarding the amount of punitive damages awarded, the trial court shall state in a written opinion its reasons for upholding or disturbing the finding or award. In doing so, the court shall address with specificity the evidence, or lack thereof, as it bears on the liability for or the amount of punitive damages, in light of the requirements of this Chapter. (1995, c. 514, s. 1.)

Chapter 1E

Eastern Band of Cherokee Indians.

Article 1

Full Faith and Credit.

§ 1E-1. Full faith and credit.

(a) The courts of this State shall give full faith and credit to a judgment, decree, or order signed by a judicial officer of the Eastern Band of Cherokee Indians and filed in the Cherokee Tribal Court to the same extent as is given a judgment, decree, or order of another state, subject to the provisions of subsection (b) of this section; provided that the judgments, decrees, and orders of the courts of this State are given full faith and credit by the Tribal Court of the Eastern Band of Cherokee Indians.
(b) Judgments, decrees, and orders specified in subsection (a) of this section shall be given full faith and credit subject to the provisions of G.S. 1C-1705, G.S. 1C-1708, G.S. 1C-1804, and G.S. 1C-1805 and shall be considered a foreign judgment for purposes of these statutes. (2001-456, s. 1.)

Chapter 1F

North Carolina Uniform Interstate Depositions and Discovery Act.

§ 1F-1. Short title.

This Chapter may be cited as the "North Carolina Uniform Interstate Depositions and Discovery Act." (2011-247, s. 1.)

§ 1F-2. Definitions.

The following definitions apply in this Chapter:

(1) Foreign jurisdiction. - A state other than North Carolina.

(2) Foreign subpoena. - A subpoena issued under authority of a court of record of a foreign jurisdiction.

(3) Person. - An individual, corporation, business trust, estate, trust, partnership, limited liability company, association, joint venture, public corporation, government, or governmental subdivision, agency, or instrumentality, or any other legal or commercial entity.

(4) State. - A state of the United States, the District of Columbia, Puerto Rico, the United States Virgin Islands, a federally recognized Indian tribe, or any territory or insular possession subject to the jurisdiction of the United States.

(5) Subpoena. - A document, however denominated, issued under authority of a court of record requiring a person to:

a. Attend and give testimony at a deposition, either oral or upon written questions;

b. Produce and permit inspection and copying of designated books, documents, records, electronically stored information, or tangible things in the possession, custody, or control of the person; or

c. Permit inspection of premises under the control of the person. (2011-247, s. 1.)

§ 1F-3. Issuance of subpoena.

(a) To request issuance of a subpoena under this section, a party must submit a foreign subpoena to a clerk of court in the county in which discovery is sought to be conducted in this State. A request for the issuance of a subpoena under this act does not constitute an appearance in the courts of this State.

(b) When a party submits a foreign subpoena to a clerk of court in this State, the clerk, in accordance with that court's procedure, shall promptly open an appropriate court file, assign a file number, collect the applicable filing fee pursuant to G.S. 7A-305(a)(2), and issue a subpoena for service upon the person to which the foreign subpoena is directed.

(c) A subpoena under subsection (b) of this section must:
(1) Incorporate the terms used in the foreign subpoena; and

(2) Contain or be accompanied by the names, addresses, and telephone numbers of all counsel of record in the proceeding to which the subpoena relates and of any party not represented by counsel. (2011-247, s. 1.)

§ 1F-4. Service of subpoena.

A subpoena issued by a clerk of court in North Carolina under G.S. 1F-3 must be served in compliance with G.S. 1A-1, Rule 45(b) of the North Carolina Rules of Civil Procedure. (2011-247, s. 1.)

§ 1F-5. Deposition; production; inspection.

Rules 26, 28, 30, 31, 34, and 45 of G.S. 1A-1, the North Carolina Rules of Civil Procedure, apply to subpoenas issued under G.S. 1F-3. (2011-247, s. 1.)

§ 1F-6. Application to court.

An application to the court for a protective order or to enforce, quash, or modify a subpoena issued by a clerk of court under G.S. 1F-3 must comply with the rules or statutes of this State and be submitted to the court in the county in which discovery is to be conducted. Where a dispute exists between the parties to the action, the party opposing the discovery shall apply for appropriate relief to the court in which the action is pending and not to the court in the state in which the discovery is sought. (2011-247, s. 1.)

§ 1F-7. Uniformity of application and construction.

In applying and construing this Chapter, consideration shall be given to the need to promote uniformity of the law with respect to its subject matter among states that have enacted the Uniform Interstate Depositions and Discovery Act. (2011-247, s. 1.)

Vision Books Order Form

Fax Orders:	1-980-299-5965
Phone Orders:	1-704-898-0770
E-mail Orders:	www.visionbooks.org
Mail Orders:	Vision Books, LLC P.O. Box 42406 Charlotte, NC 28215

Shipp To:
Name_____
Address_____
City_____State_____Zip_____
Phone_____Fax_____
Email_____@_____

Bill To: We can bill a third party on your behalf.
Name_____
Address_____
City_____State_____Zip_____
Phone___(_____)_____Fax_____
Email_____@_____

Pamphlet Number ($15.00 Each)	Qty	Total Cost
_____	_____	_____
_____	_____	_____
_____	_____	_____
_____	_____	_____
_____	_____	_____
_____	_____	_____
_____	_____	_____
_____	_____	_____
Full Volume Set 1-92	**92 Pamphlets**	**1,380.00**

Free Shipping Shipping & Handling on Full Volume Orders
Add $1.00 Shipping & Handling per pamphlet $_____

Total Cost $_____

Thank You for Your Support. Management!

DID YOU ENJOY THIS BOOK?

Vision Books, LLC would like to hear from you! If you or someone you know has been fasely imprisoned, we would like to hear your story. If the 'North Carolina Criminal Law and Procedure' has had an effect in your life or if you have suggestions, we would like to hear from you. Send your letters to:

Vision Books, LLC
Attn: Staff Writers
P.O. Box 42406
Charlotte, NC 28215
Email: staff@visionbooks.org

Order Additional Copies:

Fax Orders:	1-980-299-5965
Phone Orders:	1-704-898-0770
E-mail Orders:	www.visionbooks.org
Mail Orders:	Vision Books, LLC P.O. Box 42406 Charlotte, NC 28215

www.ingramcontent.com/pod-product-compliance
Lightning Source LLC
Chambersburg PA
CBHW071404170526
45165CB00001B/175